C is for Cat

Frank Manolson DVM was a member of the Royal College of Veterinary Surgeons. He practised in the United States, Canada, England, Italy and Central America.

Frank Manolson

C is for Cat

the care of your cat from a-z

PAN BOOKS London and Sydney

First published in Great Britain 1965 by Studio Vista Ltd
This edition published 1979 by Pan Books Ltd,
Cavaye Place, London SW10 9PG
© Frank Manolson 1965, 1979
ISBN 0 330 25641 6
Made and printed in Great Britain by
Cox & Wyman Ltd, London, Reading and Fakenham

Foreword

Cat lovers tend to make the subject very mysterious. They hold really long, heated discussions on the origins of the breeds. In fact they often can't make up their minds what constitutes a breed. It doesn't matter. They're nice people and they don't do any harm. I hope they'll forgive me for over-simplifying their favourite subject.

In this book I divide domestic cats into four sorts. The first three are purebreds. They are the orientals (Siamese, Burmese, Abyssinians, Havanas and Foreign or Russian Blues), the long-haired or Persians (divided into breeds according to colour), and the short-haired (also divided into breeds according to colour and called British or Domestic according to which side of the Atlantic you live). The fourth group includes the sort of cat most of us usually keep. It's neither long-haired, nor short-haired, nor oriental, because it hasn't been too discriminating in its choice of grandparents. Nor if it's left to its own devices will it be fussy when selecting a mate. It's the common cat and each representative has some of the characteristics and some of the virtues and a few of the drawbacks of its purebred aristocratic cousins.

Of the wild cats I only cover those that are commonly domesticated. I do this only to discourage the practice. The civets are included because they are regarded as precursors of our modern cat.

The rest of the book is simply a substitute for five years of university. If you read this book you don't have to bother about studying anatomy or physiology or bacteriology or virology or anything. You don't have to attend lectures or clinics or laboratories. You don't have to go out and gather experience and acquire a sense of judgement. This book does it all for you, and it does it painlessly. It simply points out each and every occasion when you need to consult your local veterinarian. If you really think that you can treat your own cat out of a book I pity you a little and your cat a great deal.

This book is for Joan Drummond-Hay of London who did much of the real work on it; for Margaret Knott of Windsor (not Ontario) who kept a practice at bay so I could work on it.

Foreword to revised Pan edition

For Margaret (now not Knott) Manolson.

A few general hints

Allow a kitten to explore a kitten-proof area of his new home before you offer him food. Do remember that shy kittens will immediately retreat into inaccessible retreats behind fridges, up the chimney and under the stove. After four or five hours he will feel more secure. When he's settled in you can feed him, and he'll go to sleep content and happy.

A kitten may be reassured during his first nights in a strange home by a hot water bottle (well wrapped) and a clock with a dull, fairly loud tick.

Don't stroke cats' fur the wrong way unless you know them very well. Most hate it.

Don't lift a cat by the scruff of its neck or by its middle so that the legs dangle. Support it completely so that it feels secure, and don't pinch or squeeze.

A cat who swishes his tail back and forth rapidly is considering action. If he lays his ears flat – watch out!

Don't handle a cat while your hands still smell of another animal. The odour of other animals will frighten a cat, particularly if she's a female and in season.

If you hate brushing and combing don't get a Persian.

The old rule of thumb about feeding cats is 12g ($\frac{1}{2}$ oz) of food (of which four-fifths should be meat) per $\frac{1}{2}$kg (1 lb) of body weight per day.

Don't borrow or lend cat baskets. You may be borrowing or lending disease.

You can collect a sample of your cat's urine by tipping his litter tray at a slight angle. Wedge a board (not quite touching the bottom) across the tray, and keep the litter at the upper end. The urine will trickle through to the lower corners.

Sometimes unnecessarily bandaging one or more healthy paws will distract a cat enough so that it will leave the necessary dressings around an injured ear or tail alone.

In an emergency you can bathe a difficult cat by dumping him into a canvas or denim bag with his head outside. Put the soap in first. Allow the water (at body temperature) to seep through the bag. Rub. Rinse. Rinse again. And again.

If you suspect that a cat has fleas, look for them at the base of the tail. You can often find them there when they're not easily seen elsewhere.

Don't waste your time defleaing a cat unless you disinfest the house at the same time.

A cat that is absolutely riddled with fleas may be treated by dunking him in a bag with powder. Do his head first. Then put him in the bag, leaving his head out. Soothe him for fifteen or twenty minutes. Afterwards comb cat. Boil bag. Apply iodine to your scratches.

Some cats won't play with catnip-impregnated rubber mice. They chew them to bits. Solution? Don't buy the things!

You can dry-shampoo a cat by rubbing him with Fuller's earth or coarse dry cornmeal. Then comb and brush.

Sometimes the only signs of an accident are broken claws. There may be internal damage as well, so get the animal to a vet.

Get everything laid out before catching your cat at medicine time. When giving liquid medicine give small quantities. Allow lots of time for swallowing *and* breathing between gulps. When you give pills, touching the lips with a moistened finger will encourage swallowing.

A cat who gets filthy through illness may lose all interest in living. At such times proper grooming is not merely advisable – it's vital.

Be careful of collars. They may become nooses.

Don't postpone those grass pots because you can't get proper seed. Plant rye or oats or even leftover seeds from the budgie.

Catnip, like whisky and good friends, improves with age.

If your cat must live a confined life, provide him with a window porch from which to view the madness below. Screen it in. Furnish his terrace with a cushion and a pot of grass.

If you love your dog don't think it's cute if he chases cats. He may win the fight but he might lose an eye.

Whatever lotion or ointment you stick on a cat it will promptly lick off, so be certain the stuff isn't poisonous.

See that your cat has a favourite pillow or blanket when you leave him at the boarding kennel or hospital.

Take every precaution in handling an injured or ill animal, no matter how well you know him. The pain will make him forget his manners, and he'll revert to claws and teeth.

Your cat is never too old to be inoculated against feline infectious enteritis, but if you keep postponing it, it might be too late.

If you don't agree with anything in this book write to me (care of the publishers). I'm only too willing to learn. I hope I'm not being petty if I suggest that the price of a postage stamp these days is more than the author's royalty on a book of this size. Don't expect a reply or a consultation by correspondence if you don't enclose a self-addressed stamped envelope. I must also point out that free consultations are worth slightly less than cost. Most do more harm than good.

Abortion (*induced or artificial*)

Although there may be good reasons for aborting mismated bitches (say, for example, if a Boxer mounts a wee Poodle), I can't think of one valid reason to abort a cat. It's just as well, because the hormones used may cause more harm than the pregnancy.

If you don't want your cat to have kittens, have her spayed. It may be done at any age.

Abortion (*natural*)

I suppose miscarriage would be a more accurate term. It's a very rare condition and you're unlikely ever to see it. The causes of abortion or miscarriage are rough handling or travelling in advanced pregnancy, accidents, infections and malnutrition. The first indication to the owner is the appearance of a dead kitten. The mother may appear quite normal and placid. Most owners (even experienced ones) panic into heroic harmful measures. Don't poke or prod, and don't get out the brandy bottle. Leave the cat in a small, quiet room. Provide her with a blanket and a bowl of water and leave her alone. Peek in after half an hour or so. If she's not straining, and it's after midnight, leave her alone till next morning. If she is distressed or straining, phone your vet. He'll probably ask you to put her in a basket and take her along to the surgery. Often a caesarian is necessary to remove the remaining foetuses. If it's the second time running, your vet may advise removing the ovaries and the uterus at the same time.

Abscess (*boil*)

This word comes from the Latin verb meaning 'going away'. If the body has some poison or some object it doesn't want, it pours its blood into the flesh surrounding the poison and hastens it on its way. The white cells of the blood try to wall off the area and move the offending substance towards the skin.

Every abscess is like a miniature war. The offensive armies are the germs. The defending armies are the white blood cells. The battle

9

generates heat, the battlefield swells with the corpses of the slain, and the surrounding area feels the pain. Far fetched? Not at all, if you have had the good fortune to have seen it all under the microscope, and had it explained by an imaginative pathology professor, as I did.

The practical application of this knowledge is simple. Don't squeeze a boil in any circumstances. All you are doing is to break down the body's wall of defence. You are shoving the poison back into the system.

How do you recognize an abscess on a cat? The area will be swollen, it will feel warm, it will be painful, and if you can see the skin it will be red. What to do? Get a deep bowl, fill it half full of warm water, add a few tablespoonfuls of salt, get a clean rag and soak it in the warm salt water. Squeeze the rag and then hold it against the infected area. When it loses its heat soak it again and repeat the process. Do this for ten or fifteen minutes. Dry the area and leave it alone. If the abscess is on the legs or feet soak the whole limb. Repeat in four or five hours. When the abscess is about to come to a head, take the cat to your veterinarian. He will decide if it should be lanced, or bathed until it opens on its own. He will also decide if penicillin is needed to clear it up once and for all.

Why not use penicillin or some other antibiotic right at the beginning? We often do, but usually in those abscesses that are extremely painful or near an eye or over a joint. With most abscesses it's really better to assist the body with gentle heat, and then, when it has done the work no medicine can do, deliver the final blows with modern antibiotics.

Once an abscess has burst, home aid consists of bathing the area as outlined above, using hydrogen peroxide instead of salt for the first few moments. The hydrogen peroxide helps bubble away the pus. More important, it neutralizes the odour. The cat will be more likely to leave the area alone. You finish the bathing with salt water.

Generally it's best to keep the area open and draining for some days. If you allow it to heal before all the poison has drained out the germs will usually start multiplying again, and a week or so later the poor creature will have a new, larger, deeper abscess.

A big gaping hole round an abscess is never sutured. It simply wouldn't heal.

Never bandage over an abscess. That tends to drive the poison into the body instead of drawing it out.

Now for some complications of the above simple rules. It's not always easy to recognize an abscess – even for the veterinarian. Sometimes a thing looks like an abscess and turns out to be a tumour. Sometimes a swelling that has been diagnosed as a tumour turns out to be an abscess. Lesson? If after a day or two of bathing the thing doesn't come to a head, you'd better get professional help.

If the abscess is round the eye or along the jaw, don't mess about with home treatment. You can bathe an abscess caused by a rotten tooth and draw out lots of pus, but the poor cat will still have toothache. Obviously the only cure is to locate the offending tooth, and pull it out. Needless to say it can't be done (at least humanely) without a general anaesthetic.

An abscess in or around the ear can be very painful, and should be treated professionally as soon as possible.

Abscesses between the shoulders should be treated with antibiotics right from the beginning, because they may drain down into the body. So should abscesses over joints, because the pus may invade the joint and cause a permanent crippling. Abscesses on the tail don't respond well to bathing. The infection just seems to invade the whole tail and, if neglected, amputation may be necessary to save the animal.

Neglected abscesses may invade the body and set up a blood infection (pyaemia) or an infection of the chest (pyothorax), both of which are critical conditions.

Finally, some tom cats simply can't avoid getting scratched and infected and abscessed every time they go out on a date. The only real cure is radical surgery. I mean castration. It can be done at any age, and is really much kinder than letting the old boy wander into situations that he can't get out of. If your answer is that castration is against nature, may I suggest that nature doesn't provide veterinarians and penicillin and doting owners to nurse its losers back to health? Often the ageing and the ailing crawl into corners and holes to die slowly.

Abyssinian

Your chances of getting an Abyssinian cat in Abyssinia are about nil. We are told the wife of an English army officer found one cat there which seemed to her to be a direct descendant of the sacred cats of ancient Egypt. Her name was Mrs Lennard, and she brought the cat back to England in 1869. That one cat (and no one seems to know if it was a tom or a queen) is reputed by some to be the founder of the breed that we now call Abyssinian. Other authorities state that the Abyssinian is a British product manufactured by breeding and selection from, Ticked Tabbies.

They were established, and shown as a distinct breed in 1883 at the Crystal Palace. Right from the beginning lovers of the breed aimed at producing a cat that would retain the physical characteristics of the ancient Egyptian. They have succeeded very well except in one particular. They rarely produce specimens without bands of white on the face or chest.

It's a long, lithe, Siamese-looking smooth-hair, and its colour is various shades of ruddy brown. The golden-reddish browns are very beautiful indeed. Its ears are sharp and large, and its eyes green, yellow or hazel. Incidentally, each individual hair is ticked, that is, composed of bands of colour.

Unfortunately the modern Abyssinian has few of the mental characteristics of its ancient Egyptian progenitor. We are told that those cats were aggressive and arrogant. They hunted and some, we are led to believe, even retrieved. They were used as guards. One authority says that they rode into battle on their masters' backs and sprang at the adversary. You can believe as little or as much of that as you like, but I think we must accept that the ancient Egyptian cat wasn't a retiring introvert.

The Abyssinian, though not a quiet cat, is cautious. He surveys his territory, and if it's acceptable he'll let loose. He'll never move in and assume control without gauging his escape routes first. In this respect he's more like the European cat. He's a friendly beast who loves activity in the outdoors. Too many owners restrict him, and he suffers accordingly.

One of the delightful characteristics of the Abyssinian is the way they'll explore an object with their paws rather than their noses. It's also a dangerous practice, and more than one has been burnt while investigating a cigar. Home aid consists of applying lanolin or butter, and bandaging the paws while you are getting to the vet's. If one doesn't do this the cat will lick and bite the injured paw until it's bleeding.

Do I like the breed? I'm crazy about them. I wish there were more about, and I wish they were cheaper. They're not likely to become less expensive, because for some strange reason more males than females are born.

If you are a rich Englishman import one from America, where the best specimens are bred. If you are an American write to the various clubs and pay what they ask. Abyssinian breeders anywhere are genuine fanciers, and aren't in it for the money.

Medically, Abyssinians are no different from the tough Siamese around the corner, so you need not fear that you will come up against special problems.

Twice-a-week grooming is sufficient. Start when he's a kitten, so that he'll think it's just part of life's routine.

PS: I hope I don't upset too many people if I state that in the last two decades I haven't met a single enthusiast who hasn't had a lot of breeding problems. I think the breed is beautiful but I guess I've met the wrong people with the wrong strains.

Accidents

If you are a cat lover, but simply can't stand the sight of blood, here is the one essential thing you need to know to help a cat that's had an accident. Get a basket, or a box, or even a cardboard container, and place it over the cat. It's simple enough to do, and you needn't look while you're doing it. The reason this is absolutely essential is that cats will often drag themselves off after an accident. They'll hide in a corner until they either die or are somewhat better.

If you're not afraid of the sight of blood or suffering, what do you do? Exactly the same thing, except that you *place* the animal in a container so that you can carry it to a table and light and bandages. Remember that a cat in pain will scratch at you, so grab him firmly and transfer him quickly. If there's a great deal of bleeding you might attempt to stop it (see *Haemorrhage*), but other than that I think any attempt at first aid will cause more harm than good. Whatever you do, don't try to splint a broken limb or bandage a fractured jaw. The cat's struggles will almost certainly do more damage than your splints will do good.

Summary: Get the cat in a basket and take him to the vet.

Adoption

It's usually very simple to get a nursing queen to accept strange kittens, particularly if they're about the same age as her own. Quite often she'll even accept puppies or rabbits. The trick is to collect a bit of the mother's milk in a small saucer. Rub the orphans with it. Introduce them into the basket when the mother is out. Keep a sharp eye for the first few minutes to make sure she accepts them. Sometimes two or three trials are needed. It may be necessary to remove all the mother's own youngsters before she'll accept the strangers. Cruel? Try to tell this to the people who insist on breeding from purebreds so delicate that they can't rear their own young.

13

PS: Two further tricks adopted by professional cat breeders from shepherds:

1, Take the hides off the mongrel kittens and carefully tie them on the valuable purebred orphans.

2, Don't introduce the orphans till the foster mother's teats are painfully full. At that stage she will accept any form of relief.

Advertising

The people who practise this art tell us that it is the yeast that activates the dough of our world. Cats consider advertising the way to define the limits of their world. Their method of advertising is rather direct. They urinate along the boundaries of what they consider their territory. Strange cats who move inside that area will usually be fought off.

When a cat is moved to a new home he may forgo his clean habits and urinate along the sides of the new rooms. The reason is fright at the strange surroundings. He doesn't yet know what his territory is. He starts exploring and defines the limits of what he is sure of by urinating along its borders. You can help him get used to his new outdoor area (provided he has confidence in you) by going out of doors with him, staying with him while he does his business and then encouraging him back in. Of course, you mustn't let him out for the first three or four days because he may try to find the old home. Meanwhile, you must be careful where you step.

Age

One can only guess at the age of a cat after the permanent teeth are up. In middle age the teeth may yellow a bit or show signs of wear, but some cats retain a gleaming set into old age. Unlike dogs, cats generally don't grey as they age. They do, however, lose flesh, particularly around the eyes and along the back, and some old cats are very gaunt indeed. An average life span is around ten or twelve. Some age prematurely and die at seven or eight. Others stay agile and fit into the venerable twenties.

Allergy

This must be a very rare phenomenon in cats. I've seldom seen a condition in a cat that could be described as allergy, and I've never seen them with hives or shingles (a not unusual condition in the dog).

Many people, though, think they are allergic to cats, and will start scratching or break into bumps if a cat comes near them. I think that some of these allergies are in fact caused by either cat fleas or the short dead cat hairs that seem almost mobile by the way they creep up under one's clothes. The fleas, of course, have only jumped over to have a quick look. Cat fleas can't live on people, but they can cause a sensitive skin to itch. Many people only become aware that their cat had fleas when it dies or strays away. The fleas, after a few hours, get desperate and will seek any body warmth.

Some people have a mental allergy to cats. They just dislike them. As it's a completely irrational prejudice, they can only give you irrational excuses for their dislike.

But, of course, there is a very small minority who do have a genuine allergy to cats, as some other people have to strawberries or tomatoes. These people claim that cats know this and seek them out. I think it more likely that cats, being simple, straightforward creatures, just can't understand why anyone shouldn't like them, so they make a special effort to show how nice they really are. What advice can I offer to allergic humans? Pretend you like them, and in typical perverse cat fashion they'll probably leave you alone. And sometimes, too, you may find that you rather like them after all.

Amputations

There are some fractures and other conditions in which, despite all the miracles of modern drugs and surgery, the whole limb must be removed. If a leg has been run over by a heavy wheel and crushed out of all recognition, what can a surgeon do to save it? Many cats hide after accidents or fights. A simple infected fracture becomes a complicated gangrenous one. Occasionally we see such injuries some days or weeks after they have occurred. The whole area is simply a festering mess endangering the life of the animal. Sometimes a fracture that appears quite simple when first seen proves resistant to all treatment. Most owners are quite rightly hesitant about approving an amputation, but usually agree when it's explained that only an amputation will save the animal's life. One thing that bothers them, though, is why the whole thing must be removed if only the end of the leg is affected.

The reason is a mechanical one. One can't attach pegs or artificial limbs to cats. The bit of remaining leg would just be an extra weight to be swung uselessly. This is true even of the front limbs. Most veterinarians are agreed that the stump wouldn't be useful for feeling or lifting.

The operation itself is straightforward and usually without complications, provided the infection hasn't gone too far. The cat is generally kept on penicillin or other antibiotics for some days afterwards. The stitches come out in about ten days.

Do cats have the spasms of pain in the end of the limb that no longer exists? We can't know for sure, but these pains have been described most vividly by human amputees, and we must assume that they occur in the cat. Certainly some cat amputees have miserable moods, and all we can do is to suggest that you should be extra patient. If he seems to be miserable for more than a few hours, better take him back to your veterinary surgeon.

How well does a cat get along on three legs? Very well, usually. They can eat, sleep, walk, play and even run. Climbing, of course, becomes a manoeuvre that must be calculated carefully. A cat amputee can't escape as quickly from his enemies, and your garden or yard must be provided with convenient escape hatches for him. Otherwise he can live a normal life. You must not overfeed him. His decreased activity will start him on the overweight trail, and if you indulge him at all he'll eat himself into cripplehood.

Finally, I must mention those rare cases in which two limbs have been injured beyond repair. I believe the only humane solution is euthanasia, but some people insist that their pets will be happy dragging themselves around on two limbs. I agree with the vast majority of my colleagues who refuse to amputate two limbs, and suggest euthanasia as the only kind and sensible solution.

Anaemia

The cat is weak and listless. Its gums are pale. Even the slightest activity starts its ribs heaving and its heart pounding. What should you do? Absolutely nothing except keep the animal quiet, calm and warm. What will your vet do? He will try to determine the type of anaemia and the cause. Almost always this requires the assistance of the laboratory.

It may be an *acute anaemia* due to internal bleeding. It may be a *chronic anaemia* due to a vitamin deficiency, an abscess, enteritis or even a cancerous growth. It may be an anaemia due to *bone marrow damage* resulting from radiation burns or poisoning. Or it may be a specific disease of cats called *infectious anaemia*.

Am I trying to frighten you? No! I'm trying to point out how ludicrous all those 'blood tonics' and 'fortifiers' really are. Many, many cat lovers have cupboards full of the strangest dope with names like Hoodidia 4X and Garlicks Y7. Most are harmless – as long as they're left in the cupboard. But is it really fair to give them to a cat who may be suffering with anything from an abscess to cancer?

Anaesthetics

Very few human patients bite and scratch their doctors while he's applying a plaster cast or taking a bit of glass out of an eye. If they did, doctors would use general anaesthetics as routinely as vets. What anaesthetics do we use in cat practice? Practically the whole range – except chloroform, which is reputed to damage the liver of cats if not used sparingly. Usually the vet induces sleep with a quick-acting shot into the vein, and then maintains and deepens anaesthesia with one of the many available gases. A well-known veterinary surgeon, when asked which was the best anaesthetic, answered, 'The one with which the anaesthetist is most familiar.' I think that's as sensible an answer as any.

Most owners usually ask how long their animal will be 'out'. If one is using gas the cat usually starts to come round within seconds of its withdrawal, but some cats will stay drunk or drowsy for some hours. Others will come to, lap a bit of milk and then sleep round the clock. But fair warning – no matter how alert he looks when he gets home, he may still be dopey enough not to recognize you. Be careful you don't get scratched.

How long should the animal be starved before an anaesthetic? Most vets book their operations for the morning and ask you not to feed after seven o'clock the previous evening.

Are any cats special anaesthetic risks? Yes! Very young kittens and very old cats and very thin cats, and cats suffering from kidney or lung complaints are all special risks. All orientals must be anaesthetized with particular care, partly because they're thin and partly because they fight the anaesthetic so hard that one may be inclined to overdose while trying to get them under.

Incidentally – and dentists may find this interesting – some vets use local anaesthetics *after* the animal is given a general. The jaws of a cat are very strong, and its reflexes keep closing the jaws even when the rest of the body is completely relaxed. As a result one has to anaesthetize cats very deeply just to do a simple tooth extraction, unless a local is used to deaden the nerves of the tooth.

Anal glands

These are little bean-sized sacs on either side of the anus which contain and excrete foul-smelling stuff. They have no purpose at all, except possibly identification of one cat by another. At one time in the dim and distant past they may have been a defensive mechanism like the skunk's.

If you are a dog owner as well as a cat lover you may know that dogs too have anal glands, and in the dog they often spell trouble which means visits to the veterinarian.

In the cat the anal glands are very rarely a problem. I can recall only two cats with impacted anal glands, and only one with an infected and abscessed gland. This is a remarkably low incidence in upwards of twenty thousand sick cats. In an average week I should think that most veterinarians see a dozen or more dogs with anal gland problems. It all goes to prove how near perfect a creature the cat is.

Angora

A name formerly used to describe long-haired cats and then replaced by the word Persian. The explanations are so long and boring that the long-haired cat has long since stopped listening.

Ankyloblepheron

The union of the upper and lower eyelids which is normal in kittens up to nine or ten days of age. If the eyes don't unclose of their own accord, try gentle bathing with warm salt water. If they don't open by the twelfth or thirteenth day inform your vet. There is a simple operation which gently separates the lids and allows the kitten to focus on the brave new world.

Antibiotics

The family of drugs fathered by Sir Alexander Fleming. It includes penicillin, aureomycin, streptomycin, chloromycetin, terramycin and a host of cousins and in-laws. Unfortunately there is still no drug effective against viruses (the smaller germs that cause enteritis and flu). We use antibiotics in those cases to stop the body from succumbing to other bacteria while it is fighting the virus. The only antibiotic that is 'dodgy' when used on cats is streptomycin. It must be used in small, carefully gauged doses if untoward side effects are to be avoided. Some cats can't tolerate the stuff at all. Nevertheless it's a valuable drug in some conditions, so we use it where we can. The point you must remember about all antibiotics is that you can't stop and start again. One must keep up regular doses at regular times. Otherwise, as the level of antibiotic in the body drops, the bacteria develop resistant strains. The medicine is then not only useless for that case but for any other animals sickened by the same strain of resistant bacteria.

Antiseptics and disinfectants

The stuff you put on scratches and open sores to prevent them from festering is called an antiseptic. The stuff you wash the floors and walls and kennels with, to kill the germs, is called a disinfectant. Now it's only commonsense that you can put stronger stuff on floors than you can on skin, but some people simply will not read labels. What do you do if you accidentally (or intentionally through stupidity) use a too strong solution on your cat? Dilute it – and as quickly as possible – by pouring lots of water on the area. Then pause and read the label, and see if it mentions specific antidotes. If you use some preparation on your cat and within minutes it starts running around in pain or vomiting, dilute by pouring on water, put the cat in its basket and whip it off to your vet. Please try and remember to take the bottle of poison along. You may be too nervous or excited to act, but the chances are that your veterinary surgeon will be able to call on his great reserves of strength and summon up enough determination to actually read the label.

No matter what antiseptic or disinfectant you use, remember this second bit of commonsense. There's absolutely no point in pouring the stuff on a dirty surface – whether that surface be skin or wood or concrete. You are trying to kill the germs on the surface of the skin or the surface of the floor, but what you are actually doing is killing the germs on the surface of the dirt. The germs under the dirt have a great giggle, and go on getting divorced and multiplying. So the conclusion we may safely draw from all this evidence is that one cleans a surface *before* applying antiseptics. What do you clean with? Good old-fashioned soap and water. Rinse the soap off with lots of water.

Any antiseptic or disinfectant that belongs to the family of chemicals called 'coal tar derivates' must not be used on or around cats. This family includes lysol, naphthalene, carbolic acid or phenols, creolin and creosote.

The safest antiseptic to use on cats is hydrogen peroxide. Dilute it several times and apply repeatedly. Rinse with salt water.

Dettol and TPC, if diluted according to the manufacturer's

directions, are safe. Don't use too much. Hold the cat for a few minutes afterwards to let the stuff dry in and do its work before the creature licks it off. I use a fair bit of gentian violet because it dries in nicely and most cats will leave it alone. However, it's the messiest thing to handle. If you can't convince your husband that that old rug simply has to go, here is a free tip. Apply, without care, some gentian violet to your cat. A very small bottle of gentian violet will splotch a room-sized rug.

What disinfectants are safe to use around cats? Well, none are absolutely safe, but the safest are those like sodium hypochloride, which do their stuff and then vanish into thick air. The others should all be rinsed off after the disinfecting period.

Summary: Don't use coal tar products around cats. Clean surfaces first. Read labels.

First Aid: If you spill disinfectant on a cat you must *immediately* wash the whole lot off by pouring lots and lots of water over the cat. Better still put the cat in the sink and keep the tap running till the stuff's gone.

Aphrodisiacs

The best aphrodisiacs are youth and good health. Lost years can't be restored, but certainly any animal suffering from a loss of sexual desire should be examined professionally. A general infection or even a rotting tooth might be sapping its energies. Some beasts just aren't interested. In younger cats it's best to be patient and see if maturity doesn't widen their horizons. In middle-aged animals hormone injections will sometimes restore interest in the opposite sex. I rather deplore their use, because obviously the animals who are most likely to get that care and attention are highly regarded purebreds. It's quite likely that they will pass their lack of vigour on to their progeny. Carry the whole process to its illogical conclusion and you will have a strain of highly bred champions who need shots just to make the sexual grade.

Appetite

At least once a week a lady plonks a cat on the table and says, 'There's something wrong with him. He has no appetite.' The cat appears bright, sleek and glossy.

'How long has he been like this?' I ask.

'Oh, ever since I've had him. He's never been a good eater, but the last two or three months he's hardly had a mouthful.'

'Oh, come now,' I say, 'he's fatter than me, and *my* doctor says I should reduce. Tell me, what's his favourite food?'

'Oh, he likes raw liver and salmon, but he just won't touch veal or horsemeat, no matter how I coax him.'

'Tell me something else. Is he at home with you all day?'

'Him. Never! Goodness knows where he spends his time.'

So I explain to the good lady that her cat is perfectly healthy, and too clever by half. If she serves a delicacy he's fond of, he eats at home. Otherwise he goes around checking the neighbourhood menus.

The lady goes out muttering to herself, 'The neighbours must think I don't feed him.'

There's another sort of cat owner who comes in with the same complaint. These are middle-aged people who live in lonely rooms or small flats with just a cat to come home to. They spend hour after hour pressing titbits on the poor creature, and then get worried when he won't eat its meal. I don't know whom to feel sorrier for, but I do try to explain that the cat should only be fed once a day, and maybe a small breakfast if he really asks for it.

Then there are the people at the other extreme. They put some food down. The cat ignores it. They leave the food down. The next day the cat asks for its dinner, and the owner points at the same food. The cat sniffs at it, knows it's rotten, and although he's hungry he walks away. If a cat refuses food one day it should be offered *fresh* food the next day. If it still refuses it, and you are fairly certain he hasn't eaten elsewhere, you'd better keep a sharp eye on him. If he's listless as well, better take him along to your veterinarian.

If he goes to eat and obviously wants the food but does not eat, the chances are he has a rotten tooth or something lodged in his mouth.

If your cat has been missing for some days, don't allow him to eat a big meal on his return. Give him just a saucerful and repeat it in a few hours.

If you have your adult cat spayed or castrated, don't indulge his or her every request for food. If you do, you will produce a monster.

Cats with flu can often be encouraged to start eating by offering them very strong-smelling cheese or ripe hare or well-hung game.

Older animals and those in advanced pregnancy should be fed two or even three smaller meals rather than one large meal.

Finally, a cat who has just come from boarding kennels may not eat the first day. If he doesn't eat the second day I would advise an early veterinary check. Even the best run places can unsuspectingly take in a diseased cat which may have infected yours.

Arthritis

Joint problems do occur in the cat but apparently not nearly as commonly as in the dog. This may be partly due to the fact that many people just wouldn't notice a slight lameness in a cat, and even if they did they might be inclined to let the creature get on with it as best he could. People go out walking with their dogs, so even the most callous dog owner becomes aware of a limp and has it attended to.

But apart from owners' attitudes it may be that the cat has fewer joint problems because his skeleton has been left alone. Man hasn't stretched or dwarfed the limbs of the cat to any appreciable extent. One painful joint condition that does occur fairly frequently in cats is an inflammation caused by infection introduced by bites or scratches. Don't neglect it lest it become chronic and cause a permanent lameness. Treatment includes complete rest and antibiotics. How do you rest a cat? You stick him in a confined space and keep him there till he's better.

PS: There is an extremely painful form of spinal arthritis caused by overdosing with vitamins. In years gone by cod-liver oil or an exclusive diet of liver was most commonly implicated. Today there are more expensive products that must be used with even greater caution. Many successful breeders suggest that cats fed a varied diet get along perfectly OK without any supplements. Certainly they don't show the distressing symptoms that vets see in those cats that have been overdosed with so-called goodies.

Artificial eyes

Of course it's a terrible thing if an eye has to be removed. But once it's out, it's out, and the cat soon forgets about it. So should you! Be sensible, and don't put your cat through the business of fitting a bit of plastic just to please yourself and impress the neighbours. I can assure you that the cat would sooner leave bad enough alone.

Artificial respiration

A couple of decades ago when I was a student I was admitted, as a visitor, through the back entrance of a veterinary hospital. I was absolutely astonished to see a serious-looking gentleman in a long white coat swinging a cat, back and forth, by its hind legs. He stood with his legs apart, and slowly and methodically was swinging the unconscious animal through a half circle to the full extent of his reach. He was muttering under his breath, 'one, two, three, four' with each swing. At the end of three or four minutes the cat gave a gasp. The white-coated gentleman immediately moved it to a table where an oxygen apparatus was ready to flow. Soon afterwards the cat was blinking at the world which it had almost, but not quite, left.

This primitive method of artificial respiration is effective and is still widely used. You must however be sure that (i) the cat's respiratory distress is due to a genuine accident like drowning or gas, and not to a long-standing condition like pneumonia or pyothorax, (ii) there are no obstructions in the mouth or throat, and (iii) you yourself are not so nervous and upset that you can't swing gently and rhythmically. If you jerk or snap you'll do more harm than good.

With new-born kittens rigorous massaging is often all that's necessary to get them to give that first gasp of life.

With well-loved animals, people who know the method will try the latest popular method – mouth-to-mouth resuscitation.

And, of course, one can always try the simplest method of all. Lay the animal on its side. Press gently down on its chest. In and relax. About fifteen to the minute. Keep it up. As long as you can detect a heart beat there is hope.

Asphyxiation

Cats will fiddle about with anything. Some are quite adept at opening doors and getting into refrigerators and clothes hampers and desks. Some cats learn how to turn a water tap, and others how to turn a tap on a stove. I'm convinced that many cats know all about heaters, and attempt to start them on their own. I've watched my cat hit a heater in disgust after I've turned it off.

Whether by design or accident, the gas gets turned on. If there is an automatic pilot, well and good. If there isn't you come home to the smell of gas and find a distressed animal breathing in short painful gasps. His mouth will be open, and his gums, tongue and eyes will show the blackish blue that means oxygen starvation.

Don't panic. Open the windows first. Then locate the source of the gas and shut it off. Then move the animal to a gas-free room and summon help. Then start applying artificial respiration while whoever comes can get on the phone and locate an open veterinary surgery. Take the collapsed animal to the surgery, because oxygen is what's needed. Few vets carry a tank of the stuff in their bag.

There are, of course, many other causes of asphyxiation. An object in the throat or even an abscess may prevent an animal from getting sufficient air. Open his mouth under a good light. If you can't see and remove the object, get the animal to a vet. Don't apply artificial respiration unless you're sure of the cause of the asphyxiation. If, for example, it were a congestive pneumonia you would be causing pain and hastening death.

Aspirin

You often hear the expressions, 'as safe as an aspirin', or 'it's probably just aspirin that he prescribed'. Aspirin is still one of the most effective pain killers and it is used by millions of people, but whether it's safe or not depends on what you mean by safe. Even table salt can be poisonous if used in such quantities that the body can't handle it. What constant aspirin dosing can do to our bodies I'll leave to the doctors of human medicine to sort out. I will tell you, however, that a daily aspirin for a week can kill some cats. Only recently in the veterinary journals we have been reminded of this. We don't think aspirin is anything like as dangerous for the dog, but it's as well to keep in mind that nobody was meant to be a machine for swallowing and absorbing chemicals.

Whatever drugs you have in your medicine cabinet, think twice before poisoning your pet with them. If the animal is in pain get the animal to a veterinary surgeon and let him find the cause of the pain. *Summary:* An aspirin a day for not too many days can kill your cat.

Atavism

Sometimes a kitten is born who resembles neither parent but some ancestor, more or less remote. The owner thinks there must be something wrong with the 'blood' of one of the parents, and considers either the dam or the sire or both useless for further breeding. Not at all! Try them again, and you'll probably be rewarded with a litter that fulfils all your expectations.

PS: I'm afraid that in these cynical modern times one is forced to re-examine the pedigrees of the parents of atavistic kittens. Many knowledgeable and well-meaning breeders – and some who are neither – profess that their breeding policy is properly programmed even if only a small fraction of the litter is successful. As one scientist commented, 'They would have us equate the phenotype with the genotype.' Roughly translated that means, 'If it looks OK, it is OK.' One might suggest that many generations of theory, observation and experimental proof (both in animals and plants) proves otherwise. In case this comment proves indigestible to non-professional cat breeders, may I simply state that some misguided people are breeding

24

moggies to purebreds. The kittens that look like moggies are discarded. Those that look like purebreds are sold as purebreds. Even the lax Trade Descriptions Act wouldn't swallow that!

Awns

Seeds of grasses and cereals with sharp-pointed ends have a way of insinuating themselves into the spaces of the feet and the orifices of the ears. When the sun shines hot and the crops begin to ripen, take an extra long look at Ginger each time he comes in for dinner. If he's favouring one foot or twitching an ear keep him indoors. When hubby comes home from the pub ask him to hold Old Ginge while you search for the seeds. Give yourself a chance by positioning a strong light and clearing a solid table. Almost always you can find the seeds and remove them easily, provided you do it within a few hours. Later the awns start to travel and it takes a vet, a general anaesthetic and a lot of luck to find the darned things.

Bad breath

Cats live on fish and meat, and as a result their breath is strong. If you can't stand the thought or the smell of digesting meat you can choose a cow, a horse or a hamster, as a pet. You might consider a vegetarian human. I can assure you that nothing you can give or do to your cat will disguise the fact that it's a carnivore. Most people however, can put up with the occasional whiff of bad breath, which is the only unaesthetic characteristic of cats.

Foul breath is another matter, and simply must not be neglected. How can you tell the difference between breath that is merely bad, and breath that is foul? The former is merely disagreeable, but the latter is nauseating. It smells as if something is rotting, and indeed that is what is happening. Open the creature's mouth. You may be confronted with a tooth or teeth that are midway to cheese. Exaggeration? Not at all. We veterinarians see it every day. If the teeth appear healthy, then the foul breath may be caused by diseased kidneys or the indigestion that goes with flu and gastro-enteritis or one of the other infectious diseases. In all those cases professional attention is needed – not next week but that day or the next.

Summary: Bad breath is nothing to worry about. Foul breath is.

Baldness

Cats can get bald patches through fleas or eczemas or burns or just plain old age. If the cause of the baldness is fleas or mange, they grow a nice new coat as the bugs vanish. If the baldness originated with a severe burn or scald, it's unlikely that new hair will grow. The hair follicles have probably been destroyed at their roots.

The baldness of senility is irreversible. Don't let Old Charlie get wet or cold, and don't allow any upstart kitten to usurp his favourite place by the fire. If those bald patches flake or crack, a little olive or cod liver oil might just ease the soreness. Don't use anything stronger without veterinary advice, because whatever you put on will be licked off.

Balinese

I can tell you a lot about this breed because my wife has more of them than anyone outside America.

Firstly they have no more connection with the island of Bali than I do to the Royal Family. Secondly they are Siamese with long coats. Thirdly these mutants crop up everywhere but they were properly promulgated in California by an English-born lady. Fourthly there are a few people who believe they can produce them by crossing Persians or long-haired mongrels with Siamese like people who put Rolls Royce radiators on Fords.

Conclusion: if it ain't a Siamese it ain't a Balinese.

Bandaging

It's not often necessary to bandage a cat, but when it needs doing it needs doing badly, so you might just as well have an idea of how it's done.

Lay out all your materials. You'll need bandages, cotton wool and sticky tape. You'll need scissors, preferably with blunt rather than pointed ends. A pair of pointed scissors in amateur hands can be a dangerous weapon. Try and find a calm assistant, and ask him to keep his mouth shut for the two minutes it will take to do the dressing.

The most important things to remember are that all bandages must be laid flat and even. Wrap firmly but not so tightly that you interfere with circulation. Don't tie knots or use cord. Go well above and below the area you're covering. Cover the lot with sticky tape. Remember that animals have an insatiable desire to lick their wounds, and will claw, lick, bite or rub off a bandage unless they realize it's quite hopeless. We bandage right round the body, limb or head, even if it's only a very small area that needs attention. Socks or bootees on his feet (covered with elastoplast) may divert him from clawing at a bandage. You may have to make an Elizabethan collar if the bandage is round the head.

Ears Pad the ear with cotton wool on either side. Use a lot. Then tape several layers of bandage with alternating rows in front of and behind the opposite ear. Cover with elastoplast or sticky tape. Not too tight or the cat will choke.

Eyes Almost impossible to bandage properly (see *Elizabethan collar*).

Tail Place ointment on the wound. Wrap tightly with many layers of gauze, going well back and well ahead of the wound. Wrap the lot in sticky tape. Use sticky tape to anchor the bandage to the hair at the base of the tail.

Limbs Place tiny bits of cotton wadding between each toe and a large wad under the pad. Use four or five strips of bandage running down the whole limb on one side, under the foot and up the other side. Then wind another couple of layers around the limb. Cover with elastoplast and anchor to hair above wound.

Chest or abdomen Cut a large piece of cloth into a rectangle about 20cm (8 in) wide and about 30cm (12 in) long. Cut little holes in the middle and insert the limbs into the holes. The free sides come up over the back. Cut a couple of strips at each corner. Tie the strips into bow knots over the back. Aren't you clever? You've made a 'many-tailed' bandage. Isn't kitty clever? She's going to get it off before you can get to the vet's, so hurry along, please.

Baskets

A cat when frightened or even surprised will run and hide. That doesn't mean he's a coward at all – merely that he'd like to look over the terrain and choose those conditions most advantageous to his armament (lack of strength but agility and sharp, fast claws). No matter how much your cat loves you at home he'll revert to his primitive survival instinct when away, so don't be a fool and expect him to lie in your arms while trains whistle by and dogs come up ready for battle. Buy a cat basket or improvise with a box. The ideal cat basket is about ten inches high, ten to twelve inches wide and sixteen to eighteen inches long. It should have two runners on the bottom to avoid wear, and it should be ridged at the top so that the air can't be cut off during the journey. The floor should be lined with paper or a blanket so that it's smooth. If it's cold out, cover the outside with a couple of layers of paper (not airtight, of course). If you line the inside the cat will scratch them down. A wee window at both ends sometimes helps to prevent travel sickness. The basket should open at the top for convenience and be strapped right round for strength.

Bathing

Most cats don't need baths because they wash themselves constantly. Some require a bit of help in the form of combing and brushing. Remember that the only place a cat can't get properly clean is the space between its shoulder blades.

Occasionally a cat gets so heavily infested with fleas, lice or ticks that no ordinary insecticide would stand a chance. Sometimes a cat drops into a bucket of paint, creosote or glue. Obviously heroic measures are needed. Fill a flat-bottomed sink or bath tub with 6-7cm of lukewarm water. Put a thick towel on the bottom. Insert Timothy! Soap! Rinse! Drain! Repeat! And rinse thoroughly! Dry thoroughly with many towels (or a hair dryer if Tim will accept it). Then call someone to help you to apply iodine to your minor scratches and bandage the big ones that simply won't stop bleeding.

Here's a safer way of bathing old Tommy Tim. Get a canvas sack. Dump half a package of your favourite soap or detergent inside. Dump Timothy in but keep his head out. Dunk sack in lukewarm water. Up and down! Rub Timothy with folds of sack. Rinse and keep rinsing! Eventually you and Tim will be somewhat tired but somewhat clean.

A little word of caution. If a cat is really covered in some noxious substance don't mess about at home. Often a general anaesthetic is necessary to get the stuff off properly.

Beds

A cat bed should be large enough to let him stretch. It should be of smoothly planed, unpainted wood, tightly joined and easily cleaned. It should be raised a bit off the floor, and should be enclosed on three sides. It should contain an old pillow or a bit of blanket in its own sheet. The sheet can be changed and laundered. The bed should be located in a draught-free part of the house – not just inside an exterior door. The only problem you'll have with the bed is getting the creature to use it. All the cats I know have built-in selectors that tell them exactly the most comfortable place to sleep each night. They think it quite ridiculous to sleep in the same old place night after night. Quite obviously different corners of the house each have their advantages that vary with the weather. Why then bother with a cat bed? I don't, and neither do most cat owners. However, they can be useful during kittenhood. Indeed, most kittens need the security of a permanent bed until they are confident enough to realize that the whole house is theirs. During illness many cats prefer a permanent base and, of course, a mother cat wants to bear and nurse her kittens in her own secluded corner. You'd better confine her to the room where you want her to have the kittens for a day or two before the event. Otherwise you can be quite sure she'll have them on your best quilt.

PS: A rather more expensive but simpler version is as follows: In an old cardboard box place two or three old newspapers. On those place an insulated electric cat blanket. On that place a blanket filled with polystyrene granules. The electric blanket doesn't use a lot of power. Leave it on all the time. You'll find that when the central heating is off or the sun hasn't found a way through your grimy windows the cats will gravitate to the old cardboard box. The box and newspapers are easily replaced. The top blanket must be laundered occasionally. The electric thing will outlast you and the cats.

Bird catchers

I've racked my tired head for a better phrase to describe cats who, to their owners' distress, go out and capture robins, finches and other ornamental birds, and deposit them maimed and dying at their owners' feet as a gift. The cat simply cannot understand the punishment usually meted out. Maybe he hasn't brought home enough dead birds? He goes and repeats the process. I've never heard of a cure that works. Dogs will sometimes be cured by tying a dead bird around their necks, but this is almost impossible with a cat, and probably wouldn't work. Belling a cat, i.e. putting a collar with a bell round their neck, sometimes works, but most cats can learn to stalk without sounding the bell. Besides, a real bird-hunting cat will take to the trees, and a collar is dangerous because it may get caught and strangle him. Let's face it. A cat's natural instinct is to hunt, and the only way to protect the song birds is to confine your cat until the fledglings are old enough to fend for themselves. There are only a few weeks in the spring when birds are at the awkward learning stage and deserve protection. After that let nature's laws rule. One of those laws says that even though cats kill the odd bird they make up for it by killing rodents who would kill many more birds.

Bites and scratches

Most cats will snarl at strange cats, have a heated exchange of profanities and walk away with tails erect and skin and dignity intact. They know full well that in a physical encounter both are likely to end up as losers. Occasionally they get carried away by the power of their own oratory, and they find themselves some moments later shaking with fright and miaowing to be let in among humans.

The humans wonder why the cat has suddenly become so friendly. They don't notice the bit of hair that indicates the site of the damage. For the next eight or ten hours the cat will sleep, which is nature's restorative. When he wakes he will be hungry, and after eating he will start licking the injured area.

In many cases it will be sufficient to clean the wound and so prevent infection, but all too often the broken skin will become the site of a festering sore. It's at this stage that the owners first notice that something is wrong. They usually apply an antiseptic, which is the wrong thing to do. The infection has gone too deep for the antiseptic to penetrate. All it does is to slow down the body's healing powers. The proper thing to do is to bathe the area with salt water, to help draw the infection out. An antiseptic may be of value if applied *before* the scratch has started to fester. Remember you mustn't use carbolic or coal tars or phenols on cats. Dettol, iodine mercurochrome and hydrogen peroxide are all quite safe. Naturally, if it's an extensive wound or in a tricky area such as over the eye or on a joint, veterinary attention is needed. If the wound is small but the cat is off its food or gives any other indication of general illness, you simply must get it treated professionally. The veterinarian will usually clean the area, inject antibiotics and dispense an antibiotic ointment. Remember that whenever an ointment is used it must be used sparingly and the surplus wiped off. Otherwise the cat will lick it and make itself sick.

When a dog bites a cat the injuries are usually severe and just bathing the area isn't good enough. Usually dressings and antibiotics are needed.

If a cat bites or scratches you the commonsense first aid is to wash the area thoroughly. If it's a deep wound better see your doctor. If you're handling strange animals every day your chances of getting bitten or scratched are pretty good. Don't forget your tetanus shots. If you're working in quarantine quarters you should be done for rabies as well. Don't worry. Modern shots may not be completely painless but untoward reactions are highly unlikely. If you or the doctor suspects that you are hypersensitive you may be accorded a seat in the waiting room for a boring hour or two while your body absorbs the stuff.

Some people react with great swellings to even the slightest cat scratch. They are best advised to keep a cat that doesn't scratch.

Finally, there is a specific virus disease of humans called cat scratch fever. If I thought I had it I'd see my doctor. I advise you to do the same.

Bladder

This is the bag that stores urine inside the body until it's convenient to get rid of it. Your ideas of convenience may differ from those of your cat. Those differences are usually reconciled by house-training. In the cat that's usually a simple matter of pointing out the tray or opening a door to the garden.

Most cats, once they get the idea, are fastidious to the bursting point. Also they prefer to keep their private business private. Therefore a condition which would be noticed within hours in a dog often goes for days in a cat before its owner notices that something is wrong.

There are two common conditions which may mess up the bladder of a cat. One is cystitis, which simply means inflammation of the bladder. The cat may dribble small quantities fairly frequently. It may continue to strain after it has finished. It may give a small squeal of pain while it's urinating, and it may constantly lick at its hind end. The urine itself may smell badly, or it may be tinged with blood.

Some vets say that the condition is seen more commonly in spayed females.

As it's a painful condition your vet should be notified within hours. Remember it's probably gone on for days before you noticed it. He'll decide if it's a simple cystitis or if it's secondary to an infection elsewhere. He may attempt to press out a small amount of urine, which he'll test. He'll inaugurate a course of antibiotics and urinary antiseptics. In most cases he'll discharge the patient as cured within a fortnight.

The other common affliction is bladder stones, and, as you know, many species of animals and many people may have pain and blockages caused by these accumulations.

No one seems to know why these deposits form in the urine, but form they do. In the cat they're usually very small sandy bits. Sometimes as much as a teaspoonful of the stuff might accumulate in the bladder without causing a stoppage. In fact the female cat may form

31

a fair bit of sand, but because of her relatively large urethra it seldom causes trouble. The male, however, has a very tiny passage in its penis through which the urine must travel. It doesn't take much in the way of solid material to plug it up tight. Strain as he will, the cat cannot urinate. The bladder may get so full that it seems to fill the abdominal cavity and swell the cat. Handle it gently! Any localized pressure might burst the bladder.

In other words, if your male cat seems to be swelling up or if he is straining don't mess about with any home treatment. It is a painful and dangerous condition, and requires early professional treatment. It is one of the few conditions of cats that are definitely an emergency.

The veterinary surgeon will pass a gentle hand over the animal, and confirm that in fact the bladder is distended. He might examine the penis and see if a bit of bathing won't loosen the plug that's blocking it. Usually, though, he'll give a general anaesthetic and try to pass a tiny silver catheter. Sometimes he'll try to blast the plug with an injection of water directed through a minute needle. Occasionally all his efforts are in vain, and the urine must be released by puncturing directly into the bladder, but this is used only as a last resort. The cat must be given antibiotic injections daily. If the blockage recurs the whole treatment is repeated.

The animal will probably be kept on 'kidney' pills for the rest of its days.

Now for a few general observations. Some claim that the condition occurs more commonly in neutered males than in full toms. That may be because we see more neutered males. Others say that the condition is more likely to occur in males who are neutered at the age of two or three months rather at five or six months. In any case a cat who is neutered later is said to develop 'more bone'. Horse breeders, as you may know, like to wait a full year before having their colts gelded for this very reason. I wouldn't advise holding off on your toms till this age, but five or six months seems a fair compromise.

But no matter what you do and whether the tom is neutered or otherwise, the condition occurs all too often. You should be aware of it and learn to recognize its symptoms because it is so distressing. After the emergency treatment is outlined, before your vet will discuss with you the need and the possibility of further operations he may, if chemical tests prove the 'sand' to be a particular sort, ask you to add one per cent salt to the cat's diet. This makes it drink much more and thereby keeps the bladder flushed, but it's dangerous to use this method except under veterinary supervision.

Sadly, if the condition keeps recurring and causing increasing distress, there is only one humane solution.

Fractures or dislocations of the spine or the tail may be accompanied by paralysis of the bladder with distention and incontinence. This is quite a common complication. The cat may appear OK; he can use his hind legs but his tail and bladder are paralysed. These cases are usually quite hopeless.

PS: It has now been proved to the satisfaction of many practising veterinarians and by some leading veterinary researchers that dried foods are a major contributing factor in many cases. Those of us who believe this to be true advise our cat owning clients not to feed the stuff. Certainly in the case of neutered male cats and all cats who have had kidney or bladder trouble I tell my clients to give their supply to the dogs or chickens. Those species generally drink enough water to flush the system. May I save the manufacturers a postage stamp? Every time I say what I've just said, they write me threatening legal letters. All I can say is that it's my opinion. My clients and readers are perfectly free to buy the stuff and feed it to their cats. It's not me that's spending millions advertising. As the song says, 'Go AHEAD and SUE ME.' The publicity may make more people aware of the fact that many vets have reservations about the feeding of dry foods to cats.

Blue long-hairs

I single out this Persian breed for special attention because (a) it's probably the most popular breed of long-haired cats anywhere, (b) it can be a magnificent creature and a most affectionate pet, (c) some people claim it's a type indigenous to Persia and indeed to Khorassan province, (d) it has been demonstrably changed in the last fifty years by selective breeding, and (e) it can sometimes be, at its show best, one of the rare examples of how man can mess up nature's most perfect animal.

Please stifle your screams of rage and don't write those letters of protest. I know as well as you that the Blue is beautiful, lovable and loving. I know too how his square knit, cobby body is a marvel of physiological perfection. But why, oh why, in the name of all that's sane must his head be squashed into such an unhealthy square? He used not to have a punched-in nose. His tear ducts used to work. But now, the shorter and the squarer the head, the better Blue he's supposed to be. Oh I know there are lots of champion Blues who can breathe and who don't have runny eyes. But will you admit there are more about in the last few years who live unhealthy lives because the head is altogether too short?

I don't think the breeders have gone too far – yet. But they're on the road. Every show of Blue long-hairs should have a big notice saying: These are cats – not Pekinese!

Maybe some of you don't know what a Blue Persian is. It's a long-haired cat with a stubby body and a blue coat. Years ago the blue was a rather dark shade. Today one sees more lilac and pastel blues. Some authorities claim that the Blue Persian originated in Persia. Some say it was the accidental result of the mating of a white with a black. I don't suppose it really matters if both statements are true.

Do you think cat breeders are crazy because they often concentrate on colour to the exclusion of other qualities? I think so. But my father and my grandfather did just that, and they were cattlemen.

In one of the family attics at home there is a big old photograph of a carload of steers that won a ribbon at the Chicago International some thirty or forty years ago. 'Blue steers,' my father used to say, 'every damn one of 'em. White Shorthorn Bull and Black Angus Cows. Best — steers they ever seen in Sheecago.'

'How did they dress out?' I'd ask.

'Hell, boy. How would I know? I wasn't eating 'em. I was showing 'em.'

PS: Time marches on but some cat breeders go backwards. And they use giant steps. One used to compare the worst sort of Blue Persian to tiny Pekinese. Today one is hard put to find a Peke as deformed as many Blue long-hairs. The eyes squint. The jaws don't meet. They simply can't breathe through the tiny orifices called a nose. What would be my advice to anyone who wanted a Blue long-haired kitten? Buy a share in any nationalized industry. You can be sure it will be a disaster but millions will share your losses.

And my advice to the breeders of these monstrosities? Advertise the faults! Surely you must be conscious of the misery suffered by families who in all good faith buy a pedigree kitten and lavish all their love only to discover that there's no way it can lead a normal life. If you think that's all right, why not tell people about it? Or breed healthy kittens.

I'm not being unkind. Maybe I only see the tragedies. I'll retract this statement with apologies when I stop seeing so many.

Blue-Smoke

A rather rare long-haired breed in which the light silvery hairs of the ruff of the neck, the tufts of the ears and the flanks and sides contrast with the dark shading of the back and the deep black of the face and head. The show standards of this breed are the same as those of the Smoke, except that where the colouring is black on the Smoke it's blue on the Blue-Smoke.

Like the Smoke the Blue-Smoke is a 'manufactured' breed, in so far as it occurs rarely by accident but is produced by all the artifices and skill of the dedicated breeder. They must have been more skilled or more dedicated seventy years ago, because apparently there were many good specimens about in those days. Today one seldom sees a top Smoke, and a perfect Blue-Smoke is a real rarity.

Boarding kennels

This is being written as the holiday season is drawing to a close. As far as cats are concerned, what happens during their owners' vacation shouldn't happen to a dog. For two or three weeks they are placed in prison. Instead of a wide choice of pillows and sofas they have a choice between a slatted floor and a hard rubber mat. Their exercise area is restricted. Familiar faces don't appear. They can't escape unwelcome attention. The food is boring.

Boarding establishments vary widely. Some are under-capitalized and over-optimistic. Their owners think they can make a fortune by stuffing a decrepit hen-house full of cats. Many are old-established concerns with well-planned kennels, individual outdoor runs, spotless kitchens and experienced staff. Between these two extremes you can find all sorts of places to choose among. Generally (but not always) the price is an indication of the quality.

If you are no judge of people or value you might ask your husband or a businessman friend to inspect the place before leaving your cat. He might know nothing about cats, but he will be able to recognize a well-run place when he sees it. Are there two or three animals in one cage? Is there stale food in the dish? Is there a smell of rotting food or urine? Are the attendants wearing dirty smocks? Are any of the cats sneezing? Are the sanitary trays caked with filth? Is there fresh water in every cage? Is there a refrigerator in the kitchen? And, as important as any of these, do the staff and management like animals? Believe it or not, I know a man responsible for the running of a large animal welfare organization who tried a couple of years ago to economize by shutting off the lights in the kennels. The kennels had no windows.

The staff protested that the animals would be in darkness except when they were being cleaned or fed. The man said, 'They sleep all the time anyway, and they wouldn't know the difference.' The shocked faces of the staff told him what they thought, although they wouldn't dare put it in words. No more was heard about it, and the lights stayed on.

You find the kennel. You pay your deposit, and when the day comes you drop off your cat. Leave a favourite pillow or sweater so that he won't feel altogether strange. Don't inundate the kennel people with a list of favourite foods. It's a good opportunity to un-spoil your pet. He may be too fussy or too homesick for the first day or two, but soon he'll be rubbing at the front of the cage every time the attendant comes by.

Now there are some cats that simply should not be put in kennels. Old cats, say those of twelve and up, should not be boarded out. It may be all right if they've been going to the same place for five or six years. They know what to expect. They know it'll all end in a couple of weeks, and they've probably got resistance to the germs that thrive where cats congregate in closed quarters. But I think it's very, very risky to put an old cat in kennels for the first time. Their home habits are fixed. They'll simply pine away in the unfamiliar and often noisy surroundings. They may succumb to any mild infection that is going around, and in an old cat a mild infection becomes a serious infection.

Secondly, cats who have recently recovered from an illness should not be put in boarding kennels. They may still be capable of giving the disease to other cats, and, more important from their own point of view, their resistance will be low. They're bound to pick up anything that's going, no matter how well run the kennels are.

Thirdly, if your cat has never been allowed out of doors you are really asking for trouble if you put him in kennels. He has absolutely no resistance to anything, and stands a very good chance of coming down with flu or worse.

Finally, young kittens and purebred cats of any breed (but particularly Siamese, Burmese and Abyssinians) are special risks. They should certainly be inoculated at least one month before they go into kennels. As a matter of fact, that isn't a bad idea with any cat.

Now I simply must warn you that no matter how ideal the conditions are, it's almost impossible to run a commercial boarding cattery year after year without having an outbreak of disease sometimes. I've heard some brilliant people claim otherwise, only to hear them eat their words later. One I know is a clever businesswoman, a top veterinarian and a devoted cat lover. She spared neither time nor money getting her cattery laid out beautifully. All that science and experience could offer was used. Every cat was inoculated one month before admission. Temperatures were taken on the day of admission. Anything running a fever or showing signs of illness was refused. Daily rounds were done. Anything that was 'off' was immediately isolated. Yet even that cattery had to close while it was being disinfected after an outbreak of disease.

Am I trying to put you off boarding your cat? Not at all. Each summer thousands and thousands of cats spend a period in kennels without harm. Most come back better than they went in. But each summer some people are shocked and horrified when they return from holiday to be told that their cat has died in kennels. Dozens of people pick up their cats and find that he's a sniffling, stinking, walking skeleton. They immediately rush to the conclusion that the boarding people have been negligent. They rush off to their veterinarians and telephone their lawyers. I always explain to those distraught people that in fact the kennel people have probably been up night after night nursing the whole lot. They have probably spent a small fortune on veterinary fees and drugs and extra staff, and they probably will go in the red that year. I explain firmly that I will have nothing to do with a law-suit, and that everybody has lost by the experience. The real loser is the cat, and the only concern should be to get it better.

What do I do with my own cat during my annual exodus to the sun? I tell the four or five neighbours whom he normally condescends to visit that I'm going away. I give one of them the special privilege of feeding him every day, and tell the others that they can have the pleasure of his presence on any sofa or bed he chooses to inhabit. The first time it happened I returned to find that my sleek and active flatmate had turned into a waddling balloon. He woke only to go begging. It took two months of disciplining him and the neighbours to get his belly off the ground. Needless to say, we weren't on speaking terms during that period. His attitude was, 'The only reason I stay at all is because I find it too much of a bore to move.'

The point of the story is that if you leave the cat with friends, or if you have neighbours who come in to feed the cat, leave complete and detailed instructions. These should include not only the things to feed, but the amounts and the times. It doesn't hurt to leave your veterinarian's card with the neighbour just in case there is a problem.

Finally, an increasing number of people solve the cat problem during holidays by offering their homes rent free to anyone who will look after the animals. You'd better get animal lovers with good references. I think it's fairly simple to find people who will look after the animals properly. But the temptation of throwing a party in a strange house is too strong for most of us. A party, to be successful these days, must end with at least two dozen people unconscious under what was once a house. There's no doubt that your cat will enjoy it all tremendously. The question is, will you?

PS: Some hints for owners and managers:

1 If there is any possible escape route you can be sure a cat will find it.

2 One must impress on new staff that the one unforgivable sin is allowing a cat to escape.

3 All visitors, including children, friends of staff, inspectors and meter readers must not be allowed unless accompanied by experienced staff.

4 No outside pets allowed to visit, however briefly. They may be carrying insect passengers or fleas. In any event they'll upset the regulars.

5 Boarders who arrive loose must be placed in proper baskets immediately.

6 People who say they are going to delegate a friend to phone or visit daily while they themselves are on holiday are better told to find an establishment they can trust. Nice ones can be told the truth. You'd rather spend the time looking after the cat.

7 If the first (and often only) telephone query is 'How much do you charge?' it's easier to say you're fully booked. Use the same answer for people who want to leave their cat for Christmas Day because the mother-in-law who usually looks after it has a puncture in her wheel-chair.

8 On the other hand, people who want to know every detail about the size of cages, the diet, heating and veterinary arrangements are usually concerned about their pets and turn out to be worth-while and trouble-free customers. Provided you tell the whole truth.

9 Don't try to compete with the cheapest. Try to be the best.

10 Regular hours for deposit and pick-up are not only more convenient for management but are much appreciated by cats in residence. They say to themselves, 'I can hear visitors arriving. It must be ten o'clock.' How would you like your own napping routine interrupted at capricious intervals?

11 Don't worry overmuch about the owner's list of dietary cat fads, unless prescribed by their vet. Few cats eat the first day in kennels if they're not familiar with the place. About one in ten refuse food the second day. If they refuse on the third day try with a mouthful of something really special. Once they start eating they find it difficult to stop. Then switch to the routine diet.

12 If the owner requests heat it's usually because the cat is used to it. Provide it around the clock or not at all. Otherwise you can be sure somebody will forget to turn the switch at the appropriate time.

13 One should only provide a small heated bed with preferably a polystyrene granule-filled blanket. The rest of the cage and run needs no heat – but much of it should be protected from the elements. The cat can choose for itself. Elderly and indolent cats may spend most of their time in bed.

14 Many successful establishments make a minimum charge equivalent to three nights' stay even if the boarder is only in for one night. The reason is that the time spent on reception, collection, scrubbing the cage, disinfecting utensils and bookwork doesn't vary much with the length of stay.

15 Conversely many people are surprised that there is no reduction for long stays. Of course every cat is an individual and reacts differently but most start to get a bit bored after six or eight weeks. Unless given extra attention they simply pine away. After a year or two (I knew one hapless boarder whose ultimate home was decided only after three years of divorce litigation) they require real coddling. And time these days is money.

16 A couple of hours of soft background music at dusk helps many house-orientated cats settle down comfortably for the night.

17 Long-haired cats require daily grooming. Neglected cases may require a general anaesthetic by the vet and two hours or more of careful trimming and combing by an experienced attendant. Ask your accountant how much you have to charge to avoid losing money.

18 Don't accept telephone bookings. Say you'll send them a form. They send it back with a non-returnable deposit and the certificate of inoculation against enteritis. Don't accept any cat whose owner claims, 'It's had its jabs but we never got a certificate.' The 'jabs' may have been antibiotics for an abscess.

19 State in big writing on the form that any cat sneezing or showing any signs of flu will not be admitted under any circumstances. If their owners have a valid certificate showing that the cat has been inoculated against cat flu I would be doubly vigilant. One virulent

carrier can wipe out your business. And cause incredible suffering to perfectly innocent cats.

20 The first commandment must be: 'Thou shalt not keep too many cats in too small a place.' The temptation in high season is to accept just one or two more than the place can properly accommodate. It works in hotels that cater for people. Those that don't like being crowded can complain. Cats suffer in silence. But you can be sure that if you return Sniffly Sarah rather than Sleek Sylvia, her owner's husband will be a heavyweight boxer who doesn't believe in litigation.

Bonemeal

One of the many by-products made by the people who spare us the job of slaughtering our animals is bonemeal. They grind and cook, or maybe they cook and then grind, all the leftover bones. They make two sorts. The fertilizing one is cheaper and smells. The feeding kind should be clearly labelled 'suitable for animal consumption'.

Cats who refuse milk will benefit from a pinch or two of the stuff two or three times a week. Growing kittens, pregnant and lactating females, and fracture cases should have a pinch every day. How big a pinch? The label should tell you. Generally it's somewhat less than a teaspoonful. Sprinkle it on the meat, or mix it through the food.

Bonemeal in quantities up to a tablespoonful (or even two if the cat will take it) is a useful 'binder' in mild cases of diarrhoea. Needless to say, you don't try it for a couple of months before getting the animal professional attention. If the motions aren't firming next day go and see the nasty vet with the horrid needles.

PS: It still has all its old virtues but it's becoming almost impossible to buy. The finely ground stuff called boneflour is obviously just as good but cats don't like it unless it's really well mixed with the food. Why not get an attachment for your cake mixer and grind your own?

Bones

I don't know if cats are more sensible than dogs, or if cat owners are more sensible than dog owners. I suspect that both are true. In fact, we veterinarians are seldom confronted with cats who have bowel stoppages or worse because they've been eating bones. Occasionally we're presented with a cat who is in great distress because it has a bone lodged in its mouth or throat. Usually the poor beast is drooling, shaking or pawing at its head, or making pitiful attempts to retch the thing out.

If it's in the mouth, wedged between the teeth, it's usually just a second's work to pull it out. One gets the forceps laid out first, and then a strong light focused on the area where you hope to hold the cat. One person holds the struggling front legs. The other pries open the jaw, looks and fishes. If one quick dart with the forceps doesn't get it, then an anaesthetic is necessary. That is because the cat is in such a panic anyway that a prolonged struggle would just wedge the bone more solidly. Under general anaesthetic it's simple to extract a bone that's in the mouth or the upper throat. Those that get lodged lower down require surgery of a rather skilled order, because the whole area is full of arteries and veins and nerves all placed there to prove that the vet slept while the anatomy professor lectured.

Repetition: If you suspect that your cat has a bone in its mouth get a strong light, tweezers or pliers and an assistant to hold the cat. Pry its jaws open and locate the bone. Then you and the cat and the assistant relax for a moment. Then take the tweezers in your right hand, open the upper jaw with your left and grab the bone. If you can't get it take the cat to the vet.

Brandy

This is probably the most important medicine in your feline first aid cabinet. I know that it's the only thing I've ever found in those cabinets that really helps one, particularly if it's been a long hard day. But please (and I'm being serious now) don't give it to your cat unless you've got clearance from your veterinarian. Why? Well, most people give brandy to an older cat which has collapsed. One of the common causes of collapse to an older cat is dehydration (drying out) caused by kidney disease. Brandy at that time can do nothing but harm.

Bread

Outside France white bread is nasty stuff. Cats have to be very hungry before they'll glue their insides with the stuff. Good quality bread made from unbleached flour will interest some cats, particularly if it's toasted. They like the crunchy quality. However, bread (like biscuits and crackers) is primarily a titbit or a light breakfast. The cats I know take a half-hearted bite out of sheer boredom.

Burmese

There are at least four different theories about the origin of the Burmese breed of cat, but everyone agrees that the following two

41

statements are true. First, you would be very lucky if you found a Burmese cat in Burma; and secondly, the Burmese breed was developed in America.

Anyway, Burmese are an oriental or Siamese-looking beast, which is to say they are long, lithe and slim, with pointed heads, large pricked ears and slanty yellow eyes.

There are three main differences between the Siamese and Burmese breeds. The most obvious is colour. The Burmese is (as an adult) a uniform seal brown. It may shade slightly lighter on the chest and belly, and may shade slightly darker on the ears, mask and points, but it's a delicate subtle shading and there is never a dramatic contrast. In other words, the Burmese is brown.

Secondly, the Burmese is closer to what cat fanciers consider the ideal oriental type than are most of the Siamese we see today. This is probably because there are almost no back-street dealer-breeders of Burmese. Burmese enthusiasts have been vigilant in preserving the almond-shaped slanting eyes, the svelte, dainty but firm body and the slightly higher hind legs that all contribute to the breed's extraordinary attractiveness.

Thirdly, the Burmese is a more civilized cat than the Siamese. I mean that he fits into civilized society better. He's less likely to scratch the furniture to pieces or pull the curtains down, and, more important, he's just not as noisy as the Siamese. A calling Burmese queen can get you your eviction notice, but at all other times most Burmese won't keep the neighbours awake.

Otherwise Burmese have the aggressively friendly manners of their Siamese cousins, and all the other subtler Siamese attributes. The two breeds get along well together, so you can keep one of each while you decide which you prefer.

And in case brown isn't really your colour, I can tell you without violating any confidences that Burmese now come in a rainbow assortment which includes torties, champagnes and other subtle variations that experts spend hours discussing. So why not get a colour to match your wallpaper? I think your chances of getting a trouble-free brown are better simply because there are more of them about.

Buying hints:

1 Don't buy from a shop. Buy from the breeder!
2 Never, no matter how sorry you feel for it, buy the runt of the litter.
3 If a breeder has one kitten left over in a litter, he or she will often

sell it at a reduced price just to 'clear up the loose ends'. This may well be a genuine bargain.

4 If you're not very sure of yourself (and who ever is?) insist on a second opinion before finalizing the contract. If it's a question of breeding points, ask another breeder. If it's a question of the kitten's health, ask your veterinarian. If the vendor balks, go elsewhere. After all, you're buying a creature that's going to be a part of your life for all of its.

5 Don't look for bargains (except the kind you may possibly get under hint 3 above). The few pennies you save can be eaten up by a couple of veterinary visits. And, more important, you are encouraging back-alley breeders to stay in the business.

6 Never, never, never take any living creature on a trial basis. Within twenty-four hours you'll be committed to it irrevocably and, as the saying goes, for better or for worse.

PS: I'm afraid some strictly commercial breeders have moved in with a vengeance. And you can hardly blame other breeders who started with enthusiastic idealism who have decided that they, too, can use the money. I'm not passing judgement on people. This book is about cats. The fact is, however, that financial circumstances change. One leading Burmese breeder I know was supported in her endeavours for many years by her husband. I know for a fact that he loved the cats. I assume he loved her as well. He became ill and very quickly became a liability. The cats graduated from a hobby to a business. Inevitably standards deteriorated. Sad to say but today I'd be even more wary about buying a Burmese than a Blue Persian.

I think my major complaint is that queens who are obviously neurotic and who would never have been bred twenty years ago are being used to satisfy the insatiable top end of the so-called pet market.

Caesarian section

An almost commonplace operation today compared to thirty years ago. With the improvements in feline anaesthesia and surgical techniques there's very little risk in the operation provided the queen is brought along within a few hours of her first futile strainings. So, please don't watch her trying until the small hours of the morning and then decide you need help. If a queen starts straining, or if you see the waterbag and a half-hour later there's still no kitten, you'd better telephone your vet and explain the situation. Remember, few veterinary establishments keep a surgical team on tap around the clock. It may take an hour or two to round the boys up and brew some strong coffee.

Sometimes it's not possible to save the kittens, and sometimes the surgeon finds such a putrid mess inside that he removes the entire uterus in order to save the life of the cat. You pretty much have to leave both these decisions to your vet.

The stitches come out in about ten days' time. The kittens' eyes are opening about then, and they're getting to be lively little brutes. Make sure their claws are trimmed so they can't open up the incision. *PS:* Now it's considered a much quicker and easier operation to remove the lot while doing a 'Caesar'. Quite obviously most surgeons would rather finish it once and for all. It saves at least one row of stitches and reduces the risk of internal infection. If you have a queen whose lines you reckon highly you must say very clearly to the nurses that if at all possible you want to breed her again. Provided the surgeon agrees that the queen will be able to produce further litters he'll sweat the extra three minutes required.

Calcium

Necessary for proper bone formation and particularly important for growing kittens and pregnant and nursing queens. Feral cats get their calcium from bones. Many modern animal nutritionists tell us that we should allow our domestic cats to decide which bones they can chew and swallow and which are dangerous. Most people though prefer not to take any chances, and they scrupulously fillet everything before it goes into the feeding dish. I won't argue with them but I must point out that unless the cat is drinking lots and lots of milk it is probably deficient in calcium. As most orientals won't touch milk, they, even more than other cats, need calcium supplements. In what form? You can get pills or high-priced supplements, but good old-fashioned bonemeal (q.v.) is as good as anything. This is particularly important for kittens from weaning (or before) right through to adulthood.

Calico

Isn't it a nice word? The Americans use it a lot. What they mean is tortoiseshell and white.

Canker

Many people think this is a specific disease of the ears for which there is a specific cure. They are encouraged in this belief by a

44

multitude of products widely advertised as canker cures. Some are powders, others are pills and the rest are ointments and lotions. The only things they have in common are the optimism with which they're advertised and the cheapness of their manufacture. It would appear that you can throw almost anything into a bottle, advertise it as a canker cure and find a ready sale. It's even more ludicrous when you consider that the disease it's supposed to cure doesn't exist. What is canker? It's simply ear trouble. A cat may get a seed or a fly trapped in its ear. It may have ear mites. It may get bitten on the ear by another cat. It may have an abscess in its ear. To the uninitiated and to the selfish drug pedlar all these conditions are canker. What good can you do if you pour powder down an ear that has an abscess? None at all, and you may inflict pain and postpone recovery. Obviously you must find out the cause of the trouble before you attempt treatment (see *Ears*).

Cannibalism

Cats who aren't used to constant human companionship may eat their own litters if disturbed while whelping or shortly afterwards. So don't disturb a cat which has just given birth. If you can't bear the suspense arrange a peep-hole some days in advance of the blessed event, but really you'd do best to imitate the mink and fox breeders. They stay away and hope for the best. I'm not suggesting that you should just leave a semi-wild cat all to herself. She may have need of human help. But if she goes off into a corner of the garage, don't approach or disturb her. If a few minutes or a couple of hours later you hear the tiny sounds that mean kittens, or if you catch a glimpse of them from a distance, then all's well. If you approach them all you're doing is disturbing the female just to satisfy your own curiosity.

PS: I'm happy to say that I'm reinforced in this advice by a conversation I overheard between my wife and an elderly cat breeder.

Wife, 'What sex are they?'

Cat breeder, 'Good heavens! They're only four weeks old. If there's one thing I've learned in sixty years of breeding it is never to look at a litter until they come and look at you.'

Carbolic acid and coal tar derivates

These should never be used on cats. If accidentally spilled on a cat, dilute the stuff by pouring on lots and lots of water and washing the whole lot off. If accidentally swallowed, pour strong salt water or mustard down the cat's throat to make it vomit. Wear gloves while you get on with the job because speed is important and there's no time for subtleties.

Carthusian

France is such a strange country. Not only do they speak French but they have a unique cat. Other breeds are rash upstarts by comparison. The Carthusian, or Chartreuse, was known and described as a distinct type two centuries ago.

It's a massive, strong, well-muscled cat with a broad jowly head and yellow to orangy gold eyes. His coat is short, and so dense that it's almost woolly. It's all one shade of either grey, grey-blue or blue.

In the home he's a gentle, affectionate, slow-moving creature. Although he always seems to be in repose he's an energetic and courageous ratter. Oh yes, a cat does need courage to catch and kill a rat. Some rats have killed cats. In fact, some people say that a cat who has a full-time job as a rat catcher is unlikely to survive three years!

Don't confuse the Carthusian with the Russian Blue (which is really a slim Siamesey sort of cat) or with the British short-hair Blue. The latter has a closer, finer coat, and a body that, though strong and closely knit, is neither so massive nor so well muscled as the French. But it's the Carthusian's huge 'bull' head which puts him unmistakably in a class of his own.

You can't spend very long in France without seeing a Carthusian. You could live years in Britain and not be aware of the existence of the breed. How wide is that Channel?

Castration

The removal of the testicles from the male. In England it's more polite to refer to the operation as 'neutering'. In farming districts everywhere it's called 'cutting', or sometimes 'gelding' or 'geldering' by people who don't mind ugly words.

When the testicles are taken out the animal gradually loses its male characteristics. Tom cats start to smell like tom cats when they are four or five months old. Their urine has a strong, penetrating odour. A week or so after the operation they lose this smell and the other subtler attributes of masculinity.

What are the advantages of keeping a castrated rather than an entire tom? First, he won't stink up the place. Until you've smelt an area in which tom cats urinate you can't properly appreciate what a blessing this can be.

Secondly, many tom cats spray their urine. They can be lavish or discriminating depending on their mood. I have seen big, strong, sensible men throw away a mattress rather than try to deodorize it after a tom has used it to advertise his presence. Neutered toms can have unpleasant lapses, but generally they are easily and completely housetrainable. Those lapses, when they do occur, are never as disastrous as those of the tom.

Thirdly, tom cats who are not caged will spend much of their time out roaming the neighbourhood looking for obliging females. They will come home between adventures to stoke up on food and sleep.

Fourthly, tom cats get into fights with other tom cats, and, as you know, they can't win them all. Every other tom cat a veterinarian sees is torn or bleeding, or abscessing as a result of a fight. One sees some remarkable old toms, so scarred and mutilated that you wonder if they have any recuperative powers left at all. A few stitches, a couple of shots of penicillin, and they're ready to hit the trail.

Why aren't all tom cats neutered? Obviously the best of the pure-breds are kept for breeding purposes. These are the royalty of the cat world. They live in semi-confinement, but are available for public viewing or stud. Their prime purpose in life is to propagate what the cat breeders in their collective wisdom consider desirable characteristics.

The vast majority of tom cats are left as toms simply because they're wild and wily enough to escape human interference. These are the cats born under the floorboards on farms, timber-yards, factories and docks. They'll accept food and even friendship – but at a distance, and only when they're quite sure of an escape route. They are in fact wild animals, and their domestication requires almost as much patience as that needed to befriend the undomesticated species. Friends who have succeeded tell me it's worth the effort. They gain a friend who is affectionate but not dependent, and they are privileged to observe the daily life of one of the few creatures that haven't been degraded by skyscrapers, automobiles and tin cans.

A small minority of people keep tom cats as pets through ignorance. In the slums of all big cities many people just don't know about castrating cats. If you explain the advantages they are only too willing to have it done.

An even smaller minority of people keep tom cats as pets in the city because they have thought it all out and think it is the right thing to do.

What are the medical advantages of keeping a tom cat? Some

veterinarians believe they are less prone to bladder stones, but this is difficult to prove statistically. One thing that *is* certain is that tom cats don't have as many skin complaints as neutered toms. Neutered toms, like neutered females, often get eczema – and severe, long-lasting eczema for which one can find no reason. Some of these respond to hormones, and for this reason we must assume that the condition is related to the lack of sexual organs. Fortunately these 'non-specific' eczemas occur in a small minority of neutered animals.

Some people believe that neutering a tom makes him fat and lazy. This is nonsense. Overfeeding makes any animal fat. A neutered tom on a proper diet can maintain his trim figure into old age. Laziness and sleeping in the heat are attributes of all cats. A tom is more likely to spend his time at home resting than is his neutered brother. He has more reason to.

As patients on the table, I prefer toms to neutered males or females. The tom is tough, patient and usually cooperative. One rarely sees a nervous, jumpy tom. They know they are ill, and seem to understand that they must undergo the indignity of the examination and the painful job of the needle. They will almost never scratch or bite without giving you fair warning. I wish I could say the same of all feline patients.

As in-patients tom cats are quite unacceptable. They upset the other patients. They cause employees to resign. Their noise drops real estate values in the locality. It's impossible to rid the place of their stink even after they leave. For the same reason it's almost impossible to find a boarding establishment willing to take a tom.

To sum up, it is more convenient and sensible for most people to have their tom cats neutered.

Tom cats can be castrated at any age. The operation itself is simple enough when done on a young animal. At about three months of age each testicle is little larger than a pea. A clean incision over each sac, a slight pull, and it's done. Even in very young toms the law now requires that a general anaesthetic be administered by a qualified veterinary surgeon before the operation is performed.

In some young toms only one testicle descends. Veterinarians usually advise waiting for some weeks to see if the other one will come down on its own. If it doesn't, a rather complex abdominal operation is indicated. Although it's a serious operation it must be done, because monorchid cats, as they are called, can be misery itself. They have all the disadvantages of the full tom, and none of the advantages. There is absolutely no point in removing the one testicle that has descended and leaving the other inside. In other words, wait for both to come down. If one stays inside, arrange for the operation.

After six months the operation itself requires much more skill and care. The testicles are much larger then, and their blood supply must be carefully tied off, or the animal may haemorrhage and die.

After the operation he should be kept indoors for two or three days and encouraged to drink lots of fluids. There are no skin stitches to come out, so return visits aren't necessary unless your vet tells you.

Gradually the male hormones will disappear from his body, and he will become a true neuter. He will no longer forgo food and comfort in order to follow the female in heat. He won't consider other toms as deadly rivals. His old scars will heal over.

Some toms who are neutered late in life never give up the wandering habit. They've forgotten what it was they were looking for, but they keep on looking all the same.

Catgut

This is the stuff that surgeons use when they want sutures that will dissolve in the body. Catgut is made from the intestines of sheep. These strands of sheep gut were originally used as strings on an Italian musical instrument called a kit, which was a sort of a Model T violin. Kitgut doesn't really sound right, so they started calling it catgut. Lord Lister was the surgeon who first used the stuff, and no one has come up with anything better.

Catmint, catnip

Nepeta cataria is the scientific name of an Asian plant that grows well in both Britain and America. It has a hairy, grey stem, stalked leaves and white down or fuzz over all. Its delicate white, crimson-dotted flowers appear midsummer.

The stems and leaves contain a chemical called nepetalactone which cats absolutely adore. They love to roll in it and get their fur covered in it. They don't seem to want to eat the stuff. Some people say that it has an aphrodisiac effect on cats but most authorities say it just makes them feel jolly and gay. It has the same effect on all cats right from lions down to stray tabbies. It can be used to entice and capture wild cats or move caged cats from one cage to another. It is incorporated in various playthings made for cats like rubber mice. Cats can be trained to use a scratching post by putting catmint in holes drilled into a post or board.

Catteries

The essentials are light, freedom from draught with good ventilation, dryness, a source of heat (not kerosene heaters or other spillable inflammables), and adequate space. An outdoor run (properly enclosed) is not absolutely necessary, but for lengthy visits or for permanent boarders ensures good health. A space between each kennel and run minimizes the risk of disease spreading. Cats don't mind at all living among dogs (provided there's a solid partition between them) and it's a good idea from the disease point of view to alternate dogs and cats in a boarding set up. Before you build it's a good idea to visit and if possible work for a week or two in a well established cattery (see also *Boarding kennels*).

PS: May I modify those opinions? I now think that dogs and cats don't mix well in a boarding establishment. The reason may be as simple as the fact that dogs bark. Cats, like musicians, don't like discordant sounds. I also now believe that where cats are concerned, small is beautiful. You can board twenty or thirty quite effortlessly. Double the number and you quadruple the chances of trouble. The larger the individual cages the better. But no matter how large they are if there is direct air contact you can be sure that if one cat has flu most will go down with it. Outdoor runs may please the owner but boarded cats simply don't run! They bask. I think they like the space provided by a largish house, the warmth of a small bed and all of it totally secure from all other creatures except for the lovely person who brings the grub.

Cheese

Cats that can't smell because of flu or other respiratory infections will usually refuse food. After a few days some of them, though recovering, seem to lose all interest in life. Try them with some smelly cheese. A ripe flowing Camembert or a really nasty Blue might just penetrate those blocked passages and restore a lost appetite.

Healthy cats, if they like cheeses at all, usually prefer those that have been tamed into submission.

Cheetah

Reputedly the fastest creature on four feet and certainly among the most beautiful. I know they can be domesticated, if by domestication you mean that one can be reasonably certain not to wake up in the creature's stomach. I seriously doubt whether they ever make satisfactory pets. Why do the dealers in these exotic animals usually ask vets to remove the big tusk teeth? Also I don't know any pet Cheetahs that can be let off their leads and be expected to return home. (Doubtless some irate readers will tell me of several they know who do the daily shopping and absolutely adore children.) And another thing! Some are absolutely unhousetrainable, and most have more than occasional lapses. I know I can't cite facts and figures to prove this. But I would advise you not to buy a secondhand rug from a Cheetah owner. What have I got against this big hunting cat? Nothing at all! On the contrary I respect him enough to let him lead his own natural existence. I believe the only people who should be allowed to import them are serious naturalists and zoo-keepers who aren't motivated by the big profit.

PS: Sorry I forgot to mention that unlike other cats but like dogs the claws of the Cheetah do not retract. This is true of the dewclaws as well as the claws in the feet. One vet who had several in his charge in the days when some people were trying to develop Cheetah racing as an alternative to Greyhound racing reported that their dewclaws were 'more dangerous than a razor blade'.

Chewing gum

Some cats taste it through curiosity and then panic when they find they can neither swallow nor expel the stuff. Children sometimes use their pets as a convenient repository for the odd bit of gum that's surplus to their immediate needs. In most cases it's easily removed. But if the cat is in distress and clawing at it, or if it's stuck on the eyes, you'd better go along to the vet. Don't explain. He's seen it before.

Children

Children should be told that they can hurt kittens, and cats can hurt children. If they're careful with the kittens it's all right to stroke them but not to carry them about. One of the commonest causes of fractures in kittens is being dropped from a child's arms. Sometimes children fall on a kitten and do irreparable damage. After the kitten is five or six months old it can generally look after itself in the home, but is not up to the hazards of the great outdoors. The children should be told that they definitely cannot take Kittykins to Marylou's for tea. Marylou's bull terrier might just spread Kittykins on toast. Sometimes children will take a kitten for a ride in the baby carriage with baby. They return half an hour later with a really marvellous assortment of sticky candy and absolutely no idea where baby and the pram might be. Your chances of finding baby are pretty good but Kittykins might have lost herself completely.

What about explaining the sickness or death of an animal to a child? I suppose it varies with the circumstances, but most people think it's best to tell the truth – but gently and without undue emphasis on the tragedy of it all. Most children seem to accept that birth and sickness and death are all part of the natural order of things. I knew a doctor's wife who was faced with the dilemma of explaining the illness of the family's pet budgie to her ten-year-old daughter, within weeks of the death of their old poodle *and* the old cat. She finally decided that she couldn't. She told her daughter that Budgie was lonely and therefore she was sending her to board out her days with other budgies, which is what, in fact, she did.

A veterinary colleague of mine arrived home one evening and saw that his son's pet rabbit was dead. He knew that his son was terribly attached to the rabbit, and in some distress he went inside to discuss with his wife how best to explain it. They were in the midst of the discussion when the back door was thrown open by the son, who flung the corpse on the floor and announced 'The rabbit is dead'.

The most appalling examples I can recall of parents who show callous disregard for their children's feelings are those who send an aged pet along to a welfare clinic with an accompanying note saying 'Please put this cat to sleep. Make sure the boy gives you the money'. In one case the staff made a mistake and forgot to tell the boy to 'Just leave the cat with us and we'll look after it'. He sat in the waiting room patiently for a couple of hours waiting for his cat. Finally someone noticed him and the girls, in much embarrassment, came to the vets and told them the problem. One of the vets came out and carefully explained to the boy that his cat was very ill but they would take him in for a few days and see what could be done. He wasn't to be too optimistic because the cat was very ill. Could he get his mother to phone? The boy returned the next day and we told him his cat had died. The mother never phoned. What would you have done?

Most cats are particularly gentle with children, and will only scratch if they're hurt. Children shouldn't be allowed to mess about with a cat in advanced pregnancy or one who is nursing her litter or who is ill or injured. And many cats, when they reach a venerable old age, just don't want to be handled at all. They have earned the right to snore undisturbed.

Chinchilla

I know this is a furry animal native to South America. It's also a kind of rabbit. It's also a breed of long-haired cat which many people claim is the most beautiful of all. Its distinctive silvery colour is the result of the blending of its pure white undercoat with the sharp black with which each hair is tipped. In other words, it's a white cat ticked with black so that it looks silver. The Silver Tabby is not a ticked cat. Each hair is either silver or black, hence it's a silver cat with black markings. Follow? The Chinchilla is further enhanced by the possession of emerald green eyes. At their showring-best nothing else in catdom can approach a Chinchilla, but remember they don't look that way without proper grooming, so if you're basically lazy forget the idea. *PS:* My wife's cousin is an enthusiastic Chinchilla breeder. She tells me she spends about five hours a day grooming her assorted dozen. The cats look terrific but her husband looks a bit neglected.

Chloroform

This anaesthetic is safe for humans and horses, less so for dogs and rather toxic for cats. However, as it's non-inflammable, and therefore less likely to cause accidents in inexperienced hands, it is widely used for euthanasia of cats. If used in the proper way it is as humane a way of inducing sleep and then death as we know. What is the proper way? The cat is placed in a large container with a screen through which air flows freely. If the cat can breathe normally it won't panic any more than it does when placed in its usual carrying basket. A few drops of chloroform are placed on a rag, and the cat gradually gets dozier and dozier then falls off to sleep. It's a gradual process. When the animal is asleep more chloroform is added and the air hole closed. The sleep gets deeper, and death ensues.

Civets

These are creatures with tapering tails and short legs. They look like a cross between a cat, a weasel and a racoon. They are supposed to look about the same today as they did ages ago, back about the middle of the evolutionary scale. They interest us because the several species of civets and our modern domestic cat share common ancestors.

Civets are found in Africa and India and in the Middle East. A game warden's wife in Africa rears many orphaned creatures. Among them is a civet. She informs me that it eats meat and fruit and is partial to banana and paw-paw. She found it abandoned when it was about two weeks old, and raised it on one of the packaged milk formulae. Up until the age of eight months it was very friendly and stayed close to home. At that stage it still mewed like a kitten.

Subsequently it started wandering at night (it's a nocturnal species) and like an errant husband kept coming home later and later. The front door is kept open and food left in the corridor. When it does show up (usually between two and five in the morning) the good lady hears it eating and steps out to say hello and gives it a few pats. However, its miaows have changed to snarls and it dislikes being handled.

By the time this is in print the civet will probably have shoved off to find a mate and perpetuate its kind.

The same lady informs me that civets wouldn't make good pets, and that as far as she knows the only people who keep them are some citizens of Arabian countries who cage them and extract a strong musky perfume from their anal glands.

I'd like to acknowledge this sensible lady by name, but unlike show business, in parts of the new Africa any publicity is bad publicity.

Claws (*torn*)

If you watch cats climbing walls or digging into concrete seeking a fast escape you wonder why they don't injure themselves more often. Can you grab a branch to break a fall without cracking a fingernail? I know none of us are as young as we once were. But even in our prime none of us can match the oldest, fattest, most pampered Persian. Nevertheless even the agile cat has accidents, and when they happen they are quite as painful as ours. A broken claw will cause lameness, swelling and often infection of the nail-bed.

Home aid is simplicity itself. Bathe the foot in salt water. How do you do it? Clear the table. Get a flat-bottomed bowl. Half fill it with warm water. Dump in a few tablespoons of salt. Then, holding the cat by its shoulders and front legs, place the injured foot or feet in the bowl. If the water isn't too hot or too cold there will be no violent objections. The slight squirm or hiss which any normal cat will give (just to assert his individuality) can easily be coped with. A frightened cat should be soothed. A bully of a cat should be held a little more firmly and told in a gruff voice to stop his nonsense. Do this two or three times a day. Dry the foot. If it's a bad injury smear the foot with medicated ointment and bandage the whole area (see *Bandaging*).

If it's very painful, or if the whole pad looks red and sore, you'd better not take any chances of the infection travelling. Your veterinary surgeon will probably inaugurate a course of antibiotic injections and dressings. How long will it be before a nice new claw has grown? It varies. In a week or ten days the soreness will have gone, and in another week you and Theophilla will have forgotten which foot it was.

Claws (*trimming*)

Many people come in and ask to have their cats' claws clipped. They've been told it should be done, or they own a dog and know that its claws need trimming, or they're fed up with the furniture being scratched to pieces. We usually explain that it doesn't do much good. The cat will still want to sharpen his claws. And the more one trims them the more they'll grow and the more dedicated he'll be in sharpening them. That is unless one cuts right into the quick which is painful and dangerous. It's dangerous because although the trusting creature will let you cut the quick on one claw, if you try a second he'll scratch your face. Quite right he is to defend himself against such stupidity. There are only three periods when claws need trimming. Firstly, when the cat is still a kitten, to protect the mother's tender udder and its brothers and sisters from over-zealous play. Secondly, after long periods of immobilization or dressings, during which the claws may grow round in a circle and penetrate the flesh. Thirdly, when the cat gets too old to exercise and properly sharpen his claws. Any cat of eleven or twelve should have its claws examined routinely. If they are curling round take the creature along to the vet. The old boy's probably got other things that need doing at the same time.

Cleft palates

If a kitten doesn't settle down and sleep after suckling, have a look at the roof of its mouth. The two sides may not have joined. There will be a space in the middle. If it's only partially separated the kitten may go on for a few days before you notice that it's not getting enough milk. If it's a complete cleft you will hear the kittens crying within twenty-four hours. That space opens into the nasal cavity, and they can't build up the negative pressure necessary for suction. In fact, in severe cases (and in these often the whole litter is affected) the milk simply drains out of the nose.

It's possible to correct the condition surgically. The two sides are sewn together. However, there is strong evidence that the condition is hereditary, and most owners agree that euthanasia is the only sensible solution.

Don't scrub the queen from your breeding programme. The fault may well be with the tom.

Coccidiosis

This is an intestinal disease. Infected animals and birds have a long lasting, bloody diarrhoea. It's one of the nightmare diseases of chickens and rabbits, and every poultry keeper knows all about it. It's caused by a microscopically small, round parasite of which there are several species. Three sorts can infect cats. Fortunately it's not a common problem, except in the occasional cattery where sanitation is a filthy word. Your own vet may be too polite to tell you, but if you've got coccidiosis in the place you'd better start scrubbing. Don't forget to boil all the feeding dishes between each meal. Of course there are medicines that will help, but they're not nearly as important as a proper programme of sanitation.

Codeine

Don't give it to your cat, because you can't possibly know what effect it might have. Some few cats will give a grateful purr and settle into a deep painless sleep. Most cats will go off their heads and crawl up the walls. The same goes for morphine and all its derivatives.

Collapse

The animal is lying flat out and breathing in short shallow gasps. Don't attempt any home first aid, and whatever you do don't pour things down his throat. In most cases of collapse in the cat effective treatment includes an intravenous drip and oxygen. This is best done at your vet's surgery. Transfer the cat gently to his basket or a box. Lay him out comfortably. Don't smother him with blankets and don't fuss with him. Phone the veterinarian to warn him you're on the way.

There are two kinds of collapse where home treatment is imperative and might save the animal. The first is *Heat stroke* and the other is *Electric shock* (see below).

Collar-bone

Unlike dogs, but like people and rabbits, the cat has a vestigial collar-bone. I hope you don't find this fact as uninteresting as I do.

Collars

Some people insist on collaring cats, despite warnings that they can easily get caught when cats move into the strange places they do. If you simply must collar your cat use one with the elastic bit that stretches and prevents choking. Best of all – don't use a collar at all unless the cat is on a lead attached to your hand.

The collar shouldn't be so wide that it rubs or so narrow that it cuts. Leather properly cared for is better than plastic. It should be saddlesoaped weekly.

The clip of the lead which you attach to the collar should have its opening at the side not at the end. That way the strain of the lead isn't likely to weaken it. The kind that slides open is safer than the spring kind. The latter may catch on the animal's ear or leg. In order to release it you have to press the spring clip which increases the pain and drives the animal into a panic. I've seen some caught so tightly that one had to resort to a general anaesthetic to release them.

Colour

Anyone who has ever picked up a book on cats will know that the main difference between different breeds of cats within the three breed groups (orientals, Persians and short-haired) is colour. It may be coat colour or eye colour or both. Now, I don't think that colour is a bore but trying to describe a colour with words certainly is. And, to attribute widely different behavioural characteristics to breeds that are identically the same in all respects, save that of colour, presupposes that one's readers are quite unobservant.

Will you accept as stated, that, in addition to the breeds mentioned in this book, there are a couple of dozen others who differ each from the other only in the coats they wear?

There are Blacks and Whites and Creams and Blue Creams and Reds and Silver Tabbies and Brown Tabbies and Mackerel Tabbies. There are Blues and Blue Tabbies. There are Red Tabbies which some people call Marmalade and others call Ginger. And there are Spotted cats and goodness knows what else.

Some are startling. Some are subtle. Almost all are beautiful. And most are right in your neighbourhood for all with open eyes to see.

Colour-point long-haired Cats

These should be typical Persians with Siamese colouring. For many years the Americans have had a long-haired Siamese which isn't the same thing at all (see *Balinese*). If you like Persian temperament and solidity but enjoy subtle Siamese colours, put your name on a breeder's waiting list.

Colour problem

The problem with colour is that quite often nature doesn't like those colours that some people prefer. Man breeds white cats, and nature makes many of them deaf. Man messes about making his Siamese paler and paler, and nature makes them frailer and frailer. In other words, man tries to impose his colour prejudices on a species, and too often, in the process, he'll overlook the really important things like health, vitality and longevity.

Am I preaching against colour prejudice? No! Not at all! After all, even Mother Nature is prejudiced. I'm just pointing out which way she's prejudiced, so that you'll know whom you are fighting.

Conjunctivitis

Inflammation of the membranes of the eyelids. It may be a simple local infection involving only one or both eyes, or it may be a symptom of a general illness. A bit of dust, a scratch, smoke or fumes may all cause the eyes to smart and water. The cat will often rub at the affected eye and make it worse. A safe way of relieving the irritation until you can obtain proper treatment is to bathe the eye with liberal amounts of salt water. Use a teaspoon to 6dl (1 pt). Boil and allow to cool. Keep Kitty in a subdued light (see *Eyes*).

Constipation

If your cat is normal one minute and the next minute he starts straining you can assume that his trouble is *not* constipation. Constipation is a condition that almost always starts slowly and gradually gets worse over a period of days. The cat may strain a bit, it may vomit, but often the only signs you will notice are a general mopiness and lethargy. If it's only a mild constipation and the cat is still eating, a dinner of raw liver might just do the job. Cats who are used to a lot of room will often get constipated when they are put in a kennel cage. That is because they lack the best tonic of all – exercise. Overfed and overweight cats don't move more than they can help, and they are subject to mild attacks of constipation. Dieting is what's indicated, but some owners just won't listen.

Some elderly cats like some elderly people have a tendency to mild blockages. Actually it's just a kind of slowing down. Often a bit of whole-bran mixed with the food or some of those granules they dish out in geriatric wards makes all the difference between ease and constant discomfort.

Sometimes a diet that is too dry or lack of drinking water will cause constipation. Twenty-four hours of starvation, lots of water and a tablespoon of oil will usually start the motion going.

Sometimes a cat will have a mat of hair blocking its anus. Wet the hair and tease it apart. If it's really cemented down use the scissors, but be careful!

Generally speaking, most cases of constipation are mild, and are easily corrected by a few simple measures. Starvation, lots of fluids and a bit of oil will do the job. Use liquid paraffin, or mineral oil or olive oil but never, never use castor oil. If it doesn't work, don't let the condition drag on for days, because either it's not constipation at all or it's such a firm blockage that only a vet can get it out.

If a cat has recurring attacks of constipation over a period of weeks or months, and they can't be explained on the basis of diet or exercise, then you must be prepared to subject him to a series of veterinary examinations. The cat may have a tumour, an atonic bowel or a huge enlarged colon. He may have broken his pelvis before you got him, and it may have healed so badly that it obstructs normal defecation. Whatever the reason, it must be found in order to treat the condition properly.

Finally, may I add a castigating note? Many cases of constipation are due to constant dosing with oils or other laxatives. If the gut is always coated with oil it can't digest the food properly. If you find yourself giving your cat a dose of oil twice in the same month, you'd better consider seriously whether you really know what you're doing.

Convalescence

This is the period of recovery between illness and health. It's not a dramatic event but is a gradual process, the length of which varies according to the patient and the illness. A kitten with a minor illness may be up and bouncing in a day or two. An aged cat with nephritis may never regain perfect health. As a general rule, for all but the most minor of ailments you'd better consider the recovery period to be a minimum of two to three weeks. During this time the cat should be confined, and any signs of relapse should be reported to your veterinary surgeon. Remember, too, that a cat that has been weakened by one ailment is likely to come down with everything else that's going around.

Many people seem to have a 'Let's get it all over with' mood when their animals fall ill. The tom has been badly injured in a fight, or the queen has had a difficult parturition. In the middle of treatment they request the veterinarian to operate on the animal so 'that it won't happen again'. They seem surprised when we say that we'd like to see the animal fully recovered from the illness before undergoing an anaesthetic and an operation.

Cord

Most kittens and many cats find string and thread and fishing lines irresistible. They'll pounce, and tug and chew at it. When you arrive home Old Stinkypaws is clawing madly at the stuff which is stuck in his throat. Get some help, and place the cat on a table under a strong light. Often with a little patience you can unwind it. Don't tug. It may be attached to a needle which is wedged in the gullet. If you can't see the beginning and the end of the cord, you'd better get to the vet. Often a general anaesthetic, X-rays and surgery are necessary to get it out. Similarly, if you are greeted by a distressed animal with a bit of cord hanging out of its anus you simply must not tug at it. You may evert the bowel or worse. Cut off all but an inch of the cord so that the cat will be less tempted to bother it. Pour lots of olive oil down the creature's throat. If it hasn't passed through (carrying the cord with it) in a matter of hours, you'd better take yourself and pussy to the vet's.

Cryptorchid or monorchid

A condition where one of the testicles fails to descend into the scrotal sac. Normally they both come down at three or four months of age. It is commonly discovered when a person brings their tom in for neutering. We usually ask to see him in a month's time, and if it's still not down we play the 'wait and see' game for another two weeks. At that point a shot of male hormone is sometimes used to try and nudge it on its way. If that doesn't work an abdominal operation is usually necessary to locate and remove it. The operation is quite a serious one, as the vet may have to roam all the way from the kidneys back to the bladder before finding it.

There's absolutely no point in removing the one external testicle and leaving the other inside. The cat would still have all the disadvantages of the full tom.

Finally, monorchids should not be used for breeding purposes, as there is evidence that the condition is hereditary.

Cyst

A collection of fluid enclosed in its own 'cyst-wall'. They may occur anywhere on the body and for many reasons including some we don't know. One of the commonest sorts is found on cats' ears. It is usually the result of scratching. One simply must not neglect an ear-scratching cat (see *Haematoma*). Cysts may occur around the eyes. Usually they're found on the edges of the lids. If they irritate they must be surgically removed. Some long-haired cats of advancing years get the oddest cysts on their backs. We usually advise leaving them alone unless they bother the animal. Cysts which occur between the toes are rather rare in the cat. These interdigital cysts, as they are called, are often the result of some foreign object like a grass seed. When the seed is removed the condition clears. Home aid for interdigital cysts consists of bathing the foot in warm salt water, but don't poke about. Just bathe. Some old toms get cysts on the testicles. We leave them alone unless they appear to be getting larger. Some females who behave oddly have cysts on their ovaries. When and if the condition is diagnosed the vet usually advises an operation to remove the lot. Some females get clear fluid-filled cysts in the mammary glands. They can be removed surgically but have a tendency to recur and become troublesome.

Never attempt any home treatment on any cyst. Puncturing them with needles or painting them with iodine at best only postpones proper treatment. It may make them larger and deeper. In other words leave them to the vet. They're not an emergency so don't ring at midnight.

Dandruff

Scurf or scales formed by the flaking of dead skin cells. Cats who constantly lie in front of the fire may have dry lifeless coats. Don't disturb the poor dears. Just get out the old brush and see if you can't groom some life into the old hide. The coats of cats who are ill lose their lustre. They go dull, and the skin gets dusty. Grooming helps, but the real restorative is complete recovery from the illness. Some scurfy cats regain their skin tone when fat is added to their diets. Margarine made from vegetable oils is considered better than animal fats. But, of course, that opinion is largely based on evidence gleaned by the manufacturers who are far more interested in the human market. One wonders where those sleek big cats buy the stuff. Finally, some cats, like some people, just have to live with those unsightly bits.

DDT

The miraculous powder that made at least one physical aspect of the last war more comfortable than the first. DDT is safe for men and safe for dogs, but it's poisonous for cats.

Deafness

Some cats are born deaf. These are usually white cats with blue eyes, although occasionally this sort of congenital defect is seen in white cats with pink eyes. These cats can and do compensate wonderfully by developing their other senses to an acute pitch of perception. Even so, the claims of those people who promulgate the defect by breeding these cats must be considered as sophistry – if not cruelty.

Cats may go deaf temporarily as a result of an ear infection or a really bad bout of flu. Usually the hearing returns as the condition heals. Cats with long-standing neglected ear infections may go permanently deaf. Some years ago veterinarians reported cases of deafness following the use of streptomycin. It was widely discussed and the safe dosage laid down, so now this sort of deafness doesn't occur.

Some cats go partially or completely deaf with the advancing years. Older cats should be encouraged to stay at home and avoid the contingencies of traffic and strangers.

Death

It's difficult to tell the exact moment of death. In fact, doctors debate which delicate tests should be legally valid to determine death in the case of people who lie comatose for weeks, and are kept alive by machines which artificially sustain breathing. In the case of animals it's a simpler problem, because we seldom resort to artificial breathing for more than a few hours.

As death approaches the pulse weakens. Many cats stretch themselves out violently just before they die. Respiration ceases, there is no corneal reflex and one cannot detect a heart beat. Gradually the body grows cold.

Declawing

There is a fairly simple operation to remove the claws of cats. People ask to have it done after they've watched three successive sofas disintegrate into shreds. The thing is you must train a cat from kittenhood to scratch only those furnishings that your mother-in-law loves and you hate. If you don't have hateful furniture you must provide a scratching post. Let the creature sharpen its claws on nothing but the scratching post. I know it's a difficult job with some cats. Many Siamese particularly seem determined to scratch the whole world into manageable shreds.

People who advocate the declawing operation say that it does absolutely no harm. The cat can walk and run and climb just as well without claws as with them. They're quite right. The only thing they forget is the primary purpose of claws – namely defence. A declawed cat is quite helpless in a tight corner. Are you quite certain your cat will never have to fight its way home?

PS: I must add that although the operation is simple the period of convalescence is both long and painful. I'm absolutely convinced that many cats never recover from the trauma of the operation. This surgical interference with nature is almost impossible to defend. If people are intense about furniture they should buy objects not cats.

Dehydration

This is one of the most serious symptoms in many cat diseases, and must be corrected within hours if life is to be maintained. The body's tissues lose their fluids through diarrhoea, vomiting or a very high fever. Dehydration is one of the usual symptoms in feline enteritis, and one of the prime causes of death in that disease. I have seen cats, particularly Siamese, become bone-dry within hours. Quite often they respond dramatically to injections of fluid. Within minutes, as one is watching, the dull eyes begin to glisten and the animal takes a new interest in the life it has almost left.

How can you tell if an animal is dehydrated? Lift the skin of its neck. If it's soft and pliable and rolls back into place, that's fine. If it's dry and leathery and just remains where you pull it, the animal is dehydrated. Touch its gums. If they feel sticky and dry then you're certain.

What should you do about it? Rush the animal to a vet. If there isn't a vet for miles around you can try to find a nurse or doctor who will pump salt water (sterile saline, please) or glucose water (the same again, please) under the skin, or if they're very clever, into a vein. If you can't find a professional you just might manage to hydrate the drying and dying creature by giving it a very slow enema consisting of a teaspoon of salt to a pint of water. Whatever you do don't force liquids down its throat. It will probably just vomit and die. You can, of course, comfort by squeezing just a bit of liquid – a drop at a time – into the parched mouth.

What can you do to prevent the condition? First, have your cats inoculated against enteritis and don't forget the booster doses. Secondly, don't attempt any home treatment for vomiting or diarrhoea that persists into the second day. Thirdly, provide all animals with a readily available supply of clean drinking water.

Dermatitis

Inflammation of the skin. It may be caused by anything from fleas to mange, or the application of strong drugs, or simply feeding the wrong things. I think the first step in all cases where the cause isn't obvious is to have a good look for fleas, and eliminate them. Bland calomine lotion may soothe the sore areas until you get the animal to a vet. Apply it very sparingly to the skin. Don't plaster it on the hair. Rub it in gently. Hold the cat while the stuff dries. Then gently brush it off. Remember, whatever you leave, the cat will lick off. If the sore area is dry and scaly, you can soothe it by applying cod-liver oil or olive oil. Whatever you do remember that dermatitis is just a symptom. Until the underlying cause is determined and eliminated you won't get rid of the inflammation.

Dewclaws

Those little extra paws and claws partway up the inside of the foot. I don't know if they were meant to be thumbs or teacup handles, but they're of no use to the cat. Occasionally they cause trouble.

If kittens are born with double dewclaws or great big hanging ones ask your vet to have a look when the creatures are still a few days old. He may advise a simple operation to remove them. Later the operation is more serious and requires a general anaesthetic, careful ligaturing and several dressings.

Sometimes the dewclaws grow in a circle and penetrate the flesh. We see this commonly in older cats, in cats recovering from a long illness, and in fracture cases that have been bandaged or plastered for a few weeks.

Treatment consists of cutting off the penetrating point. Don't try it yourself unless you're absolutely certain which end is which. This can be more difficult than it sounds.

Neglected cases that have become infected require bathings, dressings and antibiotic injections.

Memo: Check the dewclaws of elderly cats at least once a month.

Diabetes

If your cat drinks and drinks and eats and eats, but steadily loses weight, it may be suffering from diabetes. It's a disease of the pancreas, a long pale gland lying beside the intestine, which normally secretes a substance called insulin that helps in the digestion of food.

In the human and the dog it's fairly easy to diagnose diabetes. One gets a sample of urine, and sticks a bit of chemical paper in it, and if the paper turns blue that indicates sugar. Sugar doesn't belong in the urine. The normal body turns sugar into energy, or in the case of lazy types like me into fat. In diabetic cases the body can't convert the sugar, and it passes out of the body. No matter how much food the body takes in, it steadily wastes away.

Why is it difficult to diagnose diabetes in the cat? Well, simply because it's so difficult to get a sample of urine. Most cats simply refuse to oblige by urinating into a bowl. It's almost a major procedure passing a catheter in a cat. So what does one do if diabetes is suspected? If the cat normally uses a tray, one tries with a dry tray. But most cats will refuse to use a sandless tray. Try one with neutral washed sand. After the cat urinates one plunges the test paper in the sand. If it indicates positive one goes on with blood tests and all the other paraphernalia. Many cats, though, must be hospitalized if one suspects diabetes.

How common is the disease? Some veterinary authorities say that it occurs in the cat four times as often as in the dog, but how they arrive at this figure I don't know. Certainly it's not a rare disease.

Treatment involves daily injections of insulin. Difficult? Not really. You'll soon get the hang of it, and your cat will accept the daily jab as part of the price he pays for his dinner. For humane reasons you must learn how to sharpen a needle properly. A good needle is almost painless. A blunt one is cruel. Is that too obvious a statement? Lots of animal lovers use a needle with a point that resembles sandpaper, and they wonder why the beast hides when it sees the syringe.

If your cat has diabetes, don't let him outdoors unless you have a huge, safe garden. Why? Diabetics, when injured, heal very slowly. For the same reason one usually advises against breeding diabetic queens. What would be a minor complication in the normal cat could be fatal to a diabetic.

Summary: A cat that eats well but loses weight should have its urine checked for sugar.

Diarrhoea

Please memorize this simple lesson. Neither you nor your cat can starve to death in a day or two or three. The natural treatment for diarrhoea is starvation. Rest the stomach and the gut, and the body to heal itself. End of lesson.

Diarrhoea is a condition when the faeces flow from the body in liquid or semi-liquid form. Those motions may be any consistency from watery to thick blood stained clots. I know it's not the best sort of after dinner activity, but it's helpful if you can look and describe with some accuracy what they do look like. It's even more helpful if you can scoop some up and put it in a clean jar.

If it's a kitten that's suffering from the condition your vet will probably examine the sample under the microscope to determine if worms are the root of the trouble. He won't immediately prescribe for the worms because the worm tablets would be too harsh for the inflamed intestines. First he'll attempt to soothe and heal. When the diarrhoea is properly under control the animal can be safely wormed.

If it's an adult that's suffering your vet will want to know if he's vomiting as well. If so it may be feline infectious enteritis or one of the less dangerous infections. In some cases he'll ask you to starve the animal for at least thirty-six hours while his injections are doing their work.

Older animals that are subject to diarrhoea, on and off, over a period of months may have a tumour (see *Lymphosarcoma*).

Sorry! I didn't mean to make diarrhoea sound so serious. Often it's the result of a simple little tummy upset caused by a bit of unusual food or overfeeding. Twenty-four hours of starvation, a bit of kaolin, and kitty is as right as rain.

Diet

This is an impossible subject to cover in a few lines, but I'll try. At least I can give the general idea and point out the common mistakes.

Young growing animals require the most care. Before weaning they should have been introduced to solids. By the time they are weaned they will gravitate towards the feeding dish as eagerly as towards the mother. When you acquire a kitten it will want four or five meals a day of which two or three will be milk and baby-cereals. The other two or three will be shredded meat or flaked fish. Gradually, over a period of weeks the meals decrease in number and the emphasis switches to meat or fish in all their forms.

By four months the kitten will be on one solid meat meal, a breakfast of milk (really rich double strength, powdered or concentrated) and cereals; and a midday snack of literally anything if it demands one. By six months breakfast and supper should be sufficient. They must of course be large enough to satisfy the growing appetite. The supper should be a great lot of meat (up to 100–125g (4–5 oz) if it's a large energetic beast) but the breakfast need be no more than a saucerful of biscuit (the feline sort) mixed with a bit of concentrated milk.

Gradually, supper becomes the mainstay of the diet and breakfast a sort of take it or leave it affair.

Cats simply cannot handle a lot of roughage whether it be starches or green vegetables. The emphasis must be on animal proteins. I prefer to feed my cats on meat. Others, equally trained, prefer fish. All agree that cats need about fifty calories a day per 450g (1 lb) of body weight. An easier way of reckoning it is 12g ($\frac{1}{2}$ oz) per 450g (1 lb) of body weight. A cat weighing 7kg (121 lb) will want about 175g (6 oz) of food a day. 100–125 (4–5 oz) should be meat or fish. The rest can be cooked starches (potatoes, peas, or broccoli for that matter) or milk or biscuit or titbits off your table.

With that general guide in mind may I add a few bits of advice.

First, the milk should (if at all possible) be double strength (see *Milk*). Secondly, you simply must add calcium to all meat or fish diets. You may use calcium pills or bonemeal. Thirdly, cooked meats and fish, and this of course includes tinned sorts, are deficient in vitamin B. Add yeast to the diet. Fourthly, if you vary the diet from day to day you are less likely to create deficiencies. And finally if you are worried that you're not on the right track consult your vet. He'd rather prevent a condition than treat it.

Dieting and special diets

Your vet may prescribe a special diet for your cat in some conditions like diabetes, kidney disease or overweight. Cats are most particular when it comes to food and they can be creatures of habit. If you suddenly switch from raw liver to cooked noodles they'll simply refuse to eat. The trick is to ring in the new by disguising it as the old. One gradually switches over or down as the case may be.

For example, if your meat-eating cat must be switched to noodles and other starches you mix a bit of noodle with the meat for the first meal and increase the noodles over a period of ten days until it's mostly noodles. Always put a bit of meat on top to get her eating. You may have to continue this appetite teasing for a month or two.

If you are told one day that Gorgeous Gussiandra is really nothing but a fat slob, don't throw away the refrigerator and install a greenhouse. If you attempt to feed her on lettuce Fat Gussy will move in with that awful butcher down the road.

The way to keep her happy is to cut down from 400g (14 oz) to 375g (13 oz) and then to 350g (12 oz). Over a period of two months you'll have her down to 180g (7 oz) of food a day and she'll be able to see her own tail for the first time in years.

Digitalis

This old-fashioned drug is still saving lives. Thousands of heart patients, both human and canine, live relatively normal lives with the aid of this derivative of the foxglove plant. We don't see many cats with heart condition where the drug is indicated. In those few we do see we are unable to use it because cats simply do not tolerate the stuff.

Dislocation

Of course any joint can be dislocated if enough force is used, but in cat practice we commonly meet with only two sorts. Both are usually the results of a long fall or an automobile accident.

Dislocation of the jaw is easily recognized. The jaws are fixed in one position, generally with the mouth ajar. There may be a fracture as well, in which case the front parts of the jaw will be slack and movable. Don't mess about washing off the blood. Put the poor creature in a basket and take it to the vet. No point in asking the vet to come to you because he'll need all the facilities of his surgery to get the thing back into position again. After puss comes home she'll be happier with broths and milk for a week or two.

Dislocation of the hip is a little more difficult to recognize. The animal may be only intermittently lame, but usually it's completely off the affected leg. Any handling of the limb causes pain – even more pain than a fracture. The examination itself usually includes a general anaesthetic, because it's difficult to feel and X-ray a cat who is in pain and still has three legs and a strong mouth with which to express its feelings. I mention this because many people object to one anaesthetizing their animal as part of the diagnostic procedure.

'Why does he need an anaesthetic?' they ask.

'Because I'd like to feel the joint.'

'But what's wrong?'

'I don't know yet.'

'So why does he need an anaesthetic if you don't know what's wrong?'

Treatment of course includes pulling and pushing the joint back into place. If, as often happens, the ligaments have been badly stretched or ruptured, any untoward movement will knock the joint out again. That is why some vets insist on hospitalizing these cases for up to a fortnight. Others try splints, and still others trust to the owner's good sense to keep the cat in a restricted area for some days. Nevertheless, despite all efforts, some pop out again and the cat may have to resign itself to forming and living with a false joint.

Dislocation of the kneecap is one of the nightmares of some particular breeds of dog. It is so so rare in cats that up to twenty years ago many vets, including myself, had never seen a case. At that time it was a condition we knew existed only because it was described in the veterinary literature. At that time it was confidently asserted that 'slipping kneecaps' could not be associated with any breed or strain of cat. Today one is bound to record that it is not unusual to see whole litters of tiny Foreign Whites and Blue long-hairs so afflicted. Happily the cat is such a resilient creature that most can cope. The only lesson some of us may learn is that it's really wicked to breed creatures who can possibly pass the condition to the next generation.

Disposal

What does one do with the body of an animal who has been part and parcel of one's life for a dozen years? If you have a large garden or a bit of woodland, burial is usually the best answer. If you don't, the problem appears difficult. Some people are so distressed that they wrap the body in newspapers and drop it in the garbage bin. This is not only unsanitary, unsatisfactory and shame-making – it's illegal. Take it along to your local vet or to an animal welfare society. They're geared to look after such problems.

Docking

This is the archaic practice with which many dog breeders in this so-called enlightened era try to improve the appearance of some breeds. They chop off the tails because they think it makes the dogs more beautiful. In some countries they even chop off bits of dogs' ears for the same reason. Thank goodness cat owners leave well enough alone.

Dogs (*advice from mother*)

You can't tell a dog by its size. It can be smaller than us or as big as a man. They usually smell and sometimes stink. If they're happy they wiggle their hinds and waggle their tails. If they're angry they snarl and growl and bite. If you meet an angry dog you must arch your back, stick your hair out and hiss. They will then put their tails between their legs, run back to their humans and start whining. Occasionally one meets a very bold or stupid dog. You must then climb the nearest height and hiss at him from above. He'll soon go away. If you're actually cornered by a dog you must scratch his eyes. Both he and his human will learn that cats aren't to be messed with.

If you live with a dog you'll know that they can be great fun even if they're not as subtle or as supple as us. They're a little slow in housetraining, and are sloppy eaters and noisy sleepers. They make good companions even though they wear their hearts on their tails.

If a new dog is brought home better avoid him for a day or two until he realizes whose house it really is.

Domestic short-hairs

How chauvinistic can one be? In Britain these cats are referred to as British short-haired, and on the Continent they're called European short-haired. Americans and Canadians are quite happy calling them Domestic short-haired. In case you hadn't guessed it's a cat with a short dense coat. And like the vast majority of cats everywhere it has a well-knit body and a broad rounded head and small ears that are slightly rounded. The only exception to this body type is found in the Manx (see below).

Like Persians and orientals, the short-haired pedigree cat (oh yes, they're bred and registered and shown with as much care as any other purebred) is divided into breeds on the basis of colour. There are Whites and Blacks and Blues and Tabbies (Silver, Red and Brown) and Creams and Tortoiseshell and Tortoiseshell and White, and I'm sure I've forgotten one or two. But it doesn't really matter. All you need do if you're interested is drop into any fair-sized cat show. You'll meet a half-dozen people who will talk about the virtues of the pedigree short-hair as long as you're willing to listen.

It's really a shame that more people don't because these cats have all the virtues and resiliency and toughness of the common cat but have a bonus in the form of the most sleekly beautiful of all cat coats.

Grooming isn't the chore that it is with Persians and they're easier to live with than orientals because they're less demanding. In short you simply can't go wrong if you choose a kitten from among this group of pedigreed cats.

Drinking

Many people think that cats belong to Drinkers Anonymous. The truth is that many cats are secret drinkers. They refuse that lovely bowl of 'fresh' tap water but find some old puddle or rain barrel around the corner.

The scientists tell us that young cats consume about ten per cent of their body weight of water each day. As they get older the percentage drops to seven and then to about five. Actually this water may be in the form of drinking water, or it may be the moisture in a sloppy diet.

Don't get out the measuring cup! Just change the water in the bowl each and every day and let Napoleon please himself.

Drooling

Cats may salivate excessively through excitement or fear. This sort of drooling lasts only as long as the tension that produced it. Another sort of transient drooling is that caused by the administration of unpleasant medicines. Most cats, for example, just can't stand the taste of Epsom salts and will froth a stream of saliva if you attempt to give them even the smallest amounts. If an antibiotic capsule accidentally gets crushed in a cat's mouth the animal will froth and drool in a most alarming fashion. I've had some hysterical phone calls from normally placid people when this happens. I try to keep them on the phone for about five minutes by which time the animal is getting over its distaste.

Another sort of drooling is that caused by an object wedged in the mouth or between the teeth. If you can't find and remove the object take the cat to your vet.

Decaying and tartared teeth may set up a drooling that starts mildly. In a day or two or three it develops into an unpleasant stream. Don't sit there and watch it get worse. Arrange for the necessary dental work.

Finally, drooling is one of the common symptoms of flu.

Dropsy

Something interferes with the circulation or the kidneys can't handle the body's waste. Quite simply the fluids get blocked. They may be blocked in the tissues or in one of the body cavities. The scientific names for the condition vary according to where the fluids accumulate. If it's in tissues it's called oedema. If it's in the abdomen it's called ascites. No matter what it's called it's always a serious symptom. If you touch your animal and it feels springy or if its tummy gradually swells into a tight drum you'd better take him to a vet. No matter how he sugars it, the truth will be bitter.

Drowning

Hold the cat by its hind legs and allow the water to drain out. Quickly examine the mouth to see that there are no obstructions. Then gently and slowly (holding the animal by its hind legs) swing it up and down through a half-circle (see *Artificial respiration*). After three or four minutes feel for a heart beat. If there isn't a heart beat you may start one by contracting the chest between your hands. In and relax. Fairly rapidly. When you detect a beat resume the swinging. As long as you can get a heart beat there is hope.

Drug sensitivity

Cats are the most sensitive patients in a veterinary practice. If one likes cats and is patient with them, they usually respond with co-operation and only a token showing of claws. They don't like needles any more than people do, but if one is gentle but firm and decisive they won't bear a grudge as many of our canine patients do. Usually by the time a cat's back in the basket he's ready to settle down and forget the whole episode. Dogs, though, may be really upset and will start vomiting. That is why, if an owner reports that his dog has been sick after an injection, we don't usually consider the drug as being the cause of the upset. But if a cat is sick following an injection, we consider very carefully whether one of the drugs we've used is at fault.

One of the common antibiotic combinations used is penicillin and streptomycin. Penicillin seems to be well tolerated by all species except guinea pigs. Streptomycin, though, upsets quite a minority of cats. Your veterinarian will tell you if your cat cannot take streptomycin, and then it is up to you to remember that fact. Remind your vet on subsequent visits.

A few cats will vomit when given capsules of aureomycin or chloromycetin. If it's a genuine sensitivity to the drug, your vet will stop it, and you must remember yet another long name that Muffin can't have.

But don't get worried about that sort of drug. Antibiotics can only be used under veterinary supervision, so you're not likely to run into the problem on your own.

The drugs that you are likely to use at home and that may cause anything from a temporary upset to permanent damage are the ones I'd like to warn you about.

Aspirin is a cat killer. Never, never give it to cats. Castor oil can cause more pain than any of the conditions for which it is used. Practically all medicated lotions and ointments in a human medicine cabinet will start a cat vomiting. Anything containing DDT or any of the coal tar drugs like creolin is very poisonous for cats.

In other words, just because it's OK for *you* doesn't mean it's OK for the cat. Better do nothing than do something that will make the condition worse.

Cats will lick and swallow anything you put on their skin or coats. Before you apply anything to a cat's body, ask yourself if it's safe taken by mouth. If you're not sure, don't use it.

Some pills are designed to be swallowed whole. If they are crushed or broken before swallowing they may cause the cat acute discomfort or pain. He will salivate and retch. His face gets covered with unsightly bilious foam. It's a most alarming sight, but fortunately it's no more than a temporary upset. Prevention is giving the pills properly, but even with experienced hands mistakes can happen.

A word about morphine and its derivatives. Its effect on cats is quite unpredictable. Some it sends into dreamland, others it sends up the wall. In fact, there is no absolutely safe and effective pain killer for cats. Some of the sedatives work fairly well, and so we usually use those if the animal is in pain. If there's a lot of pain, as in severe burn, we usually anaesthetize the cat and keep it under until we have the worst symptoms under control.

Anaesthesia is quite as safe in the cat as in the dog. Siamese are no different from other cats as regards anaesthesia, but as they are usually thinner one must be careful not to overdose. Like the greyhound, they have no reserves of fat to take up the extra anaesthetic, and an overdose goes right into the system.

Suture and ligature material is usually well tolerated by cats, and one hears of few cases of stitches breaking down because the cat's body has rejected nylon or silk or gut.

Summary:

Never give cats aspirin.

Capsules must be pushed down the throat whole.

Don't put anything on a cat's skin that is poisonous.

Better to give nothing than a drug you're not absolutely certain of.

Dyspnoea

Laboured or difficult breathing. The cat may breathe through its mouth or it may accompany each breath with an abdominal contraction.

It may be caused by anything from a simple abscess or bee sting to the most serious pneumonia or heart failure. If you can't determine the cause and eliminate it the animal needs veterinary attention. The quicker the better.

Ears

Cats are blessed with lovely straightforward ears and man has left them alone. There are only half a dozen things you need know about them in order to recognize and avoid trouble.

First, neglected kittens, particularly those commonly found in pet shops, often have the most dreadful canalfuls of mites (see *Ear mites*). Secondly, one sort of cat mange has a tendency to start on the outside of the ear (see *Mange*). Thirdly, a cat who scratches constantly at the ear for any reason whatsoever may bring the whole thing up in a blister (see *Haematoma*). Fourthly, an animal who is walking in a drunken fashion or holding its head on one side may have a very painful middle-ear infection and will need (at the very least) injections of antibiotics. Fifthly, you must never under any circumstances poke into the ear with orange sticks or probes or anything. You may clean the ear and its attendant miseries by pouring lots of oil into it and wiping the debris off as it floats out. Sixthly, too much of any treatment (no matter how bland) will make a mess of a cat's ears. They just can't stand constant medication.

Conclusion: In an emergency you can clean a cat's ears by pouring in lots and lots of oil, and I mean lots and lots. Then seek veterinary advice.

Ear mites

These are wee crawling beasts that live and multiply in the dark warmth of the ear canal. The mite feeds off the lining of the ear and in the process sets up an irritation that drives the animal to rub and scratch at the ear. The body pours fluid into the ear in an attempt to defend itself, and this fluid, plus mites, accumulates into a mass of chocolate-coloured stuff that can actually fill the whole inside of the ear.

A good percentage of kittens from pet shops are infested with mites, and it's a good idea to let the vet see them before you take them home.

The treatment is simple enough. Oil, slightly warmed, is liberally poured into the ear to loosen the debris. More oil is poured in to float the debris out of the ear. Then, with the aid of an otoscope, the vet has a look down the ear to see how much damage has been done and prescribe the appropriate ointment or drops. He will probably request one further visit in a week or ten days.

If you have a kitten that is shaking its head or scratching at its ears, the only safe home aid is pouring lots of oil into the ears. Don't, please don't, try to clean the ears with matchsticks or cotton wool or any other implement. Just pour oil down the ears. Let the dirt float out. Wipe away the surplus oil. Wear your oldest clothes because you'll get covered when the kitten shakes its head. Repeat the next day, and if the kitten is still bothered you'd better get professional help.

What sort of oil should you use? Liquid paraffin or liquid vaseline is as good as any. It's bland, light and cheap. Olive oil can be used if that's all you have. Don't waste money on expensive 'canker oils' or 'canker lotions'. Whatever you do don't use 'canker pills' or 'canker powders'. They may do more harm than good.

One more thing. If a kitten throws fits, walks around in circles or walks as if it were completely drunk, you'd better have a look at its ears. Mites may be the cause of the trouble. Needless to say, if it's that severe you'd better get your veterinarian to tackle it.

Ear resection

This is a common operation in dogs such as Miniature Poodles and Cocker Spaniels who are too often cursed from birth with ears that are pretty to look at and a joy to fondle but hell to live with. The operation is really a neat bit of plastic surgery. One cuts away extraneous folds of the outer ear and then cuts down to the ear canal in an attempt to bring it into a healthy open relationship with the unhealthy world we share with our pets.

Fortunately all cats, no matter how inbred or pampered, have ears that fit into the natural scheme of things. They look like ears and function like ears. They've not been stretched or covered with silky hair, inside and out, to satisfy some silly fad. As a result no one can say of any breed of cat, as one can of so many breeds of dogs, 'Oh, they've all got bad ears'.

Unfortunately some cats, who are long-standing cases of neglected infection or mites, scratch at their ears in a vain endeavour to lessen the constant irritation and pain. The irritated ear reacts by getting tougher and thicker. Sometimes it thickens so much that the canal is closed and the infection is trapped inside. The only solution is the surgeon's knife. But no surgeon, however skilful, can rectify months or years of neglect. Less than half of the feline patients that I have seen subjected to the operation responded satisfactorily. Admittedly my experience is limited, but I can assure you that no veterinary surgeon feels optimistic about these cases. They would much rather see them early on when they're more likely to respond to simple syringings and medication. Our lesson for today is quite simple: if a cat scratches its ears have it attended to early. Persist with the treatment till the ears are right.

Eclampsia or convulsions

In kittens these are usually minor, though alarming, symptoms of ear mites or teething or worms. Don't get scratched while attempting to move the kitten to a well-padded area. They usually last only a few seconds. If it happens a second time take the creature along to the vet.

In adults, eclampsia is usually a serious symptom and must not be ignored. In pregnant or nursing females it may be due to a calcium deficiency. In those cases an injection of calcium will save a life. A delay of five or six hours is usually fatal (see *Milk fever*).

Eczema

This is a six-letter word used to describe a nasty general array of skin conditions. The reason that no single 'eczema remedy' will work on all cases of eczema is because there are so many different sorts of skin troubles. An animal can have mange or ringworm, and it may look like eczema to the owner. He plasters the cat for weeks with somebody's eczema lotion. One day the owner too starts scratching. He rushes off to the doctor who diagnoses ringworm and asks, 'Do you have an animal, and is it scratching?'

If you'd rather treat your cat yourself, I have no objection. You must first make a diagnosis. Each sort of skin complaint is more likely to respond to a medicine that is designed for the purpose. And let me point out hastily that even with all the aids of laboratories and clinical experience and proper medications many skin complaints become chronic and more or less stay that way. But obviously the earlier proper treatment is initiated the greater the chances of success.

There are three general sorts of eczema (as opposed to specific skin diseases like mange or ringworm) that veterinarians see almost daily in the wintertime and several times daily in the summertime.

The first is *flea-bite dermatitis*, which just means that the skin is sore and red and itchy because the fleas are having a go. In all skin conditions the first step is to rid the animal of fleas and keep it that way, even if it means a daily combing and brushing and a daily clean up of bedding and sofas. Some cases are so bad when the vet sees them for the first time that the animal cannot be powdered or brushed or combed. The skin is just too sore. The cat in sheer desperation has scratched itself into a festering mass. Often daily injections of antibiotics are needed just to control the massive skin infection which is secondary to the few fleas that started the irritation. Many people simply will not accept that some cats will react to fleas as they do. They always point out that they have three (or thirty) cats and only one is scratching. I answer that millions of people wear woollen socks comfortably but they make me scratch.

The second sort of everyday eczema that vets see is called *nutritional eczema*. It may be caused by dietary mistakes, but most commonly it's caused by feeding too much fish. Again millions of cats eat and thrive on fish, but some cats break out in sores and the more fish they eat the more severe the condition. If fish is the cause of the trouble the remedy is obvious. Don't worry about the animal starving while learning to eat meat or go without. She might look miserable and miaow the house down for a couple of days, but on the third day she'll eat raw apples. Remember, please, that many tinned foods contain fish, so read the labels. If the contents aren't listed don't buy the stuff.

Another sort of eczema is *hormonal* in origin. Some spayed females and castrated males get the most elusive and persistent irritations. Some get great ugly bald patches for no apparent reason. Many respond to hormone tablets and injections. They partly replace the hormones that would have been produced had the ovaries or testicles been left in peace. It may take weeks for the results to be apparent. If the hormones do the job they must be continued indefinitely.

In addition to the above types there is a myriad of skin complaints that belie description, elude diagnosis, frustrate the veterinarian and bedevil the animal. The owner's only solace, if solace it is, is that such cases are never critical. But nevertheless the animal and everyone concerned live at a pitch of screaming nerves, and it goes on and on and on. And on.

No matter how pressing the case the veterinary surgeon will usually try the simpler remedies first, depending on the sort of eczema it is. Then, if those don't work, he'll go on to stronger and more complicated drugs. Obviously it's easier on the body if one can cure the condition with simpler drugs. Using very strong drugs on a simple condition is a bit like using a sledgehammer to mash peas. You'll get them mashed all right, but you'll make an awful mess. So string along with your vet while he gently plods through the weary weeks.

PS: I don't think I'm being unkind or unfair if I mention that some of my colleagues aren't very interested in treating cats. Of course they'll make sure that the patient isn't suffering but they'd rather be out among the cows and horses than go through the laborious business of skin scrapings and laboratory tests. I don't think it's at all out of line for the cat owner to ask the nurse or the vet if someone in the partnership has a particular interest in small animals. I also don't think it rude if there is no firm diagnosis and no improvement after two visits to ask whether a skin scraping wouldn't at least eliminate some possibilities.

Eggs

As you know, the egg is as near a complete food as there is. Eggs are just full of good protein and minerals and vitamins and maybe other things that we haven't got names for. They come in convenient, easily opened packages. All you have to do is break one into a clean bowl and your cat has a breakfast. If it's twelve o'clock noon you can do the same thing and call it lunch.

Are eggs part of a cat's natural diet? People who spend hours observing such things tells us that most cats will raid a nest and eat its contents of eggs or nestlings while waiting for the adult occupants to come home.

I think it's a good idea to give your cat an egg once in a while. If he gets ill or has tooth trouble he'll recognize an egg as an edible object which can be used to add substance to the monotonous soups and broths.

PS: Raw eggs should not be used as a *regular* part of the diet. They may dangerously deplete some vitamins. It's no big problem. Even my simple brother, Willie, can boil an egg.

Electric shock

Cats love to play with string, elastic and cord. The more it bounces the more they think it's a mouse, so they chew at it. If it's an electric cord the 'mouse' bites back – and with a vengeance. The cat leaps in the air, twitches, and lies still. BE CAREFUL! Often an electrocuted animal urinates. You may step in the urine, which is an excellent conductor. Before you do anything turn off the current. Then apply artificial respiration and have someone phone the vet.

Elizabethan collar

Presumably good Queen Liz the First wore a ruff around her neck because she thought it was pretty. Other ladies wore them because the Queen did. Today they are worn by some actresses and those dogs, cats and babies who can't otherwise be restrained from scratching at sore eyes or ears.

Take a piece of stiff cardboard. Cut it in half. Cut a wee semi-circle out of each half. Lace the two halves together around the cat's neck. That's an Elizabethan collar!

Enema

I don't know what the plural is, but singly or in series I think you'd best leave the job to your vet. The colon of the cat, particularly if it's distended, is paper thin. Any localized pressure can rupture it. If you're certain that the trouble is constipation and you simply can't get a vet, try introducing a few gelatine suppositories. Let them dissolve. Then introduce the enema tube, and by gravity alone allow the lukewarm soapy water to soak into the offending mess. Use about 6dl (1 pint). Repeat in an hour. If you're successful you'll realize why you should have left the job for your vet.

Enteritis (*feline infectious enteritis or panleucopenia*)

This is the fastest killer of any of the cat diseases. The cat seems normal one minute, and is listless and depressed the next. He sits hunched in one position. If you attempt to handle him he'll move to a more inaccessible place. He's not interested in you, his mates or indeed in life itself.

Sometimes the first thing the owner notices is vomiting, although this isn't a constant symptom. The poor creature brings up a large flood of liquid and food, followed by shorter belches of bile stained froth. There may be diarrhoea in a minority of cases.

Almost always the disease shows the following four symptoms:

1 depression
2 high temperature (up to 40°C (105°F))
3 abdominal tenseness or an arched back (which indicates pain in the tummy) and
4 dehydration and collapse within twenty-four hours.

Moral: If your cat is hunched up in the corner take its temperature. If it's 38°C (103°F) or over get it to your veterinarian straight away.

What will he do? First he'll try to confirm that it is in fact enteritis. Some cases are fairly straightforward. In others he might take a bit of blood, make a smear, and have it examined under the microscope. If the diagnosis is confirmed, what is the treatment? Well, not very different from what it would be without a diagnosis. One treats symptoms. First, absolute starvation for up to forty-eight hours. Small amounts of liquid might be allowed – but never forced. What sort? Oh, anything along the line of broths or soups or juices. Squeeze some fresh raw meat. The juice that comes out might look like blood, but it may tempt an ailing animal. Glucose in water is as good as anything, if your cat will lap it.

Injections include penicillin or the other antibiotics. Their main purpose is to keep down the common bugs that are ready to attack any body weakened by a virus. Vitamin injections, especially those of the 'B complex', and liver extract may boost resistance. Serum prepared from the blood of cats who have recovered from the disease is very expensive but worthwhile.

The best medicine, though, is the simplest. Good old-fashioned salt water (the stuff we all crawled out of long before automobiles and biology), if injected into veins or under the skin, snaps many apparently hopeless cases back to life.

Sadly, the virus is usually the winner. The mortality rate of this disease is still the highest of all cat disorders. The only nice thing you can say about virus enteritis is that if it kills, it usually kills quickly. Within a couple of days the animal's fate is sealed. But please don't let an apparent recovery fool you. Many relapse into further illness in a week or ten days. Sometimes the virus is having another go. More often the commoner bugs of flu move in to knock over a weakened constitution.

What is the point of this distressing dissertation? Simply that there exists a fairly effective inoculation against enteritis.

When should it be done? Any time from six weeks on. The full course is two injections about ten days or a fortnight apart. The kitten must, of course, be isolated during that period and for a week afterwards.

Adult cats who are going to shows or into boarding kennels should be reinoculated at least a fortnight beforehand.

There are two sorts of cats for which the inoculations are even more vital. Orientals like Siamese and Burmese seem to be more susceptible than Domestic short-hairs or Persians, and when attacked they usually succumb. Secondly – and many people won't accept this – if your cat is constantly indoors and away from other cats its natural resistance to all infections is likely to be low. You or a friend might well carry infection. In case you didn't know it, even little flies can carry germs that can kill a big cat. So don't hem and haw. Get your cat inoculated.

The inoculations are safe because the vaccine is inactivated. It must not be given, though, unless the cat is in perfect health. IT MUST NOT BE GIVEN IF THE CAT HAS RECENTLY BEEN EXPOSED TO INFECTION. A kitten may go off its food for a few hours after the injection, but most of them bounce away as if nothing had happened.

Many people believe that the vaccine is no good because their cat, though inoculated, came down with flu or pneumonia. That's like saying insurance is no good because your fire policy didn't cover your burglary losses. Enteritis is one specific disease of cats caused by a particular kind of virus. The vaccine builds up resistance to enteritis but has nothing to do with flu. Flu in the cat is more like flu in the human, for which there is still no safe effective long-term vaccine.

Summary: If you acquire an uninoculated kitten (assume it hasn't been done if there's no certificate) phone your vet for an appointment. Have it reinoculated before showing or boarding. Annual boosters are recommended.

Entropion

An infolding of the eyelids. It's fairly common in short-headed dogs who have too much skin for too little face. In cats it's rarely caused by the shape of the head. Usually an accident or a bite causes scar tissue to form, and this distorts the natural lie of the eye. The eye, instead of being gently bathed in its normally moist bed, is constantly irritated by the friction of the lids.

Medicated ointments may soothe the condition, but seldom do they effect a permanent cure. The eye gets scarred and ulcerated, and it becomes obvious to even the most reluctant cat owner that radical surgery is necessary.

A tiny, carefully calculated portion of skin is removed, and just enough tension put on the union to pull the lids back where they belong. Obviously, few of them heal perfectly, but in most cases there's a decided improvement within a few days, and in a couple of weeks the eye itself (now relieved of constant friction) starts to heal.

PS: I'm afraid we're now seeing almost as many cases in some breeds of cats as we expect to find in Chows and Pekes – and when man actually produces a painful deformity one case is too many. Come on, you breeders of runty Foreign Whites and malformed Blue Persians, prove me wrong and we'll celebrate together. One constructive suggestion: If any animal that has the tell-tale scars of an entropion operation was automatically disqualified, the incidence of the condition would fall dramatically within two or three generations.

Escalators

One of the additional complications of modern life to ensure that we need never use our legs. Most pet owners know enough to carry their Siamese up and down those moving stairs. Even so, we are occasionally presented with an animal who has been caught and badly torn. Usually it was accompanied by a child or by a servant with limited experience of animals. They just didn't think that the poor creature wouldn't know when to step off the contraption.

First aid consists of a pressure bandage to control the bleeding. Don't attempt to strap the broken bones. Get the cat into a box or a basket. Almost always those accidents happen in densely populated areas and usually during business hours, so it's not difficult to find a veterinary surgery that's going full blast.

Memo: Explain to your cat-walkers that Samuella simply must be carried into and on to and out of all mechanical contrivances.

Etiquette

Cats are usually considerate creatures. They are clean to the point of fastidiousness. They hesitate before waking one up, but if they have to they try to do it gently. If they don't really feel like being good company they don't hang about and make bores of themselves. They just go to sleep. If they don't like you they don't pretend that they do and then say nasty things behind your back. And they always give fair warning before they strike.

Their table manners are exemplary. They say please before, express pleasure during, and say thank you after a meal. They then wash carefully so that the furniture doesn't get greased with leftover stickiness.

They always prefer to do all their private business in private – if people let them.

If insulted they don't lower themselves by retaliating. They walk away with upright tails and dignity intact.

How many dogs do you know with such good manners? And how many people?

European Wild Cat

A larger, fiercer version of the alley tabby, in Britain he's found only in Scotland, although there have been some unconfirmed sightings in Wales. Lest you think he's just a tabby gone wild the zoologists tell us that he belongs to not only a different genus but a different family from his domestic cousin. He has a higher forehead and a bushy, bushy tail. That's evidence enough for the Court of Taxonomy. No one has domesticated a British Wild Cat, even though several young kittens have been captured. It has now been proved that *Felis Sylvestris* (as it's called) can and does interbreed freely with our domestic cats. And there is some evidence that the offspring are fertile. We may have in the wilder areas of this green and fertile island an emergent new sub-species.

Of possibly more interest to lovers of domestic cats is the observation recorded by a naturalist who reared an orphan litter. They refused all milk formulations. He and the other attendants despaired. Quite by accident a small dying bird found its way into the cage. The kittens who were so young that they couldn't see fought over it and consumed it in its entirety. The litter thrived.

Since that report was first published, many breeders have offered all forms of meat to young kittens who for one reason or another don't seem to thrive on milk alone. Amazing how many prove that they are truly carnivores!

Euthanasia

Some people come in and casually, as if they were ordering a packet of cigarettes, ask the vet to put their animal to sleep. 'Why?' we ask. In an offhand tone they reply something like, 'Oh, he's getting old and he made a mess on the rug', or, 'We thought we'd try a dog for a change'.

There's no point in trying to talk them out of the idea of 'getting rid of the cat'. Sometimes one can convince them to hang on to the animal for a few days while efforts are made to find it a new home. More often these people are so insensitive as to insist on their 'rights'. It's 'our cat' and 'we want it put to sleep'. Strangely enough, in law one can do nothing about it, so the animal is put to sleep. If one vet were to refuse, they'd just think he was a nut case and go to another. Or they'd do what thousands of others do: they'd simply dump the cat somewhere to fend for itself.

There are even some people who in this day and age will kill a cat by drowning – and I'm talking about adult cats. Consider it as you will, it's better that the vet concerned should just mutter under his breath and get on with the distasteful job. Maybe one day we'll have societies civilized enough to require that a prospective cat or dog owner should be worthy of that responsibility. You can't run a car without a licence because you might kill someone, but anybody is allowed to keep, and kill, a cat.

Some people go to the other extreme. They have lived with their cat for a decade or more. Each has added a dimension to the emotional depth of the other (which is what satisfactory relationships are meant to do). Then, one day, the cat miscalculates the strength of an adversary, or the height of a wall, or the speed of an approaching car. The animal is taken to the vet and examined. The damage is found to be irreparable. The vet is certain that the animal, if it survives, will live in constant pain. He advocates euthanasia. The owner recoils in horror. One doesn't order the execution of an old friend. The vet explains his reasoning. The owner usually says, 'I don't care how much it costs', as if that would mend the broken body. Again the vet gives his reasons, and often adds, 'Leave him with us for a few hours. Think it over. You'll agree it's the only kind thing'. Most owners will go home, take a stiff brandy, discuss it with the family or a friend, and phone in their permission to go ahead. Usually they're back in a few weeks with a delightful new kitten, 'who is nothing at all like old Mandikins, but doesn't she have the most perfect blue eyes?'

But there are some people who, no matter how hopeless the condition or how painful its effects, absolutely refuse to have the animal put down. They'd keep it going for a few pain-filled days or weeks by dint of constant nursing. It's a nerve-racking experience for them, and hell for the cat.

How are cats put to sleep? One has a choice of methods. If the animal is placid and experienced help is available, an intravenous injection is the quickest method. It's the same sort of injection one would use for inducing anaesthesia before pulling a tooth. One just gives a larger dose. With nervous cats it's often better to use chloroform. As long as they're getting a good flow of air while the chloroform is introduced, it causes little distress and absolutely no pain.

Chloroform is the method used by many welfare societies who have the unpleasant task of collecting and 'disposing' of dozens of unwanted cats every week. The employees who do it must of necessity do it mechanically. If they thought about it much they'd go off their nut. I know the whole business is deplorable, but as long as people are allowed to throw kittens out of doors when the mother stops feeding them, so long will the problem and its present solution persist.

Eyes

The eyes of the cat are highly developed and extremely efficient. Unlike the dog, the cat hunts mostly by sight. No matter how bright the day or how dim the night the pupil of the cat can instantly adjust. Thus the cat can generally outsee its prey and its adversaries. It's not so good, however, in focusing on still objects. Mice must know this by instinct because they'll often freeze at the approach of a cat and be overlooked. The blank unwavering stare of the cat which some people find so disconcerting is simply due to the fact that cats blink less than other animals and man. They don't need to blink because they have a third eyelid which comes up and clears the dust and moistens the eye. Cats can't swivel their eyes as well as we can. Instead they swing the entire head. If you've ever observed a cat watching an elusive object you'll know how fast those head movements can be. Cats' eyes don't shine in the dark. They do, however, reflect any available light. Finally (and only the owners of affected dogs can appreciate this) the eyes of the cat, except for a few highly bred short-headed Persians, haven't been messed about by man. Thus most cats are spared the whole host of operations that are done to restore the natural eyes the creatures had before they were turned into decorative objects.

There are only a few bits of commonsense you need to know about your cat's eyes, which will ensure that you don't do harm when you attempt to do good. Don't stick unused bits of ointment into eyes. Even if they're labelled as being expressly for eyes they may be the wrong sort of ointment for the particular condition. For example cortisone eye ointments may actually retard the healing of an ulcerated eye. Many ointments date rapidly and lose their efficiency. Others may actually be contaminated and introduce infection into the eye. The safest procedure is to simply bathe the eyes until you can get a diagnosis and the proper ointment. What do we use to bathe eyes? Teaspoon of salt to 6dl (1 pint) of water. Boil. Allow to cool. Store in a closed container.

You may have to use the above solution in those *emergencies* when some oaf drops cigar ash in a cat's eye, or to help float off bits of grit that are driving the cat to distraction. For pussy or *inflamed eyes* the same solution may be used to clean the eyes before applying ointment or drops.

85

The vast majority of eye infections don't actually originate in the eye but are *extensions or reflections of illness elsewhere*. For example most cases of flu are accompanied by sore runny eyes. One must treat both the flu itself and its localized manifestations. So if you bathe your cat's eyes for a day or so and there's no sign of improvement you'd better get along to the vet and find out where the real infection is.

Blocked tear ducts and *overflow of tears* is an all too common condition in Persians. Over a period of months the face gets stained and an ugly sore eczema spreads down from the eyes. Although one can control the condition for a time it usually recurs. However unsatisfactory you find this state of affairs you simply must repeat the treatment each and every time it does come back. If you just forget about it the face will end up an ulcerated mess. I suppose we'll see the condition more often if the present tendency towards Pekinese-faced Persians persists.

Cataracts: Those things that some elderly people and dogs get that makes the eyes look like clouded glass. Cataracts are rare in aged cats but they do occur in cats of all ages for many reasons. There is an operation to remove the clouded bits which often improves the vision considerably. Needless to say this is a specialized field of surgery, and your vet will arrange for a specialized colleague to assess the case and do the operation.

Progressive retinal atrophy: Night blindness is usually the first symptom of this distressing condition that progresses to blindness. Fortunately it's not the common problem in cats that it is with some breeds of dogs. Nevertheless there is an inherited form of the disease that we see from time to time. It's a condition for which there is no cure. One should not breed from affected animals no matter how valuable they are.

The third eyelid or *nictitating membrane* may come up and partially cover the eye. The first time an owner sees it he, or she, becomes most alarmed. It may be merely a sign of fatigue. It may be a sign of nutritional deficiency or worms. However, it may equally well be something serious. In other words it's not an emergency but if it persists beyond a day or two you'd better get professional advice. No point in bathing meanwhile. It simply won't help.

PS: Recently this condition has been commonly reported as an accompaniment to chronic diarrhoea. At this moment no one has come up with a real answer to the problem. One recent report suggests that if it's treated with all modern medication it lasts six weeks. Untreated it clears up in under two months. Despite that sort of cynicism one should check for the obvious causes like improper diet, parasites and environmental poisons. Quite obviously any sort of old-fashioned 'binding' medicine like kaolin or charcoal given in moderation can't do any harm while you and your vet try to determine the cause. Incidentally, one of the drugs commonly used to control diarrhoea in people (even young babies) sends many cats absolutely loco. Apparently it's chemically related to morphine which simply doesn't agree with most cats.

Eyes of kittens usually open about the tenth day. If they don't open by the twelfth day you'd better take them along to the vet. If the kitten's eyes are crusted with matter take them *and* the mother along. They'll all be happy together in the basket. You'll save a trip if the mother happens to need treatment as well because often eye infection in kittens is a result of some infection in the mother. Until the mother is cured there is little point in treating the suckling kittens. Older weaned kittens, particularly those about ten or twelve or fourteen weeks of age are very susceptible to flu and other infections. They won't ever get properly over a setback at this age so at the first sign of trouble get professional treatment.

Eye removal

Surgery on and within the eye is more difficult in the dog than it is in man, and it is even more difficult in the cat. In the cat the muscles are very fine, the socket is narrow, and bleeding can be an uncontrollable flood. Also, we occasionally see eye conditions in the cat that don't respond to treatment as do those of the dog. We are often forced to advise removal of the eye as the only way of preventing further pain or saving sight in the other eye.

The operation is fairly straightforward, but the anaesthesia is complicated. A tube is introduced into the trachea because a mask can't be used when one is working on the head. Unlike the dog, a cat can't be easily tubed unless its muscle contractions are stopped with one of the paralysing drugs. The drug that paralyses the muscles of the throat also paralyses the chest muscles. This means that you have a few short seconds in which to get the tube in and start mechanical breathing. I've never seen a death caused by this, but that's only because veterinarians know how critical the timing is and they get everything set up beforehand so that accidents just aren't allowed to happen.

The operation involves about half an hour of slowly snipping down and separating the muscle attachments of the eye until it is held only by a stalk consisting of the huge optic nerve and the accompanying blood vessels. These are tied off. I have seen grown men cursing or sweating (depending on their temperament) as they tried to get these ligatures tightened. The vessels lie on a little wee stalk at the bottom of a socket that is too small to admit more than one finger. Try tying a knot with one finger in a slippery matchbox and you'll have the idea. Anyway, if that ligature is tight the operation is virtually over – and over safely. A few skin sutures bring the new 'lids' together, the cat is kept on antibiotics for a few days, the stitches come out in a week or so, and soon the whole area is covered with hair and old Tom learns to swing his neck to see offside objects.

And in case you hadn't guessed, many people rename their pet after the operation. What? Nelson, of course.

False teeth

Many old ewes and a very few valuable guard dogs get fitted with false teeth. Cats don't because they don't need them. A cat uses its teeth to cut and to tear, but not to masticate.

Tell toothless old Penelope to choose her friends wisely and never pick a quarrel. Cut her meat into small, swallowable pieces. She won't miss those rotten old teeth a bit. Even if she doesn't look quite so beautiful, she'll smell ever so lovely.

The reason I mention this is because many owners postpone urgent extractions because they think their cat will starve without teeth.

Feeding

The stuff you actually put in the bowl is covered under *Diet*. How and when to feed is something you have to work out to suit your own convenience, and not that of the cat. Many cats like to have a stroll and a gossip about three in the morning. They run into the neighbourhood bore and, my God, she talks and she talks and before you know it's six o'clock and everybody's just starving. Everybody except you, that is, because you're just sleeping. Does that deter old gadabout? Not at all! If he had his way you'd be up and slicing tomorrow's steak into cat-sized bits. So, don't be sentimental and foolish. Train him from day one that he gets fed at regular hours of *your* choosing. At all other times he's miaowing up the wrong tree.

When a cat's food is put down you leave him alone to get on with it. Nobody likes to be watched while savouring mouthfuls. Similarly Old Piggy-Kittens must learn that while you're eating he must wave his tail elsewhere. In fact well-mannered felines should know that they are not allowed above chair level in the kitchen and dining room.

Feeding bowls should be solid, heavy and easy to clean. They should be broad and flat rather than narrow and deep. After a reasonable time they should be picked up and soaked. Whether you wash them in soap or in detergent they should be rinsed with clean water and allowed to dry on their own. I simply can't understand how people who are otherwise quite fastidious can eat or drink from utensils that taste of detergent. Cats refuse to and, of course, they're quite right.

Feet

If we went around without shoes most of us would be lame most of the time. Shoes, although they're expensive, uncomfortable and smelly, do protect us from the bits of glass and grit and metal that most cats learn to avoid almost by instinct. A cat crazed by fear or by the opposite sex may land with full force on some sharp object. He comes home limping. Look at his feet first, because that's where most lamenesses originate. Before you put him on the table do three things. Get your assistant lined up because few cats will let you examine their feet unless they are held firmly. Get your light in position because you'll need it if you're to see anything at all. And thirdly before you pick the cat up make sure you know which leg he's lame on. Amazing how many people (myself included) will start examining a cat's foot, and after ten minutes of finding nothing realize that it's the wrong foot. Once the cat is on the table he'll often (whether out of fright or perverseness I cannot say) put equal weight on all four feet and express equal displeasure whichever one you handle.

What will you find? The pad may have a small open cut. If it's clean, bathe the whole foot in warm salt water, dry it, apply a bit of antiseptic ointment and bandage the foot. Repeat in two days. Two days later it should be healed.

There may be a broken claw. If it's a fairly clean break treat it as above, but you'll have to repeat three or four times.

The pad may have a bit of grit in it or a sliver of glass. Bathing will ease it out. Often these cuts are best left open.

If the foot is extremely painful to the touch it may be fractured, or it may have been bitten deeply and infected. Such cases, of course, require professional attention. The ones that are most often neglected but may be the most dangerous are those in which only a tiny prick is visible. These are called puncture wounds, and the infection may be

89

deeply embedded. Daily injections for some days are part of the usual treatment.

When bandaging a foot you must pillow the pads with bits of cotton wool, or else you can cause worse pressure sores than you are healing. Wind the bandage well up the leg. Lay it flat so as not to cut off circulation. Cover it all with sticky tape, or Kit will have it off before breakfast. Don't leave it on for more than two days. If you're not sure of your technique, change it daily. If you wake up in the middle of the night and think it might be too tight, phone your vet to come and change it. He'll be delighted.

Feral

This is a word meaning wild or untamed or uncultivated. It is often applied to the domestic cat. I will agree that the domestic cat is untamed, but it is neither wild nor uncultivated. I think some people think it is feral because it is capable of looking after itself. It is the only animal that has retained its freedom despite thousands of years of domestication. Is that one of the reasons you prefer cats?

Fever

Anything over 30°C (103°F) is a fever, and must be considered as a serious symptom (see *Temperature*).

Fights

You can usually separate two cats by dumping a pail of water over the pair of them. The same harmless shock will usually allow a moment's respite in which a downed cat can escape from an attacking dog. If you don't happen to be carrying a pail of water you can try throwing your coat over the combatants. A fur coat is a particularly valuable confuser. Whatever you do don't attempt to separate fighting animals with bare hands. If you have nothing to wield or throw, you can run very quickly between them. The force of your legs will separate the animals and allow the loser to escape.

Fish

Being a prairie boy I was brought up to believe that fish was the horrible stuff you ate when you couldn't afford meat. I still prefer meat, and so do many cats. Some cats, though, have been indoctrinated through habit into eating nothing but fish. It isn't natural. Certainly in the feral or wild state there are many more hunting cats than fishing cats. Although I imagine that when the salmon are running even the most passionate of hunters would dampen a lazy paw.

Most 'cat experts' say that the suitable fish are white and non-oily. Everyone agrees that the fish should be fresh, and most people agree that it should be cooked and boned. Some people feed raw fish, and don't bother about removing the bones. They claim that the cat is clever enough to fillet his own fish. I guess lots of them get away with it, but vets see those cases which don't. Many vets, too, believe that too much fish in the diet may cause or aggravate eczema.

Many cats which are fed on an exclusively fish diet stink. Being sensitive creatures, they don't like to smell badly, and I can't imagine how their owners put up with it.

Your vet may recommend increasing the amount of fish (and other white meats) if your cat is suffering from one of the kidney conditions.

And finally, to refute everything, may I remind you of the cats of Venice. There one runs into pockets of sleek fat creatures who are obviously thriving and propagating on the remains of fish that smell even worse than the canals.

Fish hooks

Kittens, as you will have observed, will follow any material down to its mysterious source. Adults will do the same thing, albeit with more caution. Do I really have to advise that fishing tackle and cats are best kept apart?

Another common source of fish hooks is fish. A single barb or the whole head of a hook is often broken off. Some venerable fish contain so much metal that you wonder how they keep afloat. Most cats are fastidious eaters and will avoid the bits that contain the metal, or they'll delicately pick the flesh off the hook. But accidents do happen, and when they do they are most distressing both to the unfortunate victim and to the panicked observers.

The cat (unlike the dog) doesn't usually paw or claw at its throat if there's something stuck there. He usually hunches up and keeps gulping. If there's professional help available anywhere in the area the only sane thing to do is to get the cat in a box or a basket and transport him to the vet. Under general anaesthesia most offending objects are easily removed.

What to do if there's no such thing as a vet or an animal loving doctor in your part of the bush? First, confine the cat. The beast in his panic is quite likely to run off and hide himself for a couple of days. Secondly, gather together your materials. An assistant, or preferably two, a strong light, a sharp knife, narrow-nosed pincers, a towel and two neckties are what you need.

Roll the cat tightly in the towel, leaving only his head outside. One assistant holds the cat in the towel. Pry the jaws apart and get your second assistant to hold them open with one necktie around the lower jaw and the other around the upper.

Focus the light and locate the hook. Try to figure out which way the barb is pointing. Never pull it out. Push it out. Otherwise you'll tear everything into a bloody mess. You may have to cut over the area, but your incision will do less damage than a forceful pull. Sometimes you can cut the offending barb, and it will then slide out.

Remember that after your crude butchery the cat's only instinct will be to run off and hide. Don't let him out until his confidence in you has been restored.

Today's lesson: Fish hooks should be pushed out, not pulled out.

Fits

These are upsets of the nervous system which can take many forms. Usually the animal starts with a slight champing of the jaws. The champing becomes faster and more intense. Sometimes the tongue appears lifeless and locked outside the mouth. The animal may go through paddling, walking or running motions. It may fall over locked in a fixed, frozen spasm.

Please, whatever you do, don't panic. Any animal having a fit cannot recognize you, or anything else for that matter. Don't soothe it. It can't hear you. Don't pat it. It can't feel you. Throw blankets down to minimize the chances of its hurting itself, and do nothing else. You'll almost certainly get scratched or bitten badly if you try to handle a cat while it's having a fit. You cannot possibly do any good. Most fits pass in seconds or minutes. A veterinarian can give injections that may lessen the severity of *succeeding* fits, but no one can inject a cat in time to shorten a fit while it's actually taking place.

Kittens occasionally have fits because of worms or teething problems. Sometimes an overdose of a strong worming pill will cause a fit. Sometimes ear mites will cause fits. Take the kitten along to your veterinarian (after the fit is over) and let him try to ascertain the cause.

In an adult a fit is almost invariably a sign of a more serious disorder, and I'm afraid that many of those that I've seen – particularly where the fits increased in frequency, duration and severity – have proved fatal. One recommends euthanasia if the cause is something incurable like a tumour or one of the kidney conditions. Fortunately fits in adult cats are rather a rare condition, unlike dogs, where they are an all too common sequel to distemper.

A warning to people who live in countries where rabies is rampant – or even just present. If your cat or kitten throws a fit, lock it in the room and make sure your children are warned to stay out. Call your veterinarian. If there's an actual outbreak going on, call the government department that is dealing with the disease. Under no circumstances attempt to deal with it yourself.

Summary: Do not try to handle a cat while it's having a fit.

Flatulence (*gas in the bowel, breaking wind*)

This complaint is seen fairly rarely in felines, but I include it for two reasons. The first is that if it is *sudden in onset* and causes a great deal of discomfort it may be due to an obstruction in the bowel. The only safe home aid is a gentle enema. Don't repeat the process. Often surgical removal is necessary to avoid penetration of the bowel by the object and a fatal peritonitis.

The second reason I mention flatulence is because some people allow their cats to suffer with it for months. They don't know how to describe the condition politely and are too shy to say that he makes bad smells. Say flatulence! This *long-standing type* of flatulence may be due to bad food or the wrong sort of food, but more often it's due to overfeeding and lack of exercise. Put Stinky on a diet!

Fleas

Most eczemas are triggered off by fleas.

I say it ten times a day, and I haven't found a way of saying it so that people believe me. If you have a cat that is scratching or is covered in sores or has wet eczema or dry eczema, put him on a table and look until you see a flea. If you don't see one turn him on his back and look along his belly and on the inside of his legs. I can assure you that (*a*) ninety per cent of all 'eczema' cats have fleas on their bodies or hiding in their bedding and (*b*) if you get rid of the fleas you're halfway to curing the condition.

'But,' everyone answers, 'lots of cats have fleas.' Yes, that's true, but your cat is just more sensitive to fleas than lots of cats. Just as lots of people will scratch themselves raw because of one mosquito bite, while hundreds of people around them sunbathe in comfort.

What does a flea look like? It's about the size of this letter i without the dot. When you first see him he's usually stock still, and then he crawls off to get out of the light. It's fairly easy to catch them.

How do you get rid of them? Spread newspapers on a table. Put the flea powder and brush on the table. Then entice or catch your cat. Place him on the newspapers on the table and hold him with your left hand. Apply pinches of powder with your right hand to the tail. Gently rub it around. The fleas will start moving. Then carefully avoiding the eyes, the ears and the mouth, dust a bit on the head and then the neck. The fleas up there will start moving. The idea is to drive them towards the middle where you can dust and brush and comb thoroughly. If you start in the middle you drive the fleas to the extremities and the cat crazy.

Brush all the powder out. Tell your cat how wonderful he's been and shove him outdoors or give him a snack if that'll make him forget the indignity of it all. Fold up the papers and burn them. They should be full of powder and a few fleas. Then go to every spot where your cat sleeps, sprinkle it with powder and vacuum it out. If you repeat this three times at weekly intervals you and the fleas will have had enough. Remember you must brush all the powder out of the cat's fur. Otherwise it will lick it and get sick. You must catch the fleas as they drop and destroy them. You must do the bedding at the same time. If you have two cats both must be done, even though only one is infested.

What sort of flea powder? Get one put up by one of the giant companies that labels it clearly 'may be used on cats'.

One final fact about fleas. They can carry tapeworms. If your cat has tapeworms treat it for fleas at the same time as you give the pills (see *Tapeworms*).

Flies

Cats don't attract flies. Food and filth do. Don't leave leftover food about. Put a fresh layer of sand in the sanitary tray twice daily in the summertime. If the cat uses a small area you must operate a daily pick-up service. Don't spray your cat or its food, because it's not an effective way of dealing with flies, but it is a sure way of poisoning your cat.

Flu

Veterinarians call this disease Rhinotracheitis, which is a more accurate description, but the public persist in calling it Influenza or Feline Flu or Cat Flu or Snuffles, because that's what it looks like to them. It resembles the common cold in that it usually starts with sneezing and discharge from the eyes or the nose. Both diseases (the cat sort and the human sort) spread rapidly in a closed community like a kindergarten or a cattery. There is no effective vaccine against either sort, because the viruses involved just don't stimulate the body's defensive antibodies. And there is no specific effective treatment.

Please don't take the analogy too far and assume that because the human form looks like the cat form they are actually the same. They are two completely different diseases with no relationship to each other. There's an old medical cliché about the common cold that goes like this: 'If left untreated it lasts a week. If treated properly it's cured in seven days.' In the cat, let me assure you, a neglected case of flu will drag on for weeks and even months. Many of the animals affected die. Those that don't may be left with the most frightful sinus troubles which can plague them for life. If Puss comes home from holidays with crusty eyes and a runny nose, don't let a whole week go by while he loses condition. Early treatment will shorten the course of the disease. Antibiotics are used, which don't hit the virus but do prevent other bacteria from moving in. Fluids are injected to keep up bodily strength if the cat is not eating or drinking. Vitamins, particularly of the B group, are prescribed. Soothing ointments are applied to the eyes and nose. Sometimes a stomach tube is passed in order to force feed.

Home treatment – and it must be at home because few veterinary hospitals are equipped adequately to isolate such an infectious disease – includes several daily cleansings of the eyes and nose. Use a teaspoon of salt to 6dl (1 pint) of warm water. Apply the prescribed ointments, sparingly, after cleaning.

Grooming (combing and brushing) becomes more important than ever because cleanliness is an integral part of a cat's life. If he's kept clean it will retain his pride, his interest and his hope. Keep him out of draughts but ensure adequate circulation of fresh air. Encourage him to eat by trying a variety of foods. Some will regain their interest in food if offered a very strong smelling cheese or a really pungent game stew. A source of heat should be available but not fixed in a small space so that the cat can't escape it. It should be changed often enough to keep its temperature reasonably constant.

How long will he be ill? Certainly a fortnight, and possibly a month! Most show considerable improvement within a week, and the owner assumes a false optimism. They phone and say, 'He's so much better. He's sitting up beside the phone right now. He played with the dog and he bit my husband. It's a pity to give him any more needles. You know how he detests those injections.' The vet tries to persuade them that the cat may be improved but is far from cured. He's not his persuasive best, because he's holding the phone in one hand and fending off a Corgi with the other. He doesn't see the cat for a week. Then an abject owner shows up. The cat has relapsed and the condition is now solidly entrenched.

Not all cases relapse because of the owners' neglect. Some, despite all treatment and every attention, become chronic. Often the sinuses become involved. They thicken and discharge horribly. The vet may decide to trephine, which is a nice way of saying that he will bore a hole into the affected sinuses through which he can syringe the sinuses every day. Some 'flu' cats develop pneumonia, and these can be touch and go. Finally, some cats are exposed to flu and enteritis at the same time. Those that haven't been inoculated against the latter come down with both. Needless to say, they will have a very tough struggle to survive.

Summary: There is no effective inoculation against flu. Treatment must be started early and kept up until the cat is absolutely healthy.

PS: There are now several fancy names for cat flu and some even fancier vaccines. I wouldn't hazard a guess as to their efficiency but I can tell you they're expensive. More worrying is the fact that some observant vets and breeders suggest that these new vaccines may protect the cat but turn it into a carrier of the disease. In other words, they suggest that the inoculated cats may show no signs of the disease but act as incubators to spread it to other cats. This is such a complicated problem that no one can prove it, at this moment, one way or the other.

I do know that in our own cattery we will not allow a cat that has been done with the new-fangled stuff.

As far as flu is concerned we'd rather rely on plenty of space, isolation of suspected cases and early treatment. We've come to this opinion partly because we think that the big companies who we've relied on for many years – despite their capital and expertise – have not jumped on the bandwagon and partly because it's still such a debatable subject in the human medical field.

Foreign bodies

To you and your cultured friends the term 'foreign bodies' probably means the corpses of foreigners. Veterinarians, however, are peaceful beasts and seldom deal with such thrilling items. In order to add excitement to their dull lives they refer to any object that gets stuck in an animal as a 'foreign body'.

Fish hooks and fish bones and pins and needles and butcher's cord and little rubber balls become foreign bodies the minute they get lodged in a cat.

The symptoms, of course, vary with the location of the object. If it's in the mouth or throat the animal may be in constant distress. Sometimes an object can be lodged in or round the pharynx for weeks without causing distress. The only symptoms may be recurring abscesses in the area. It may gag or cough or it may paw at the area. Don't panic! Get a good light focused over a strong table. Find a friend with a thick skin or expendable gloves. Get him to hold the cat (one hand on each shoulder) while you pry open the jaws. It may be just a simple square little geegaw that's got lodged in the wrong place. A gentle push or a sharp pull might dislodge it. Pull it out, stroke the cat, and join the growing ranks of honorary veterinary surgeons. But please, if you can't see the whole object don't mess about. It may be a wedged hook or a fish bone that is properly anchored. Apply any pressure, and you'll make the problem worse. Get the stupid creature in a basket and hie yourself off to the vet.

Sometimes things get lodged further down. Symptoms vary from retching and vomiting to a simple refusal of food. Sometimes the vet can feel the object. Sometimes an X-ray is needed to pinpoint the object. Usually the vet decides that the only way to get it out is to open the cat and pull it out. Occasionally laxatives will move the thing along.

I recall one cat who had swallowed a needle. The X-ray showed that the needle was lying nicely in the bowel and the dull eye-end was pointing towards the tail. During coffee break we discussed the needle. (What do you discuss during coffee break?) In our collective wisdom and laziness we decided that it would probably move along. It did. It took two anxious days and several X-rays till the drama reached its happy ending.

What's the point of this story? Before you start filleting fish or threading needles or tying flies remind pussy of a pressing social engagement elsewhere.

Fractures

Fractures can vary from minor discomforts to serious affairs that necessitate the destruction of the animal. A kitten who fractures a toe may hobble about for a few days and then be right as rain. The owner might not even notice it. A cat who drops from a height and fractures a couple of legs and its skull will probably not survive.

Generally speaking fractures are not emergencies insofar as the shattered bones are concerned. You can do much harm by splinting a bone in an amateur fashion. If there is a lot of bleeding attempt to control it but otherwise don't mess about. Just transfer the cat to a basket, being careful not to get bitten or clawed in the process. Grab the scruff of the neck with one hand. Support the abdomen with the other. Gently lay the cat in its box, secure the lid and phone the vet.

The following is an outline of how some common fractures are treated. It may help you recognize the damage and will give you an idea of what your cat will undergo, its chances of recovery and how long that recovery will take. Each individual has different healing powers and each fracture is its own new problem.

Fracture (*scapula*)

The shoulder blade is well covered with muscle and is rarely broken. When it is broken it may set on its own particularly if there hasn't been much displacement. The surgeon may decide to sew parts of it together with stainless steel wire. He'll leave the wire in place for up to three weeks at which time the cat undergoes further X-rays and another operation to have it removed. American veterinarians prefer to splint these cases. But no matter which side of the water you and your cat live you needn't worry yourselves about this rarest of fractures.

Fracture (*palate or split palate*)

Almost never seen in dogs but seen fairly often in cats. It's usually the result of a fall. The creature lands on its feet but hits its head. I suppose it must be something similar to what happens when people involved in car accidents strike the windscreen. Something's got to give. In the human, I'm told, it's usually the vertebrae of the neck. In the cat it's usually the jaw, occasionally the hard palate and some-times both. The animal may appear perfectly OK. It can walk, talk and beg for its dinner. When dinner is served pussy takes a half-hearted nibble and leaves off. She may lap a bit out of her nostrils. Under a good light one can easily see the split. Treatment involves a general anaesthetic and sewing the opening together. Puss stays on antibiotics for a few days and on soft or liquid diets for days and days. In a fortnight, all being well, she'll be her usual aloof self.

Fracture (*pelvis*)

The pelvis is a cradle of well-muscled bones which forms the rear end of you and cats and lots of other creatures. The organs of urination and defecation and procreation are protected by the pelvis. If the pelvis is injured badly one of those functions may be affected. Although the pelvis itself doesn't move, the hind legs swivel in the sockets of the pelvis. If those sockets are knocked out of position the animal is lame. Needless to say, all pelvic injuries are painful.

Because it is so well protected a great deal of force is required to break a pelvis. Usually that force is an automobile accident. In rural areas it's occasionally seen in cats who didn't realize that cows can kick sideways.

The injured animal runs or drags itself off. When it has found a relatively secure place it will rest there − sometimes for days − and this is, of course, the best treatment for an injured pelvis. The cat will move reluctantly, and then only to drag itself into an even more inaccessible corner. Sometimes it will be able to move on three legs and occasionally, very slowly and painfully, on all four.

Veterinarians can usually feel a fractured pelvis, but only an X-ray can determine how extensive the injury is.

How can you recognize a fractured pelvis? The cat is in pain. It moves reluctantly or it drags itself or it cannot stand. In some cases the damage is so slight that the only symptoms you'll notice are constipation or retention of urine.

Now, quite obviously there is no first aid for this sort of fracture. The animal must be taken to the vet. Carry him in a basket or a box. The X-rays will show how bad the mess is, and the veterinarian will give you an idea of the chances of recovery. We don't operate on pelvis fractures because it is impossible to immobilize the patients for long periods as they do in human medicine.

Sometimes the patient is allowed to go home fairly soon. Nursing consists of giving sloppy food to prevent constipation. Raw liver is as good as anything. If the cat can't pass its water or its motion, or if there's blood in either, back to the vet you must go.

It's quite miraculous how most pelvic fractures heal. Within a week the patient is hobbling about, and a couple of weeks later they try a short spurt of running. They may be a bit crooked or a bit wobbly, but most of them get along just fine.

A female who has had a pelvic fracture should be spayed because if she gets pregnant she'll almost certainly need a Caesarian operation.

Fracture (*radius and ulna*)

Below the humerus (which is the long bone that runs into the shoulder) are the twin bones called the radius and ulna. They run straight up and down, the smaller ulna lying immediately behind the larger radius. They are about 10cm (4 in) long in the normal cat.

They may be fractured easily in kittens. We see it fairly commonly in kittens who have leaped out of their owners' arms. I think there must be many more cases which veterinarians don't see. The ulna can act as a splint for the broken radius. If only one of the bones is fractured the kitten may hold the leg up for a few days and then slowly and painfully hobble about. After two or three weeks the callus will start to form, and soon nature will have effected a cure – in some cases. Those cases in which the fracture is too far out of line for natural healing are very painful. Such cases, if neglected for too long, are most difficult to heal.

If a kitten jumps out of your arms and limps away on three legs, examine the injured leg. If it's floppy or painful, then go to the vet straight away. If it seems OK but just a little sore, wait for a few hours. If he gradually puts weight on it, he's probably just banged it too hard. If the lameness persists, better let a veterinarian see it.

Most of these fractures mend easily and without complication in about three weeks – provided they are splinted (in young kittens) or plastered (in older kittens). Some, though, may require surgical reduction, to get the ends in place and thus ensure healing.

In the adult cat a fracture is a much more serious matter, and the sooner you get professional attention the better.

Now a few things to remember about nursing fracture cases which your veterinarian may forget to tell you. If the cat starts biting the plaster off, cover it with a sock, or better still sticky tape. If at the end of a week or so he goes off his food or you smell something funny, take him back to the veterinarian. It may be that the plaster is rubbing and causing sores or worse. Do not feed the cat on the morning that you go back (at the appointed time) to have the plaster removed. Anaesthetics are dangerous if given after a meal.

Finally, and this applies to all injured cats: they are easy prey for dogs or bullying cats while they are convalescing. Keep a sharp eye the first few times he's allowed out.

Fracture (*tibia or fibula*)

The twin bones of the hind leg corresponding to the radius and ulna on the front. Fractures of these bones are usually plastered. Unless there is a great deal of damage they usually heal quite nicely in three or four weeks.

Fracture (*humerus*)

This is the bone at the top of the front leg that connects the shoulder blade to the radius and ulna. A fracture of the humerus is always serious. The animal cannot put any weight on the limb. Usually a blow that is severe enough to fracture a humerus is so severe that it displaces the fragments. In addition it's difficult properly to plaster a humerus. In almost all these fractures the animal must be caged for a day until the swelling goes down. Then a general anaesthetic is administered, and the leg is clipped and shaved and disinfected in preparation for surgery. The surgeon cuts over the bone and separates the muscles until he can see and manipulate the broken ends. He inserts a stainless steel pin right up the hollow of one of the broken ends. Then he directs it into the other broken end and manipulates until he has the two ends in proper position with the pin supporting each equally. It is a skilled laborious business. He may wire the smaller fragments into place afterwards. Then he sews the muscles back together and finally the skin. In three weeks or a month an X-ray is taken to see if proper healing has occurred. If it has, the animal has another operation and the pin is removed.

Fracture (*femur*)

The long bone on the hind leg that corresponds to the humerus on the front. It rotates in a socket of the pelvis and connects to the smaller twin bones, the tibia and fibula. Generally fractures of the femur are treated like fractures of the humerus. That is, one attempts to insert a stainless steel pin to support the weight while the bone is healing. Unfortunately many fractures of the femur occur right near the top, and there often isn't enough bone left at the top of the leg to take the pin. Each surgeon tackles these differently, but most of them insist on two months of enforced rest. Some take as long as five or six months before puss really feels like chasing mice.

Fracture (*wrists and paws*)

The very tiny bones at the bottom of the limbs heal quite nicely provided not too many are broken, and provided they haven't been knocked too far out of line. A general anaesthetic is usually necessary to relax the limb for proper positioning before the plaster of paris is applied. If the fracture is the result of a dog bite, or if it's a compound fracture that has become infected, the plaster may have to be changed fairly often so that the foot can be bathed and antibiotic ointments applied. Generally they are discharged as healed within a fortnight or three weeks, although it may be a bit longer before full weight is put on the limb.

Fracture (*or dislocation of the spine*)

I leave the most serious to the end. Sometimes the injury is obvious. The animal is in extreme pain and cannot move. Sometimes there is little pain, the animal can move but its tail and bladder are paralysed. In all cases it's a most serious business and often the only humane solution is euthanasia.

Funny or non-orthodox medicine

This includes witch doctoring, folk medicines, herbal tea doctoring, chinese grocery medicine and a host of more respectable ones backed by money, solicitors and libel suits.

Cats are subjected to more of these weird remedies than any other species save the human. This may be because cat lovers are weird. More likely it's because many people who are attracted to cats are the sort of people who question orthodoxy of all kinds. I, for one, wouldn't do anything to stifle their spirit of free inquiry. In many cases it doesn't do any harm to shove a garlic pill down a kitten's throat or fill its room with the pungent odour of boiling weeds. Incantations and chants, even when not immediately successful, are almost always amusing, and most cats find them a pleasant diversion.

The only harm that funny medicine does is that it may postpone proper treatment or discourage people from having their animals inoculated. You can push anything you like into a diabetic cat, but the only thing that will relieve it will be insulin. The only treatment that will relieve an abscess caused by a rotting tooth is the removal of the tooth. Nevertheless, the purveyors of trial and error quackery thrive. I suppose the reason they do is because most doctors and veterinarians are relatively honest. Instead of pretending that they know the 'only truth' they admit that a condition 'may' be what they think it is, and 'may' respond to the treatment.

When a condition is hopeless they will say so. Many conditions become chronic, and medicine simply has no effect one way or the other. It's precisely because there are so many hopeless cases and so many chronic cases that the funny medicine people survive. They don't attempt to compete in those fields that orthodox medicine has conquered. They just stick their greedy fingers into those miseries that are still without scientific solution. Who do you think will eventually cure cancer? The hocus-pocus people or the doctor? (See also *Quacks*.)

Gerbils, Butterflies, Hamsters, Budgies and Canaries

More advice from mother: These are tiny delicacies kept by the off-spring of our humans for our amusement. Most are kept in secure prisons. After two or three days they become a bit of a bore. One should, however, take the odd glance. Occasionally the children forget to lock the gates. Pounce immediately! They can advertise those tinned foods as much as they like, but there is no substitute for the real thing.

Geriatrics

The branch of medicine which deals with the care of the aged. As more and more of the infectious diseases are controlled by modern antibiotics and vaccines, more and more cats, like people, have a greater chance of reaching ripe old age. Many cats are vigorous and active at twelve years of age, but most start to slow down before that. By fifteen even the most vigorous creatures exhibit degenerative changes. After all, even the best machines show wear. Sometimes the wear is uneven. One must have the creaky parts serviced regularly. I would suggest that, no matter how well an ageing pet appears to be, regular check-ups are essential. Often your vet can detect an important change in its early stages when there's a better chance of effective treatment.

It's important to avoid dangers and stresses and changes. Allow the ageing cat all the exercise it wants, but make sure the gates are closed. A marauding dog is only a nuisance to a vigorous young cat, but can be fatal to an older cat with slow reflexes and tired muscles. Make sure the old boy can get back inside when he's finished his stroll. It doesn't hurt a young cat to get wet or cold, but an extra half-hour out of doors may be a prelude to pneumonia in the aged. If the weather is nasty you'd better consider reintroducing Old Tom to the indignity of the sanitary tray. He may resent being treated like a kitten, but gradually (if grudgingly) he'll accept its convenience. Some old cats can't control themselves all night long, and for these a sanitary tray is essential no matter what the weather. How many eighty-year-old people would get up at 3 a.m., go downstairs, stand suspiciously at the door for several minutes to make sure there were no dangerous strangers about, and then dart into the cold night air? What would they do if they returned a few minutes later to find the door locked? It's amazing how many people expect an ageing cat to do exactly that, night after night, and in all weathers. If the old boy makes one mess indoors they come screaming into the surgery the next day, complain that he's 'dirty', and demand that he be put to sleep.

Consideration for an ageing cat includes the right to privacy. No cat likes loud noises, but older cats, like older people, detest all noise. They just don't have the patience and fortitude. If you're throwing a party for your children and their delinquent friends, allow puss a dignified retreat; if Aunt Adenoid and her brace of Great Danes are down for the weekend, inform them politely but firmly that Puss has the run of the west wing *and* the tropical conservatory, and he simply must not be disturbed.

Boarding aged cats is very tricky. They're too set in their ways. The most comfortable kennel may upset them to the point of physical illness. Even if they don't mind the place they may come in contact with some disease. With the lowered resistance and resiliency of old age they may succumb. Best to leave your old cat at home and get a neighbour to drop in to do the necessary.

If your ageing cat has had a bout or two of constipation your vet will outline a bulk-making diet. Generally this will include sloppy lighter foods and exclude concentrated heavy foods. He may advise raw liver once or twice a week. He may ask you to add small amounts of all-bran or other cereals to fill out the meat. He'll certainly ask you to avoid tinned foods that contain more than five per cent ground bone. He may recommend a really sloppy tinned food that contains a fair bit of broth or soup. He'll remind you that liquids of all sorts, but particularly water, must be available at all times. He may advise bi-weekly doses of mineral oil, or he may dispense one of those bland bulk-making powders.

Many ageing cats have kidney diseases. After the acute phase is over your vet will outline a 'kidney diet'. Generally this includes white meats like fish, veal, chicken or rabbit, and excludes red meats. He will ask you to try and get the cat to change its normal preference for meat to a grudging acceptance of starches. Pasta in all its forms can be tried. Spaghetti, macaroni, ravioli and noodles can all be sauced up to appeal to a cat's fastidious taste. Just douse the stuff in straightforward chicken broth or meat juice or mix in a bit of tuna fish, juice and all.

Many older cats require vitamin supplements. The ones usually dispensed by your vet will be heavy in vitamins A and B but low in C and D.

Grooming becomes more important with age. It helps the cat to retain its interest and its dignity. Also it prevents hair-balls, which may be fatal to the older cat.

The teeth of older cats should be seen by a vet at least twice a year, and preferably more often. He may be able to keep them healthy without resorting to anaesthetics, which is a major procedure in the aged cat. He may ask you to clean them at home with either salt water or one per cent potassium permanganate.

Any skin condition should be seen early on. If allowed to become chronic it may never be cured, because the regenerative powers of the aged are limited. Some older cats with skin complaints benefit enormously from hormone injections and pills. They seem to get a new lease of life. They put on weight, and they grow a lovely sleek new coat.

Check the claws at least once a month. They may grow round and penetrate the flesh. Your vet will show you how to trim the points.

Of course no amount of care can turn a cat into a kitten. Some drugs can slow the changes of old age, but none can stop the march of time. The commonsense approach is to consult your vet each step of the way. Take advantage of all the advances that medicine has made. But remember that there comes a point where the medicine changes roles with the body. That point is reached when the drugs no longer enhance and sustain life, but life itself is little more than a vehicle for the assimilation of drugs. Long before that point is reached you should have had that final consultation and agreed to euthanasia.

Gestation

This is the duration of pregnancy. It's usually sixty-two days, but may be as many as sixty-six. Mark the mating date on your calendar, and assume that the first mating has been successful.

Naturally ma wants more vitamins and proteins and minerals during this period. Cats who normally eat only dinner will eagerly gulp breakfast during pregnancy. This can be a bowl of rich condensed milk with added vitamins. Sprinkle a bit of bonemeal or boneflour on her dinner at least twice a week. In late pregnancy many cats develop cravings for really fresh fish or meat. Keep Freddie the Budgie and George the Guppy out of harm's way.

During the last fortnight she shouldn't be allowed to roam. Meals may be decreased in quantity but stepped up to three a day. If she's absolutely enormous she may be more comfortable with four smaller meals. At the first sign of constipation call the vet.

During the last few days one should have her bed (if she has one) replaced by a kittening box. A kittening box is a large, simple, private area that is draught-free and raised off the floor. It should be easily accessible and easily cleaned, and above all it should be in a quiet area of the house.

The onset of birth is usually indicated by restlessness and a drop in temperature. Don't panic. The overwhelming majority of cats have no problems if they're left to get on with it (see also *Parturition*). *Memo:* Have your queen checked about a month before you intend to have her bred. Your vet may advise reinoculation (if she is being sent by train) or worming if there is evidence of an infestation.

Most vets like to check pregnant females about a month after mating, and again a fortnight to a week before kittening.

Ginger Cats

Most (but not all) are males – an example of what the geneticists call a sex-linked characteristic. I know of no particular virtues or faults that are associated with the colour.

Gingivitis

This is inflammation of the gums. They are sore, may bleed easily, and after a few days become ulcerating messes. It's a fairly common condition in older cats who have been on soft, sloppy diets, but it may also be seen in younger animals with nutritional deficiencies. Gingivitis may be a symptom of one of the more serious diseases like enteritis or flu.

The cat acts just as you would if you had a sore mouth. It approaches food, attempts a half-hearted nibble, but soon loses interest. It might lap broth, but refuse solids.

Your vet will probably try penicillin injections, but if there isn't a decided improvement in a couple of days he'll move on to the other antibiotics. Home nursing includes feeding nutritious broths, frequent rinses with weak salt water, and gently rubbing the sore gums with borax and honey if the cat will allow you to.

PS: Dilute Hydrogen Peroxide, which is often used on afflicted dogs and humans, makes many cats sick.

Governing Council of the Cat Fancy

Possibly the nicest body of governors anywhere. Unlike the Kennel Club (the equivalent in the dog world) it allows ladies. Indeed the gentlemen may be odd men out. All are however distinguished by an enthusiasm for cats untinged by mercenary considerations. Cat devotees expect to lose money. This may explain the fact that to many newcomers and outsiders the whole affair appears rather amateur. They also comment on the fact that cat breeders seem immune from the laws of libel and slander. The things they say about each other publicly and in print would land anyone else in jail. I say God bless them. Long may they bumble along. And so long as we have the present set-up I feel that although the odd human ego may be dented temporarily, our cats will benefit.

Grass

Cats naturally eat all sorts of vegetables and grasses. They prefer them warmed over and partially digested which is the way they find them inside their prey. They will, however, enjoy green shoots just as they sprout from the ground. If you live in Cementville you might consider buying a half-dozen pots in which to grow cat salad. What to plant? Oats if that's all you have but the grasses are better. Best of all is Cocks-foot grass (*Dactylis glomerata*). Plant a pot fresh every month and Marzipan's feline friends will be green with envy.

Gravel

It's not a very scientific word but it's descriptive enough, and it's used to denote the sand-like material that forms in the bladders of some cats. Nobody knows why, but some of us guess that cats ain't made to eat dried manufactured foods. Maybe they just can't read the advertising. Whatever the cause no one disputes that it causes a painful irritation and in male cats usually blocks the flow of urine. If left untreated for too many hours (not days) the bladder bursts and death ensues (see also *Bladder*).

Greyhounds

These are the gentlest, kindest of dogs, as far as humans are concerned. But they are one of the worst enemies of the domestic cat. Not only can most greyhounds outrun most cats, but they have an incorrigible desire to do so, and once they've caught up they can kill with one slash of their well-toothed jaws. Many kind people adopt retired racing greyhounds as pets. They are often the sort of people who will listen to reason. Explain to them that their dog simply mustn't be allowed off the lead in places where your cat strolls in complacent peace. Greyhounds should be exercised either in their owners' gardens or in parks where there are lots of dogs around, and which cats know are strictly out of bounds.

Grooming

There is no great mystery to it. You get a comb with fairly widely spaced teeth and another with narrow spaces. You get a stiff brush. You tease and comb the mats until they're no longer mats. Then you brush. The only place a cat can't get properly clean is the space between its shoulders so you pay particular attention to that. If the cat objects, you're doing it too hard. If there's no visible effect on the coat you're doing it too gently.

Of course, each cat varies in its reactions to grooming. Some jump on a stool and beg for it. Others require three leather skinned assistants to hold them down. Generally the earlier you train them to accept the brush the better.

Short-haired cats may seldom require grooming but few long-hairs do well without it. Most require at least ten minutes a day. Stretch it to half an hour and you'll realize why your husband's lady friend always looks so glossy.

If you do it over newspapers you'll have less mess to clean up afterwards.

While you're at it have a look at the toes and pads. Nip out any mats. See that there are no broken or infected claws. Have a look at the ears. Just wipe the flaps clean and don't mess about with sticks or cotton in the ear itself. Every two or three months check to see that the teeth aren't being covered with tartar.

If Pistachio comes in soaked, wrap him in a towel. After he's dry you can give him a brush down and then dinner and then he'll be ready to go out and get wet again.

Guard Cats

Some ancient civilizations, like the Egyptians, are reputed to have used cats to guard their warehouses and homes. Cats must have been much bigger or men much smaller.

Modern cats will guard their litters against intruders, or their territory against other cats, but most of them won't blink an eyelid while the heirlooms are being carted away.

Some individuals act as alarm raisers if their owners are alert enough to notice. We read from time to time of cats rousing a family minutes before any human could detect a fire. There was a story in the papers a few months back about a publican's cat who used to come down into the pub from the apartments upstairs every night at closing time. One night the cat appeared an hour early. People commented that the clock upstairs must be running fast.

After closing, the pubkeeper and his wife retired upstairs to find that thieves had stripped the place. Was the cat trying to warn them, or had he just moved downstairs because he didn't like the strangers who were moving things?

A Canadian newspaper friend assures me that the following story is true. His family summered close to the Roosevelts' holiday place in Nova Scotia. The Roosevelts had a particularly haughty strain of Persians, and in due course a kitten was presented to my friend's family. They loved and cherished the kitten, and watched him grow into a completely disdainful aristocrat. Not once in fifteen years did he take the slightest notice of the family. He ate his food and retired to his own inner world, making not the slightest attempt to give any impression other than one of contempt. His attitude was that he might have come down in life, but he'd never forgotten his origins or principles.

One morning, towards two, the cat, then in its fifteenth year, jumped on to the bed and woke his sleeping owners by pulling at the bedclothes, and pawing at their faces. It was such an unexpected occurrence that they took it seriously and looked around the house. The coal pile in the basement was smouldering, and in minutes would have been beyond control.

The next day the Persian acted as if nothing had happened. The family attempted to make a fuss of him, and he responded with his usual indifference. He lived on in the same old aloof manner, and one night in his sixteenth year he went to sleep and didn't wake.

I guess you might find a moral in that story if you're interested in stories that have morals.

Haematuria (*blood in the urine*)

This may be a symptom of kidney disease but more often it's linked with a bladder infection or bladder stones. It always a serious sign of trouble, and there is no effective first aid except rest, warmth and lots of available drinking water. In the female you can safely postpone professional treatment until the following morning. In the male cat it must be considered an emergency. No matter what time of day or night find a vet. It may be a simple bladder infection and nothing to worry about, but it may equally well be an obstruction of the urethra. This can be fatal in hours.

Haematoma

A sharp blow or a paroxysm of scratching will cause the tissues to defend themselves by pouring in a lot of blood. Sometimes they overdo it and the result is a blood blister. You recognize them as taut swellings which don't feel hot to the touch. They're not painful unless you apply pressure.

Don't stick pins or needles into these swellings. You may introduce infection, and they'll pop up again anyway.

Put a dry dressing around the whole area only if the cat is scratching at it. Don't tie it too tightly. Your vet will decide whether it's necessary to cut the whole mess out or whether it's got a fair chance of resorbing naturally.

Blood blisters of the ear are usually painful. Because they're usually the result of scratching or rubbing an infected ear, the earlier they're seen by a vet the better.

Haemorrhage

A little bit of blood can smear a large area. Almost always it looks worse than it is, so don't rush into heroic measures. You'll frighten the cat and raise his blood pressure and increase the bleeding, and you'll get scratched.

The first thing to do is place the cat in a basket or box. Then collect bandages or tear up somebody's shirt. Set a light over a table, explain to your assistant how you want the cat held, and then remove him from the basket and have a close look. If you and the cat are lucky, the wound may have started to clot. Cats seldom bleed badly, first because there's so much 'give' to their tissues and vessels, and secondly because their blood clots very quickly.

If it's still pouring or oozing, don't mess about with ointments or cleaning. Leave that for the vet later. Just wad a bit of material over the wound and start wrapping.

Take the strips of cloth and wind as tightly as you can round the wound. Go well above it and well below. Lay the strips as flat as you can.

Leg wounds are simple. Simply wrap round the leg. Pad the foot and between the paws and bandage the lot. Start at the bottom and work to the top. In that way you don't have to worry about tourniquets and whether it's an artery or a vein.

110

If it's the tail that's bleeding, roll a whole package of bandage around it – tip to base and back again. Cover with elastoplast. Anchor it to the hair at the back of the spine. Be careful you don't include the anus in the bandage.

A bleeding scrotum is difficult. Place a pressure bandage over the scrotum and anchor it with criss-cross strips over the back and around the hips.

A bleeding breast or nipple should have a pressure bandage tied in place by bandage strips going right round the body. If you're ambitious you can try a many-tailed bandage (see *General hints* at the start of the book).

The only effective first aid for a bleeding tongue or gum or lips is quiet and peace until you can get to the vet, because one needs anaesthetics and ligatures to deal with those.

A bleeding ear should be tightly padded on both sides. Wrap the whole ear firmly by winding strips of material round and round the head. Don't wind too tightly or you'll choke the beast.

Bleeding round or in the eye may be controlled by pressing a moistened bandage against it and holding it there while getting to the clinic. The cat may not panic if it can see out of the other eye.

Profuse nosebleeds are strictly not to be dealt with in an amateur fashion. Put the cat in a basket and go to the vet. Minor ones will often stop if the cat is confined (see *Nose*).

Now, the most serious of all wounds. An animal usually tries to finish an adversary by slashing the jugular or the carotid. These important vessels lie in the furrows that run along either side of the neck. It might just be possible to save an animal that's had its jugular ripped open, but I've never heard of one surviving more than a few long seconds. Certainly if the carotid were opened death would occur in a few short seconds. Sometimes, however, the area is slashed but the vessels remain intact and entire. The area bleeds freely, and a pressure bandage may save a life.

All the above are just first aid measures to minimize blood loss until you can get to a vet. He will anaesthetize the animal and methodically locate and tie the injured blood vessels. If there has been a lot of bleeding he may use an intravenous supply of blood or one of the plasma-fillers.

It's difficult to impossible to have a supply of cat blood for transfusion purposes. In a flat-out emergency dog blood has been used and has saved a cat's life. But it can only be used once. The blood of the cat gets sensitized to dog blood by the first transfusion, and a second would cause a reaction leading to death. Most vets, however, keep a supply of plasma-fillers of one sort or another, and these can be used on any species.

After the bleeding is controlled and the blood volume restored, one leisurely cleans up the jagged edges and sews pussy back into one piece.

Hair-balls

If you have a long-haired cat particularly, or a short-hair that just licks and licks, it may collect enough hair in the stomach so that it starts rolling into a ball. These hair-balls can become quite large and they are usually of firm felt-like consistency. They may cause a great deal of distress ranging from vomiting and mild constipation to complete stoppage. When we diagnose hair-balls, usually by feeling them in the stomach or intestines and confirming by X-rays, we may try to get them passed with laxatives like liquid paraffin or olive oil, but sometimes an abdominal operation is necessary to remove them. Prevention is the keynote here, and there is only one way. That is five minutes of daily combing and brushing in long-haired animals, and at least five minutes weekly in short-haired. During moulting more care is required.

Hairless cats

Some unfortunate cats, through disease or scalds, may lose all or part of their hair. Others, through some accident of nature, are born hairless. Some people, endowed with a kind of kinky aesthetics, have attempted to promulgate those cats as true hairless strains. The Mexicans succeeded by using – or so we are told – some hairless Uruguayan cats as parent stock. Actually they're not true hairless, but have a sort of downy fuzz that comes and goes with the rains. Other people in other places have succeeded in producing 'hairless' strains of all sorts of cats, including Siamese. I suppose you could call it scientific breeding or applied genetics. I call it lunacy.

PS: In 1968 the *Observer* Colour Magazine in their wisdom and propelled by the inspired and inspiring editor, Nigel Lloyd, printed an article of mine about animals. To illustrate he chose four dramatic photos of a 'Naked Cat'. It was a Rex without any hair at all. I didn't anticipate the response that he confidently predicted. Dozens of letters poured in from all corners of the globe. A few were nasty. Most wanted to know where they could obtain a hairless cat. Artists and sculptors topped the league of letter writers. Then came people who were allergic to hair.

Interestingly enough, the *Daily Mirror*'s inimitable Betty Tay had used exactly the same cat (photographed by Freddie Reed whom other photographers unsuccessfully try to imitate) to illustrate an earlier article. *Mirror* readers were horrified: quite obviously promulgating a mutant against all the odds for our own selfish needs is repellent.

To my shame as a Canadian, there is a group there producing hairless cats. I won't advertise them further. Nor would I be party to producing them.

Havana: (*chestnut brown, foreign*)

This chestnut-brown short-hair with the fine oriental body is about as Cuban as a London bobby. It was developed in England by breeding from the offspring of Siamese and short-haired, self-coloured British. Lovers of the breed say they have the advantages of both and the disadvantages of neither. Detractors of the breed don't own them so they don't really know, do they?

Heart

Busy animal clinics that see a dozen canine heart patients a week often go for months without seeing a single cat with heart disease. One recent paper written by a group of experts only described six cases. Although they looked everywhere that's all they could find. That seems curious, but let me ask you something. Why is it that coronary arteriosclerosis and hypertension are very common in man but rarely seen in any other animal? You might say it's because man lives under such stress and makes such a hash of his life by smoking and drinking and riding around in automobiles.

I'll accept that, because I don't know enough to argue. But let me ask you another question. Why do dogs suffer from heart conditions more than cats? Some people say it's ten times more common in dogs! In effect, these experts say that if you examined one thousand older dogs you would find a hundred of them suffering to a greater or lesser degree with some heart defect. If you examined one thousand cats of the same age group you'd only find ten heart cases. If you are statistically minded you might say that these figures are partly attributable to the fact that veterinarians know more about heart disease in the dog and can diagnose it more easily than they can in the cat. That's true. But the pathologists too tell us that they find many fewer heart lesions in cats than in dogs. Not only that; some cats who on post-mortem are found to have the most dreadful hearts have apparently lived completely normal lives.

So what? If you are a normal cat lover you don't need me to tell you that in all respects the cat is superior to the dog and infinitely superior to man. All I'm saying is that it's extremely interesting, and scientifically vital, to find out why cats don't suffer from heart disease more than they do. After all, in any fair-sized city there are hundreds of cats who live lives as pampered as any dog. They get overfed. They get rich foods. They are overheated. The only exercise many of them get is in the triangle from their bed to their bowl to their tray and back to the bed again. Does the cat keep in tune by stretching every time he wakes up? There are whole books on physical fitness exercises based on the way a cat stretches. Is it because dogs like sugar and cats don't? Some studies would have us believe that sugar intake and heart disease incidence are related. What do you think? Don't you agree that it would be a good thing if we could learn the cat's secret?

Finally, a disquieting note. Cats seem to get more than their fair share of aortic emboli caused by the formation of clots way back where the aorta supplies the hind legs. Nobody knows why (see *Thrombus*).

Heat (*or period or oestrus*)

This is the period when the female cat attracts and accepts the male. Unlike the bitch, the cat may have several heat periods during the year. They usually start mildly enough. The cat becomes more affectionate than usual. She rubs herself along objects and rolls around a bit in what she must think is a sexy manner. She becomes very restless, attempts to get out of doors and cries persistently. She crouches and treads with her hind legs.

Her external sexual organs become enlarged and hot. At first there is a clear discharge which may be tinged with blood. After three or four days of this it's pretty obvious to most cat owners what is happening. Surprisingly enough, though, about once a month someone comes into the surgery and describes these alarming symptoms, and usually they shake their heads in disbelief when we say she's just looking for a boy friend.

Gradually the 'symptoms' get worse, and Old Jennie goes out and starts calling all the males. She may go through a short period of just teasing. Within days you will hear the sounds of toms fighting and the squeal of delight (or some say it's pain) as each tom finishes. In nature many toms usually fight each other and then serve the female one after the other. The penis of the tom is barbed, and it must cause some sensation as it's withdrawn from the female. Whether that

114

sensation is pain or pleasure I don't know, but when it happens you can hear the female a long way off.

The heat stops with pregnancy. If the cat isn't bred she may come on heat again in a few days or weeks. That is why it's really rather cruel to keep a female cat unspayed if you won't allow her to have kittens.

Nature tries to arrange her affairs so that kittens are not born in the dead of winter, so many female cats will have a quiet period from August or September through to early spring. A cat who is run down through nursing a large litter or as a result of illness may not come on heat till the following spring. And some cats, though nursing, will nevertheless come on heat. Within days of delivering one litter they'll go out and conceive another.

Summary: An unspayed female cat will keep having heat periods until she's pregnant.

Heating

Nursing litters and orphans and ageing animals and ill animals often need additional heat. Infra-red bulbs are safe and effective provided they're placed out of the animal's reach and at the distance specified by the manufacturer (according to wattage). One must remember that they do interfere with rest and proper sleep.

Hot water bottles must be well wrapped to avoid burning tender skins. They must be changed often enough to keep the temperature fairly constant otherwise you're alternately warming and chilling the creature, a procedure more suited to a James Bond film than the sick room.

Young boisterous creatures in play may run into an open fire or knock over a kerosene heater. One installs fire-guards and bolts down heaters.

Cats who stare into the fire may get sore runny eyes. Buy a screen. Cats who lie by the fire, day in day out, may get dry scurfy skins. Install central heating. The best way I've found is to provide a small electric blanket (properly insulated) under a polystyrene granule filled sheet.

Heat stroke

If you're drinking iced tea and complaining of the heat, don't leave puss in a small airless room. If you do she'll start salivating and panting. Before long she'll lose consciousness. Her temperature will be 40°C (105°F) or more.

Don't force fluids or try artificial respiration. What she wants and wants fast is to have her body temperature lowered. Stick her in a pail or a sink or a tub of cold water or put ice packs around her. Please keep her head out of the water. It's a rescue operation not a drowning exercise.

Speed is the essence in treating the condition so do that and then try and contact a vet. He'll do exactly the same thing except that he'll keep checking the body temperature. When it's approaching normal he'll stop and try to assess the damage and start the slow building up process.

Heights (*panic and the fire department*)

Is it curiosity or panic that kills the cat? All too often it's panic, and that panic is brought on by the ill-directed efforts of people. The cat finds a new and interesting back passage. It follows the path up, and there is a roof and a ledge that display a whole new vista of the same old world. There is a small creature down below. What is it? Good heavens, it's a man. Doesn't he look insignificant? I bet he doesn't know I'm looking at him. I bet he doesn't even know I'm up here. 'Hello, down there, look at me! No, not there – over here!' Goodness, men have the most useless eyes. Ah. Now he sees me. 'Hello. Nice day, isn't it?' My God, he's shouting at me. What have I done to make him angry? Look, there's a woman at that window shouting at the man. No, she's not, she's shouting at me. Whatever have I done? What's that behind me on the roof? Another man! He's really in a state. How can I get out of here? This ledge is too damn narrow. If I go back he'll catch me, and I can't go ahead. What shall I do?

You know the usual sad ending. The poor creature falls, and is injured or killed. One seldom hears about a successful rescue from a height, but one is often presented with the unhappy victim of a hurried rescue. Don't blame the Fire Department. What can they do if some panic-stricken voice says they must send a ladder at once? If they calmly reply that the cat, if left to its own devices, will probably find its own way down, they will be accused of laziness, brutality, cruelty and callousness. In those rare cases in which the cat panics on its own and falls, they would be filling in bureaucratic forms for months. It's easier to send out the ladders.

Do I sound callous? I've seen my own cat parading up and down a narrow ledge miaowing piteously to the neighbours down below. The more he miaowed the more people came. He loved every minute of it. They'd taken him for granted for too long, and now he was conducting a whole orchestra of open mouths. The first time it happened was a couple of years ago, and he has played repeat performances from time to time since. Now most of the audience just stay for a moment or two and only the odd stranger starts screaming back at him. He still goes through the whole play, line by line, but somehow he doesn't put the same spirit into it. I think he's relieved when he can take his final bow and come back to earth.

Hernia

Our bodies are made up of tight little compartments. The heart and lungs belong in one place, and the stomach, liver and intestines in another. There's a nice firm partition that keeps them in place. Occasionally, either because of an accident or through one of nature's mistakes, the organs that belong in one place get shoved into another.

The commonest sort of hernia is an *umbilical* hernia. You see a swelling where the belly button should be. Turn the kitten on its back. If the swelling disappears you know it's a hernia. The stuff that has poked through has gone back (by gravity) where it belongs. When the kitten rights itself the swelling will reappear. Sometimes these hernias will close over on their own. More often a surgical operation is necessary to poke the guts back into the tummy and close the hole.

Umbilical hernias are seen fairly rarely in cats and more often in dogs and in hogs. Pig farmers recognize that the predisposition to the condition is probably hereditary. They don't breed from affected animals. Some conscientious dog breeders do the same. Most cat breeders, when they have the situation explained, will ask for affected kittens to be castrated or spayed. It's a rational decision.

Just to prove how perverse I am I recently heartily approved my wife's purchase of a young female Balinese with a very large umbilical hernia *and* she intends to use it for breeding. The reason? There were half a dozen other kittens in the litter and all were perfectly normal. The one she bought had obviously been damaged at birth.

There's another kind of hernia that occurs high up on the inside of the thigh. It's called an *inguinal* hernia and is rarely seen in cats. Affected animals should not be used for breeding.

Sometimes after a bad fall or a severe blow the diaphragm (the tough membrane that separates the lungs from the liver and the stomach) is ruptured. The abdominal contents flow into the lung cavity and cause respiratory distress. The animal may look all right. It may eat and drink, but it breathes very rapidly. Any exertion at all causes distress. If the animal is raised by its hind legs the breathing

117

becomes faster and more distressed. The abdominal organs are squeezing the lungs. Some vets diagnose the condition just by looking and by listening to the lungs. Others prefer to confirm by X-ray. There is only one way to correct the condition, and that is to operate. One goes in and attempts to sew up the ruptured diaphragm. I've seen experienced and competent surgeons lose such cases, so you mustn't be too optimistic.

Hip dysplasia

The hip joint of human beings and of cats and dogs is a ball and socket. The head of the femur (or long bone) ends in a ball which fits into the socket of the pelvis. The more perfectly round it is, the better the joint moves. In many larger breeds of dogs the socket or the ball or both have become flattened. The joint creaks every time it moves, and the animal becomes a cripple. It's a distressing problem in the dog world. In some breeds of dogs X-rays to determine the state of the joint are almost routine. If the picture confirms hip dysplasia the animal is not acceptable for breeding, because there is an increasing body of evidence that says the condition is hereditary.

Until just lately cat breeders have been able to congratulate themselves and their pets, and murmur sympathetically when forced to listen to the problems of the dog breeder. However, in the last year or two an increasing number of cases of lamenesses in Siamese have been diagnosed as due to hip dysplasia. There haven't been that many – as yet – but there have been enough to alert the cat world. What can I tell you about it? Almost nothing, I'm afraid. If your cat is lame and your vet X-rays it and demonstrates hip dysplasia, you'd best follow his advice and not breed from the affected animal. It may be that in the cat the condition is not hereditary. But until we're sure, one way or the other, why take a chance of promulgating pain?

History

Doctors and vets don't ask questions to fill in the time while waiting for diagnostic inspiration. An accurate history of the case is often crucial. You say, 'He has diarrhoea and he's vomiting.' The vet would like to know which started first, because in some conditions one precedes the other by several hours. Or you say, 'She just won't eat.' The vet would like to know if she approaches food but is afraid to eat, or if she's completely uninterested. The first would indicate some trouble in the mouth like bad teeth or a foreign object; the latter could mean something like enteritis.

Many people take the attitude that the vet should know what's wrong without asking a bunch of silly questions. Let me assure you that in most cases he can. But if you answer his questions accurately right at the beginning it will save a lot of time.

Holding (*while examining or treating*)

This is an art that can only be learned by experience. Until you have that experience a few bits of commonsense may help you handle your cat so that both of you emerge from the experience intact.

Put him on a strong table and place a hand on each shoulder with your fingers pointing forward. Don't squeeze or pinch but hold firmly. Reassure him by words and a scratch or two between the shoulders. If you wish to lift his head don't encircle his throat. The choking sensation will panic him as much as it would you. Place one hand over his muzzle (being careful not to crush his whiskers) and lift his head. If you pull it straight up he can't scratch you with his front feet, but watch out for his hind. You can examine his back and his tail quite easily by stroking him while you're doing it. To look at his belly and his legs you must place him on his side being careful not to bang his head as you do so. Hold him down with one hand and stroke him with the other.

A cat will only give you a limited time before its patience runs out and no power can hold it, so have everything you need ready beforehand.

Hookworms

World-wide in distribution but only a problem in warm areas. The cat usually gets infected by eating a mouse or an insect that contains the hookworm larvae. The adult worms attach themselves to the lining of the intestines, secrete a substance that prevents blood from clotting, and proceed to suck the cat's blood at leisure. When they've exhausted one area they move on down the gut. Often they do so much damage and suck so much blood that the cat becomes too weak for even the gentlest worm pills. One has to build the creature up with injections and transfusions before attempting to rid him of the worms. How does your vet diagnose the condition? He examines samples of the animal's faeces under the microscope. The hookworm eggs are quite distinctive. Anyway, don't worry unless you're drinking a mint julep under a blooming magnolia way south of the Mason-Dixon Line.

Horner's Syndrome

One eye appears smaller than the other. It seems out of focus. Its pupil is smaller than the normal eye and the third eyelid partially covers it. It may occur after an accident involving the neck or more rarely it accompanies a tumour in the area. If a tumour is the cause of the trouble there is no cure. If it's a result of an injury it usually responds to treatment but it's a long drawn out affair. It may take a month before any improvement is apparent, and some cases take as long as six months before you and the cat can forget which eye was out of focus.

Hysteria

Some too delicate orientals can churn themselves into a hysterical frenzy. Any cat suffering from a painful skin or ear infection may scratch itself into madness. A cat who is burned or poisoned may go hysterical. In all cases you must be very careful not to get injured. Throw a blanket or a bag over the animal and transfer bag and cat to a box. Often confinement alone will stop the self-torture. If the cause isn't self-evident and easily remedied you'd better go along to the vet. Often a general anaesthetic is needed just to relieve the symptoms temporarily. While the animal is sleeping one can examine at leisure and try to find the cause.

Iatrogenic

This is an unpopular word with practising physicians and surgeons and veterinarians. It is used to describe conditions caused by doctors. Pathologists, who are sometimes accused by their richer colleagues of being impractical and morbid, always have a rich store of iatrogenic cases to prove that no one can afford to be arrogant when dealing with lives. Sometimes drugs can cause far more harm than the disease they are meant to cure. Sometimes surgery can leave the patient worse than it found him. Sometimes a relatively minor ailment is transformed into a serious illness by ill-considered treatment.

Cats are particularly sensitive patients, and veterinarians who deal with them are quite aware of it. Many drugs that are tolerated well and work beautifully in dogs and people will sicken cats. As students, veterinarians have drummed into them long lists of drugs and procedures that must not be used on cats. Later, as they join the fraternity of working veterinarians, the professional journals warn them which of the newer procedures and drugs can be used with safety. Even so, there are lapses of judgement or knowledge. Many veterinarians deal mostly with cattle or horses, and, although they can handle dogs quite adequately if called upon to do so, feel that cats are too specialized and tricky. They will treat them if it's an emergency or if there's no other veterinarian available, but they'd rather not. When I was in large animal practice I always referred my friends who had dog or cat problems to a neighbouring vet who specialized in them. There were three very good reasons for doing so. The first was that I didn't have the equipment. The second was that most of my reading and work and most of my contemplative time was taken up with cattle problems. Any of us can get rusty, and as far as cats were concerned I was very rusty indeed. The third is that I really wasn't interested in cats. Any reasonable person will understand that at that time and in those conditions I wasn't really the person to treat a cat. Nevertheless, I did my best and so far as I can recall didn't lose any cases through neglect or ignorance. Is there a lesson here? I think so. Take your cat to a small animal specialist, if at all possible. If the only available vet happens to be a chap who is really more interested in virological research or public health or racehorses you can be assured that he will do all that's possible. Then, he'll refer you to a more specialized colleague. It's not that he doesn't like you or your cat. It's because he's far more aware of iatrogenics than you are.

Ice

Even in darkest Canada most cats know how to look after themselves. Occasionally, though, a pampered Persian meets a combination of wind and sleet with which it cannot cope. It drags itself home in such a state that even its greatest admirers cannot tell whether it's an icicle or a badly cooked hamburger.

Thaw him as quickly as you can without burning. Melt the frozen bits from between his toes by soaking in warm water. Get the ice out of his ears by pouring in lots of warmed oil. Then call a vet. If he's frozen, thaw him with alcohol.

Indoors versus outdoors

Rationalize as you will, the cat who goes out will be healthier and happier. Of course, it will learn independence and may become a little more choosy in deciding when to sit on your lap. If you find that you simply must have a doting dependent animal, maybe you should have a dog.

Some cats, though, are always confined. Purebreds kept for breeding aren't allowed to roam for obvious reasons. But confinement does not mean locking them in something the size of an orange crate. The fibreglass cages we provide for our confined breeding stock are high enough for a tall person to move freely and big enough for a human double bed. At one time I thought outdoor runs were absolutely necessary. Cats may have read all about the virtues of jogging, but when they're confined they prefer a secure niche to bask in while they observe the madness outside.

Cat lovers who live in tall apartment blocks have a real problem. They want a cat but hate to confine it. They know that Siamese can be trained on the lead and can be taken for walks, but they also know that Siamese can wake the dead with their cries. Some of my friends find that Persians adapt well to an inside existence, and I agree that I've seen some Persians who would rather be carried than walk – even to their food.

Right. If at all possible allow your cat to indulge his natural exploring instincts. He just wants to have a little walk and a little look around and a gossip with the neighbours. A cat-door so that he can come and go as he pleases should be provided.

If you simply must have a cat where it's impossible to allow him to go out, or if as often happens, you and your cat move to a place with no available garden, please remember that he will gradually lose his natural resistance to the infectious diseases.

I recall a Persian, belonging to a designer friend of mine, that was kept confined. He died within twenty-four hours of first showing symptoms of feline enteritis. He had absolutely no resistance, and didn't respond at all to drugs, fluids or nursing. So it's terribly important to have confined cats inoculated and booster doses given annually. And the answer to the question everyone asks: how do they get the disease? They're confined, but you and your visitors are not. People carry it on their shoes or clothing.

Some people simply will not understand that you really mean it when you tell them that the invitation to dinner does not include their recently acquired pet shop kitten. They arrive with the glow of a first-time father. They hand out the odd cigar and two months of flu, fleas, ear mites and mange. While you try to lock up your own livestock and mildly protest about the invasion, they whisper loudly, 'We thought they were animal lovers.'

Infectious ophthalmia

This is one of the many names for a distressing condition of newborn kittens. Their eyes are sore and inflamed. They become crusted with dry discharge. If untreated, the condition may lead to blindness and death.

If your kittens have gummed eyes, examine the mother. She may have a sticky discharge coming from her vagina which is the cause of the infection in the kittens. Obviously no amount of eye bathing or herbal witchcraft will cure the kittens. Mummy wants antibiotic injections, and the sooner the better. Put them all in the basket and get a strong man (or two boys) to carry them off to the vet.

Ingrowing eyelashes (trichiasis)

A few years ago I read a book. It said that cats don't have eyelashes. I looked closely at the very next cat I saw. It had eyelashes – at least on top. I suppose the book should have said that most cats don't have eyelashes. Among the rare minority that do an even smaller number have the sort that grow inward towards the eyeball. These can cause trouble. They rub against the eyeball and set up an irritation that grows worse and worse. Because Fanny Hurst, the writer, had a favoured cat who suffered with trichiasis many cat lovers became aware of this relatively rare condition. Treatment is usually surgical. The cat is anaesthetized and the irritating hairs are removed. The procedure may have to be repeated.

Injections

Some cats simply cannot be given pills. You can wrap them in rugs and wrap yourself in steel mesh and they'll end up victoriously placid while you lick your wounds. Many medicines are not as effective when given by mouth as when they are injected. Some drugs cannot be given by mouth because the enzymes of the digestive tract destroy them.

Injections are given under the skin or into the deep muscles or into a vein.

You may have to learn how to give your animal injections. For example, diabetic cats require them daily. It's not very difficult if you work out a system. Prepare everything beforehand. Clean, rinse and boil the syringe and needle for twenty minutes. Allow to cool. Then load the syringe. After you have done all that call pussy. The less time she has to wait the easier it is for her and you.

Placid cats may be held with one hand while you use the other to inject the stuff. Most cats require two people. One holds while the other injects. You can't blame them because they can't possibly associate the pain of the needle with its beneficial contents.

Today disposable syringes and needles are so cheap that there is simply no excuse for using a dull needle.

Injections (*intravenous*)

Many drugs are best given direct into the vein. It's the quickest way of getting the stuff working throughout the body. An animal that is shocked or bleeding may need fluids to replace the loss, and if those fluids are given directly into the blood stream they can be life-savers, and in a most dramatic manner. An almost lifeless body starts to perk up, and within half an hour is often ready to scratch the hand that's holding the needle.

Some anaesthetics are best given direct into the vein. The effect is immediate, and the dose can be judged according to how 'deep' the sleep is.

Until a few years ago veterinarians didn't use the veins of cats. We were quite happy using the veins of dogs and cows and horses and rabbits, but the technique for hitting the veins of the cat seemed too tricky for most of us. Why we've decided that it's really rather easy I can't tell you. Possibly more vets have learnt how to handle cats gently but firmly, which is the main part of the problem. A squirming, fighting cat simply can't be injected intravenously, because the vein is very little wider than the thickness of even the smallest needles. Once the vein is punctured wrongly it's very difficult indeed to use it before some days of healing have elapsed.

Anyway, today we casually clip the hair off the front leg, dampen the skin with a bit of alcohol, raise the rubbery elusive vein and use it to inject anaesthetics, antibiotics and life-saving fluids. Once the needle is in and the stuff flowing most cats sit there and watch the process with the same curiosity and interest that they have for anything unusual.

Often, if the owner isn't an hysterical type, we'll ask him or her to sit there throughout the process and hold the cat's leg so that it doesn't tug at the needle. If a cat has a severe bout of gastro-enteritis with lots of fluid loss through vomiting and diarrhoea, it may have to have fluids every day for four or five days. Many owners get to be pretty handy nurses in the process. When the animal starts recovering its strength we begin injecting the fluids under the skin. By that time the veterinarian, the owner and the cat are thoroughly bored with intravenous injections.

Injustice

Your cat leaves for his morning rounds and doesn't return for his afternoon snack. You go about calling for him without success. You renew your efforts that night and the following morning and for a couple of days and nights. Three days later a skeleton with some resemblance to your cat comes miaowing to be let in. In fact it is your cat. He's in a pitiful state. You rush him off to your vet and he promptly accuses you of neglect. That is an injustice.

I think too many animal lovers fall too hastily into a judgement of neglect. I'm inclined to myself if I'm tired, or if it's a hectic day. Neighbours are even more likely to condemn without justification. There's only one retort, if you care enough or are so sensitive that you must reply.

A cat remains its own master, and if one respects felines at all one allows them their freedom and hopes they can cope. When they can't you, the owner, step in, and if that isn't enough you get professional help. What else can any reasonable person do?

You can't go out and follow your cat down the back alleys and over the fences. If he gets injured and hides away for three days, there's simply nothing you can do about it. After he's over the initial shock he'll come crawling back to be fed and doctored and nursed to health.

Introducing

Never bring a new animal into your animal-filled home without isolating it for a few days to make sure it's not suffering from fleas or mange or one of the infectious diseases. Animal lovers pick up a stray or buy a pitiful kitten in a shop window. They take it home, and a few days later their family pet comes down with all sorts of horrible things.

How can you isolate a new animal? Try to get a petless friend to take it for a few days. If that's impossible, keep it in a separate room. Use separate utensils. Wash your hands after every visit. Keep a pair of slippers by the door of that room and change into them before going in. Difficult? Much less so than nursing your old pet through a new disease.

What about the social adjustment of new cats with old? There's usually a fair bit of social sniffing and jealousy and maybe a bit of spitting, just to show who was where first, but almost always an uneasy truce will be declared within a few hours. Within days they'll be real buddies when you're not watching. When you are watching the older established pet will put on a bit of a show just to remind you whose home it really is.

Intubation

This will only interest doctors. They are often surprised to learn that we intubate our patients just as they do theirs. We induce anaesthesia intravenously with something like pentothal, and slide the tube into the trachea. In most dogs it's a simple knack, and one can easily see or feel if the tube is in the right hole. The cat is a more difficult subject because they go into coughing spasms as you slide the tube in – I know one or two vets who can tube a cat as they cough, but most prefer to give them scoline, insert the tube, and squeeze the old bag until the scoline wears off. Don't try it unless a vet shows you how! A dose of scoline that would be safe for a small baby would kill a large dog.

Iron

Every pig farmer knows that milk is deficient in iron. You can feed a farrowing sow iron by the carload, and she might still raise anaemic piglets. The piglets get pale and listless, and they stop growing. It's a severe condition in pigs because they grow so quickly. Kittens grow much more slowly, so in their case iron anaemia is a much subtler disease. In fact many kittens, although they're slightly deficient in iron, manage to bridge the period until they're taking some solids. Anaemic kittens may appear just slightly dull. In most cases they simply stop growing. Your vet can confirm your suspicions by a clinical examination and a simple blood test. Don't start pouring iron tonics down helpless throats. Effective doses of iron, if given by mouth, may cause gastritis, so the stuff is given by injection. They usually respond beautifully within days. Within a week they're ready to swallow the syringe.

Itch

Ugly word, ugly feeling. An abscess, while it's forming, may be itchy. Ringworm, mange, ticks or lice may set up an irritation that can only be satisfied by a deep scratching session. The scratching spreads the irritation. The scratching gets deeper and the reaction more severe. Soon the whole area is a mess.

The commonest cause of itchiness in a cat is fleas. Have a look! I mean a good look under a strong light. If you can see the cause and cure it, well and good. If you can't, there is a likeable chap round the corner who probably can. He's called 'the vet'. Let your cat scratch itself to pieces for a week. Then phone him at midnight.

Jacobson organ

A tiny bit of tissue near the pituitary gland in which, unconsciously, the cat stores memories of smells. This built-in codifier tells the cat which reactions should go with which smells. Mice may mean dinner or aggression time, while doggy smells might mean flight, fright or all claws out.

Jaundice

This is a yellowing of the tissues caused by bile pigments getting into the blood instead of minding their own business in the digestive tract. Jaundice is not a disease, but is a symptom of liver trouble or poisoning or some intestinal obstruction. I'm told that in the human, jaundice may be a symptom of some quite easily treated condition. In the cat, however, whatever the cause, jaundice is invariably a serious business. In my limited experience. I have seen only a minority of afflicted cats treated successfully.

Jaw

Cats land on their feet, or so we are told by people who talk in clichés. They forget to add that the creatures usually strike their heads in the process. Sometimes the resulting bruises are minor. A few days on a soft, lappable diet, and Ferocious Sue is roaring to have another go on the tightrope. More often concussion and a fractured jaw are the penalties of a miscalculated jump.

A jaw that is fractured may look quite normal. The cat may drool a bit, approach food and refuse it, or show pain only if the head is handled. In other cases the cat has a drunken look. Its head is askew. Its jaw may drop lifelessly. In all cases any attempt to open the mouth causes pain. Obviously the animal must be anaesthetized, the fracture sites determined, and the bits sewn together with wire or held in place with a steel plate. Sue stays on soft foods for days and days. After a fortnight the hardware is removed.

Dislocation of the jaw is rather rare in the cat. When it does occur (usually as a result of a bad fall or a car accident), the jaw is generally snapped back into place easily, provided the cat is anaesthetized deeply enough to relax its very strong jaw muscles. But fair warning! A jolt that was severe enough to dislocate a jaw was probably severe enough to cause far more serious injuries internally.

127

Abscesses of the jaw may be the result of a scratch or an infected cut. More often the cause is a rotting tooth.

Or the jaw may be the site of a tumour. If this is the case I'm afraid, in animal medicine, we must still recommend euthanasia as the only humane solution.

Jealousy

Some child psychologists tell us that the elder child should be specially fussed over when baby is brought home. I suppose this advice is particularly applicable in those homes when there's such a shortage of love that it has to be rationed by plan and apportioned by the hour. In the pet world it's a rare adult who won't delight in a new kitten or puppy. In fact I've never heard of an adult cat who wouldn't extend its hospitality to a weanling stranger. Most cats will take special pains to ensure that the newcomer learns the routine. This courtesy may not always be offered to adults. If there's any indication that claws will be unsheathed you'd best keep them in separate rooms for a few days. Feeding should certainly be separate until you're sure of mutual acceptance.

When introducing a new baby (human) to an old cat, let common-sense be your guide. Don't leave them alone until you're certain that puss knows baby isn't a competitor but is part and parcel of the world that provides the goodies. If she shows any indication that she means to drive baby back from where she came, I'd be inclined to dump puss on the in-laws, at least until baby grows to brat.

Kerosene (*paraffin, solvents*)

Never use anything strong to remove paint or oil from a cat. You'll just be adding one poison to another.

Rub off what you can by using a series of dry cloths. Wash small areas with soap and water or cut off the matted hair.
Warning: If the cat is in pain, or if large areas are involved, rush the animal to the vet. Often a general anaesthetic is needed to remove the stuff. In severe cases intravenous fluids are needed to combat shock.

Kidneys

The kidneys are the filters of the body. The blood passes through them, the waste products are sieved out, and the blood is allowed to go on circulating in the body. The waste products and the surplus fluid of the blood form urine. I know that is an oversimplification. If you want the whole complicated story I can refer you to lots of heavy books with sentences three pages long. Anyway, if the kidneys become diseased so that they don't filter the waste products, the body will try to make up for it and ease the kidneys' job by diluting the blood. How is this done? There is only one way, and that is to drink more water. That is why, if your cat suddenly increases its water consumption, you must suspect kidney malfunction and get him along to the vet.

There's one important thing to remember while you're deciding whether or not to make the odious trek to the vet. Don't cut down on the supply of water (unless the animal is drinking it down and shortly afterwards bringing it up). Many people cut down the animal's water consumption because they think it can't be good for it. In fact, often the only thing that is allowing the kidneys to function is the increased water consumption. A veterinary surgeon may ask you to limit an animal's fluids for two or three days, but never will he recommend a permanent limit on drinking.

What other signs will a kidney case exhibit? Often if he's drinking more water he will urinate more frequently and larger quantities. He may strain to pass his urine. He may arch his back in pain.

In many cats you won't see any of these signs, simply because many cats don't drink at home. And practically all cats prefer to urinate in private. Sometimes the only signs you will notice are the odd bout of diarrhoea or vomiting, some loss of weight, a general listlessness and depression, and foul breath. Many people only take the cat to the vet when its breath has become so foul that even the most boring neighbours stop visiting. They bring the cat along and point out its rotting teeth. They take a lot of convincing before they'll acknowledge that the bad teeth are probably a result of the bad kidneys. Until the kidney condition is brought under control the cat probably wouldn't stand the anaesthetic necessary for the dental work.

The vet, after deciding that the trouble is indeed in the kidneys, will try to find out what sort of nephritis it is. He will usually get a urine sample, and he might take a small bit of blood. He may inaugurate a course of antibiotics, vitamin B injections, and possibly fluids into the veins or under the skin. When he thinks he has the condition under control, he will send the patient home.

Almost always he will recommend that these recovered cases should be kept indoors or confined to a small garden, because an accident that a normal cat would recover from would probably be too much for a nephritic cat. Even a small abscess is a serious business for a body that already has quite enough to cope with. He will probably dispense vitamin pills and 'kidney' pills, and he will give you a long talk on what you can feed and why. And he will insist that lots of water should be available at all times.

Kinks

Sometimes it's fashionable to be kinky. Sometimes it ain't. Currently a Siamese or a Burmese is allowed to have a slight kink at the very end of the tail which should be so slight that it can be felt but not seen. At one time some people considered a pronounced kink denoted a superior Siamese. I'm on the side of the squares who consider kinks to be definite abnormalities and not to be encouraged.

Lactation

The secretion of milk by the female. The breasts swell during pregnancy. A day or two before the queen gives birth the milk starts to flow. Occasionally a cat who isn't pregnant (but thinks she is) will start forming milk. Conversely some cats who have just had kittens won't drop their milk. In both cases there are drugs that may restore nature's rhythm.

During a normal lactation the queen must be fed properly. In addition to her normal food she'll want plenty of titbits throughout the day. If she'll drink milk as well that's just dandy. But if she gets diarrhoea you may have to give the milk to your husband and feed the queen the fresh broiled salmon.

Remember she's nourishing more than herself. As I write this I'm chopping the remains of a huge roast into shepherd-pie pieces. The nasty bits are going into the casserole for us. The good stuff is going down the gullet of the nursing queen standing between my feet. Because she's oriental we make sure her water bowl is clean and full.

If the teats become raw, red or cracked, a bit of very gentle massaging with cod-liver oil will ease them. It won't do the kittens anything but good. Excess hair around the teats may be trimmed.

Wean the litter by gradually increasing their feedings and decreasing their dependence on the mother's milk. At actual weaning time (permanent separation of the young) give the mother nothing to drink for twenty-four hours. That will help dry her off. If the breasts get cracked or hard you may massage them with oil. If they stay that way for more than a day get veterinary advice.

The queen may continue to demand extra food long after she has need of it. Harden your heart and save her figure.

Lameness

If a cat is only slightly lame it may be that he's just jarred himself or twisted a limb just like your middle-aged friends do during their annual picnic. If he's still lame a couple of hours later you'd better have a look. He may have cut his pad or some stupid kid might have tied a piece of cord around his ankle. It only takes a minute to look.

If the animal puts no weight on the limb it may be fractured or there may be an infected bite wound over a joint. Don't mess about at home but get the thing attended to properly.

Language and signs

Cats communicate with each other. They have a rather complex system of sniffs and delicate facial expressions. Their language is altogether too subtle for you or me, but is quite adequate for the discussions of love and philosophy or whatever it is that cats talk about among themselves.

Cats rarely use their voices when talking to each other. When talking to people they generally use their voices as well as facial and body expressions. Some people say that the cat finds the human so stupid that in exasperation he talks very loudly, just as some Englishmen talk to foreigners.

I had a cat who used to knock over the bedside table whenever I was too slow in understanding what he wanted. Doubtless you and your cat have developed a private language through the years. I hope you don't suffer as many broken spectacles and spilled drinks as I did.

The following are some common expressions and behaviourisms:

Widely dilated pupils – fright
Fluffed up tail – fright
Drooping tail – fatigue
Tail hanging but rigid – disgust
Relaxed gently swishing tail – pleasure
Lashing taut tail – warning!
Tail rigidly out behind – war declared!
Ears pricked forward – curiosity
Ears backward – warning!
Ears flat against head – war declared!
Rubbing face against object – love or desire
Rubbing whiskers sideways on object – love or desire
Touching whiskers to an object – curiosity
Tail straight up as a flagpole – indifference

Tail straight up with relaxed tip – pleasure – it's a great day
Deliberately looking away and then licking body – indifference or pretended indifference
Purr – contentment
Growl – anger
Miaow ending on a rising note – conversation opener or a greeting
Deep purr during handling or veterinary examination – pain but he can take it
Deep purr changing to a growl during examination – stop, I've had enough
Nursing cat's deep growl – warning to kittens that there's danger about
Nursing cat's deep growl ending on a rising note – warning to people and other animals to stay away from kittens
Arched back – intimidation
Arched back and flat ears – war declared!

Laparotomy

This means cutting into the abdominal cavity. The commonest operation of this sort done by veterinarians is spaying the female, i.e., removing her uterus and ovaries. Some do a dozen a day year in and year out. But because it is simple it doesn't mean that it can be done carelessly. Every operation that involves going into the abdomen requires absolute sterility.

The other common laparotomies are caesareans and locating and removing foreign bodies like needles, bones or fur-balls that are causing obstructions.

In older animals, when a veterinarian suspects abdominal tumours he may ask permission to do an exploratory laparotomy. This means that he wants to go in and have a look, and confirm his diagnosis beyond doubt. Some people get upset because they mistake exploratory for experimental. Not at all. There's nothing faintly resembling vivisection about it. If the animal has a fatal cancer it's better to know for sure, and then not let it wake up from the operation. All the animal feels is the initial needle that puts it under. Isn't that better than going on week after week with certain discomfort, possible pain and uncertain treatment? What alternative do many people prefer? They immediately rush off to another veterinarian – don't mention that the animal has undergone weeks of tests and treatment – and put the creature through the whole process again.

Laryngitis

We often see these cases very late at night. The cat (usually a Siamese or a Burmese) is brought in by a friend of the owner who is keeping it while the owner is away. The anxious friend is certain that the cat has something stuck in its throat. 'You can hear the vibrating when it miaows, and if you just touch his neck he starts choking and coughing,' they say.

They're quite right. The cat has a low raspy voice and any handling of the area causes distress. When questioned they will admit that the cat has missed its owners terribly and has kept up a constant cry for them. I'm told that a famous American folk singer yells his head off for two hours before a concert in order to be able to produce the same strained guttural rasps.

The cure includes antihistamine injections and soothing syrups if the cat will take them. If the owner is going to be away for some time one tries tranquillizers but their effects are rather variable.

There is also a laryngitis that is secondary to other infections. These usually take much longer to clear up and require long courses of antibiotics.

Leptospirosis

This is one of the three nasty diseases against which dogs get inoculated with what most people call 'the triple shot'. The other two are distemper and infectious hepatitis. Cats can't get either of these, but they can get leptospirosis. In fact some surveys show that quite a large number of cats either have it or have had it. Interestingly enough, they seem to suffer no ill effects from the disease, nor apparently do they transmit it to other animals or people. Nice pussy!

Leukaemia (*feline infectious leukaemia and feline infectious peritonitis*)

Our kids sit in front of the telly and munch crisps as they watch real men walking on the moon. They take it all for granted. There's nothing that man cannot do, they think. Meanwhile people on earth are dying of all sorts of things that we're not halfway to understanding. And so are our animals. Leukaemia in cats at this stage is classified as an interesting problem by the scientists and as a nightmare by serious breeders and cat lovers. What do we know about it? Almost certainly it's caused by a virus. The scientists think they can recognize the virus and identify cats that have been exposed and those that are active carriers. They think that the virus may cause blood disorders, malignant tumours of the lymph glands, reproductive difficulties or just a lowered resistance to ordinary infections. Some say it may cause the huge swollen bellies which we see in some ill cats and for which there is no other explanation. All are agreed it's nasty.

How common is the virus? In many papers I've read, the figure forty per cent crops up again and again. For example, in one study it is claimed that about forty per cent of all cats 'living wild' have been exposed to the virus. Another study claims that about forty per cent (or more) of a closed cattery will pick it up if one infected cat is introduced. Some ignorant cat breeders suggest that a virus that involves forty per cent of a population must be near enough normal. Surely, they suggest, if that figure were sixty per cent those who didn't show positive signs of exposure would be abnormal. Maybe in their ignorance and innocence they are closer to the truth than those in favour of imposing a rigid policy of isolation and or euthanasia in an attempt to wipe out the virus.

I simply don't know and neither does anyone else at this stage. There is reputed to be a living vaccine that is effective. But it's not yet considered safe enough for general use. I'm afraid there is simply no advice I can proffer at the moment with any confidence. The average cat owner must simply hope that his cats will have sufficient resistance to throw it off.

People with small closed communities of breeding cats are currently being told to isolate all newcomers, until they are proved negative. This is an expensive, laborious and in no way a fool-proof method. I certainly agree with the isolation, because feline infectious leukaemia (Fe.I.L.) as it is called is not the only problem that newcomers can introduce.

And what if the syndrome appears in a completely closed colony? Isolation or euthanasia? There are expert advocates for each.

I suppose (but in no way propose) that a practical compromise is the one many commercial catteries follow:

1 Any cat that is showing *any* signs of trouble is simply not admitted or is rigidly isolated.
2 Any cat in the colony that is ill is immediately isolated.
3 Any cat suffering with any condition that appears incurable is put to sleep and sent off to a laboratory for a proper post-mortem.

I'm afraid we have to wait till the scientists come up with the answers. I hope I'm not taking advantage of my readers when I suggest that there is no way they can come up with an answer to the problem unless they use animals in their research. Yes, dear, I'm talking about vivisection. I know it's frightful. But so is the fact that we know so little about this condition.

Don't tell me about your natural herbs and raw vegetables. I eat garlic in unsociable quantities, nevertheless I suffer every ailment in the medical dictionary except modesty. Please write and tell me how leukaemia in cats will be conquered without research.

Lice

You probably live a refined sort of existence and don't see many fleas. I see them every day, and occasionally they hop across for a friendly visit. Lice, by contrast, are rather scarce these days, and often I go for weeks without seeing one. One louse-infested cat, however, makes up for the barren weeks.

Usually the poor cat is absolutely inundated with the creatures. It may be weak through loss of blood. Almost certainly it will give off a rotten, musty odour, its coat will feel sticky, and its body will be covered with the marks of constant but futile scratching. If several cats share quarters they usually share the lice as well.

The adult louse is a very fast crawler, and you may not notice him. Because lice spend their entire lives on the bodies of their hosts you will be able to see the eggs or nits which are attached to the hair. Don't use DDT or bathe the animal with disinfectants. You'll kill the lice, but you may kill the cat as well.

Get a dusting powder from the vet. Put the cat on newspaper. Dust him thoroughly. Start at the head and be careful to avoid the eyes, the ears and the mouth. Then do the tail. Then do the middle. Comb and brush thoroughly. Gather up the newspaper and burn it. Repeat in three or four days and again in ten days to get all those that have hatched meanwhile.

In severe infestations, leave the whole nasty job to the vet. Some are so bad that an anaesthetic is needed to clip off hair so thick with nits that one can't tell where the cat begins and the lice end.

Licking

If you've watched a cat clean himself you know it's a relaxed sort of business even if it's not leisurely. He goes over his whole coat systematically with a routine he's worked out for himself. I don't know if there's any more rhyme or reason to the way he does his washing than there is to the way I do mine, but if he starts licking at one particular area and keeps licking, biting or pawing at it, you can be sure there's something wrong. If during his daily cleaning he returns again and again to the same area you'd better corner him, get him on a table and have a good look. It may be a small festering area. It may be a bite or a puncture wound. Some child may have wrapped an elastic band or a bit of string round his leg. He may have a tick, a colony of lice or an eczema just starting.

If it's a foreign object like a grass seed or an elastic band, you must remove it. Sometimes bathing the area will facilitate the removal of an object. If it looks like the red sores of insect bites, check the animal carefully. If you see fleas use a powder. If it looks like an abscess starting, bathe it with warm salt water (see *Abscess*). Remember, if you put an antiseptic ointment on, the cat will immediately lick it off and make himself sick. I use a lot of gentian violet (after first cleaning with salt water) on those places where an animal just seems determined to lick a wee nothing until it becomes a big something. Gentian violet has the virtue of drying in quickly, and often it will stop the irritation. Put it on just before feeding time. By the time the meal is over it will have dried in and done its work. At other times you must hold the beast for fifteen minutes to allow the stuff to dry in. Remember, gentian violet will stain everything it touches. Sometimes cutting the hair round an irritating area will hasten healing. A cat that is constantly licking at its vulva or penis should be seen by a veterinarian. It may be one of the more serious conditions like pyometra or bladder stones.

Lifting

Mother cats lift their young by the scruff of the neck, and this is the proper way to do it – until the kitten is weaned. After that the body becomes too heavy, and unless you support its abdomen with one hand its weight stretches and strains the neck muscles.

When you lift an adult cat point its head away from yourself. If you point it towards yourself the cat will instinctively claw for your clothes in order to get a foothold. Support its body firmly but without squeezing, and you'll find it won't struggle. If the cat feels that it's being held securely it will relax.

Litter Box (*or sanitary tray*)

Cats are naturally clean. If they are gently shown the litter box after every mishap, they will soon get to know what it's for. Usual size is about 20cm (8 in) wide by 30cm (12 in) long. Don't get out the slide rule. Just use your commonsense. It may be of wood, plastic or metal, and filled with paper, sawdust, sand or specially bought grit.

I use cardboard boxes that I get from the grocer's, and cut the sides down to about 7·5cm (3 in) high. On the bottom I put newspapers folded flat, and then shred newspapers on top of that, and then use about a pint of commercial grit on top of that. At the end of the week I throw the whole lot away. I encourage my cat to go out no matter how cold it is as long as it's not blowing wet, so really the litter box is just a standby. If your cat is a stay-at-home you'll have to use more grit and less paper and change more often. If you've got ten cats and they're all stay-at-homes, don't bother inviting me for tea.

Little Girls

Little girls of nine or ten or eleven walk into the clinic with the biggest, fiercest cats in London town. The cats have their front legs curled round the necks of the little girls, and the little girls ooh and aah at all the other animals in the clinic. The little girls put their cat on the table, and it takes two assistants and a vet to hold it there during treatment. The cat claws at everything available. When the examination and treatment are over the little girl picks up the cat, it hugs her neck, and out they walk. Often the little girl scolds her cat saying, 'You big silly! It's only for your own good.' The cat hugs her all the tighter.

When little girls get to be bigger little girls of twelve or thirteen, they have to bring their cats to the clinic in a basket just as you do. Don't ask me why.

Liver (*as food*)

Most cats love liver. It is delicious, nutritious, convenient and cheap. What sort of liver? There isn't all that difference nutritionally between sheep or pig liver, so you might just as well buy the cheaper. In many parts of Canada and the States steer liver is preferred and comparatively expensive, while the butchers can hardly even give pig liver away. In England it's quite the opposite. People think ox liver is tasteless, and pay a premium for pig or sheep liver. Your cat will enjoy all, despite local fashion.

Cooked or raw? It depends what the liver looks like. If it's full of those tell-tale spots that indicate parasite infection, I cook it. In the States a very high percentage of sheep livers are condemned because of parasites. I've seen lambs going down a New York assembly line at the rate of six hundred an hour, and more than half the livers were being thrown out. Actually they were condemned for human use, but allowable for animal foods provided they were cooked. Obviously, at that rate of inspection some infected livers would be missed and go through normal trade channels. In Britain and on the Continent meat inspection varies so much that it's quite possible for huge quantities of unfit stuff to reach the market. Am I being unfair? I think I recall reading somewhere that tons of corned beef were imported from a factory in South America which used typhoid infected river water to wash the tins. The factory was inspected every six months or so. I'm not out to change all the traditions and stuff. I'm just suggesting that when you get the liver home you should have a look at it. If it's a clean-looking, smooth liver give it to your hungry monster as it is. If it's got spots or pocks or irregular swellings, cook it first.

Small bits or big pieces? I give it just as it comes, and make the brute use his teeth and his jaws. When he gets old and creaky and toothless, I shall chop it into swallowable bits. Needless to say, when he was a temporary-toothed kitten I performed the same service.

Quantity? I ask the butcher for 225g ($\frac{1}{2}$ lb) and tell him I want less rather than more. Actually, about 175g (6 oz) fuels my brute for the succeeding twelve or fourteen hours. Yours might be satisfied with four ounces, or need as much as eight. It depends on how active he is, and how hot it is, and how much he's used to. If you're too wide off that margin you're either starving or bloating him.

Frequency? Twice a week is what I usually advise, but many cats only like liver once a week, and others thrive on it every other day. Liver, and especially raw liver, has a laxative effect, and feeding it too frequently will cause loose bowel motions or diarrhoea. Some owners say that they feed their cats nothing but liver because they refuse everything else. I advise them to put down veal or beef or fish or tinned food. If they refuse it, pick it up and put it in the fridge. Then try again in five or six hours. After a day or two it's surprising how many cats decide they like lots of different foods.

There are some patients whom vets put on a diet that is primarily liver. These include Persians who keep forming hair-balls and ageing Siamese who get great constipated masses in their colon on a normal diet. Animals that have intestinal operations or a slow growing tumour may be helped along by a diet that is mainly liver.

Finally (and I hope this boring repetition has some effect) any animal with diarrhoea should not be fed liver while it is ill, and for at least a week after it is cured.

Liver disease

Cats have more than their fair share of tumours of the liver, but only rarely do they suffer from other liver complaints. I think the only thing I can say about liver troubles in the cat is that they are so complex that most veterinarians (and I put myself at the top of the list) would like to know far more about them. They are usually so difficult to diagnose that by the time one finds the root of the trouble it's too late. Why bother to mention it? Simply to point out the futility of those universally advertised liver tonics. If they did any good at all vets would be the first to use them.

One of the few symptoms that is really significant of liver trouble is jaundice. The bile backs up into the system and causes the typical yellowing of the gums and eyeballs. Need I say that this is a very serious sign? Even with the most expert of professional attention the animal is likely to die. But do give it half a chance and don't mess about with somebody's herbs.

Loneliness

My Oxford Concise defines lonely as solitary, companionless, isolated, unfrequented. You can define it as you like, but you must know that as our society gets more urban and more mobile the family unit gets smaller and people who formerly had a place within the family find themselves living alone. It wasn't so many years ago that solitary aunts and uncles and ageing grandparents lived under the same roof with a couple and their growing family. In much of Latin Europe and Latin America and in other so-called backward places you still commonly find four generations living as a family unit. There're lots of drawbacks, but there's one big advantage: those societies have fewer people who feel cast-off and lonely.

Many people who, for one reason or another, live alone find it increasingly difficult to meet companions or make new friends. Some of them, in a surprisingly short time, seem to lose their ability to communicate easily. They can go through the formalities of work and shopping, but become awkward at a personal level.

How did this sociological treatise creep among the kittens? Simply because any veterinary surgeon who treats any number of small pets is confronted daily with people whose main object of love is their pet. Is it pitiful? Is it despicable that so much time and attention should be lavished on an animal? Would you laugh at such people and tell them not to be ridiculous? Tell me, then, how often do you visit your lonely relatives? No, not your rich Uncle Jack, but penniless Aunt

Odorifera? Well, let me tell you a secret. Aunt Odorifera has got ten thousand in gilt edged, and every damn penny is going to the cat.

Lungs (*as food*)

These are bulky, rather fibrous organs, from the butcher's point of view, and they don't rank very high with the nutritionists. However, in Mediterranean countries they make some delicious dishes out of lungs, and the cats relish the leftovers. In urbanized societies lungs seldom find their way to the butchers' shops. They're usually minced down and added to the tinned stuff which the advertisements tell us is so delicious. Anyway, if you have a cheap source of lungs and the patience to handle the bulk, your cat may find them a welcome change.

Lung disease

Cats are prone to pneumonia and pleurisy and other sorts of chest trouble. They may be primary conditions or secondary to something like flu or enteritis. I know that pneumonia no longer seems to be the terrible word it was thirty years ago. But despite all the new anti-biotics it can still be a killer. Unfortunately many of these cases are infectious and so they cannot be hospitalized. Home nursing includes confinement in a very small area. The lungs need to be rested. Any exertion postpones a cure. So get out the sanitary tray and keep the door closed.

Don't force some old cough syrup down the patient's throat. It may neutralize the drugs your vet has prescribed, or it may contain codeine. Codeine will drive the cat into insane activity which isn't really the way to rest the lungs.

Lymphosarcoma (*malignant tumours of lymphatic tissue*)

They may occur in any organ of the body or as a generalized condition which we call leukaemia. In the cat they occur mostly round the liver, the spleen, the kidneys and the bowels. Even in its localized form the blood picture is usually pretty significant.

Those that occur in and around the bowel are one of the commoner tumours that kill cats.

I'm told that they occur less frequently in the dog, and are even rarer in the human. Lymphosarcoma of the bowel can occur at any age, but we seem to see it mostly in the four to eight-year-old range. The cat usually has rather mild symptoms at first. It may have a bout of vomiting or a bit of diarrhoea or a tendency to constipation. It may refuse food and have a slight temperature. A day or two of starvation, a bit of oil and they seem to recover. A few days or a couple of weeks later, and the symptoms recur. One feels the tummy very carefully and gently. Sometimes you can actually feel the slightest bowel or glandular thickening. Sometimes, especially in fat animals, one can feel nothing, and sometimes in advanced cases one feels the rather big lump that spells 'serious and hopeless'. One X-rays just to make sure that the lump isn't a piece of rubber or part of an old sock.

If the case is diagnosed early on, a clever surgeon might be able to cut the lump and its neighbouring glands out cleanly. But personally I have never seen a lymphosarcoma in a cat that didn't terminate fatally within weeks.

Usually, when the vet has more than a vague suspicion that a lymphosarcoma is present he advises a liquid diet for a few days. He may then anaesthetize the animal and palpate the relaxed abdomen. He may send a bit of blood off to the lab where some clever myopic boffin will fill out a slip stating that 'the differential count does not exclude the possibility of a malignant tumour'.

Many vets advise their clients that the sensible procedure is an exploratory operation. They want to open up the abdomen and have a look. If it proves to be a growth, they won't allow the animal to wake from the operation. I think it's a humane procedure. The alternative is to nurse the suffering cat for some weeks through increasing distress and pain to certain death. If there were a really effective pain-killer for cats I wouldn't be so adamant about the desirability of an early diagnosis and decision — see also Leukaemia (Feline Infectious Leukaemia).

Maine cat

This is a big solid cobby, who developed all by himself in New England. We're told that he started as a domesticated Angora or Persian from the old world, went feral in the Maine Woods and through natural selection developed into the hardy long-coated cat of today, who is equally happy whether hunting in the snow or lying by the hearth. In other words he's a domesticated long-hair who is hardy enough to withstand a northern winter. His undercoat is not so luxurious as that of his show cousins. He can manage to keep it mat free without man's help. His tail ends in a point rather than the bush that most long-hairs sport. He comes in all colours but rich tabby predominates from which he gets his nickname of 'Coon' cat. The breed is solidly established and neither the cat nor its many admirers seem to mind that it is not officially recognized. *PS:* Today there are almost as many breed societies in America as there are cats. Lots recognize the Maine Coon cat. I am given to understand that many of the pedigrees attached to these cats are as poetic as those casually dispensed at some Irish Greyhound auctions. Needless to say with the admixture of pure Persian, regular grooming graduates from a luxury to a necessity.

Mammary tumours

These are growths that occur on the chest and abdomen around and between the nipples. They are seen most often in entire queens who have never been allowed to have kittens. As there are relatively few cats in this category, mammary tumours aren't nearly the problem in cats that they are in bitches. However, they do occur, and some have been reported in spayed queens and even the odd one in male cats.

Mammary tumours on the cat simply must not be neglected. Those small hard lumps should be seen by a vet within a day or two of their appearing. They can grow very quickly, and even if they don't the cat will be inclined to open them up with her rasp-like tongue. Sometimes early radical surgery is successful in removing them completely. Sometimes even early cases spread faster than the knife can cut.

Summary: Any lump on a cat's chest should be seen by a vet within a day or two.

Mange (*notodectic mange*)

A skin disease caused by a small mite with the big name *Notoderes cati*. It starts innocently enough with a small bare patch on the edge of the ears or on the face. Then the feet and the neck go bald and get crusted with grey material. These areas are terribly itchy, and the cat scratches them into festering sores. Gradually, if left untreated, the skin wrinkles into hard ridges. Your vet will suspect mange in any skin condition that starts around the face or feet. It may be so typical that he'll have no doubt as to what it is, or he may wish to confirm by taking a scraping of the skin and examining it under the microscope.

Treatment includes cleaning the whole area, applying the specific medicine or medicines, and generally cleaning up everything, with particular emphasis on your own hands after each application. Although the cat mange mite can't properly live on humans, he can cause an ugly itchy mess before he realizes he's lost his way.

Manx cat

The rabbity cat from the Isle of Man. He has a short back, long hind legs and as for a tail he has none at all. His hop though sloppy is quite fast enough to catch all but olympic quality rats. Of course it's difficult to express all the nuances of emotion without a tail but people manage somehow and so does the tailless cat.

Because the Manx is a natural mutation that has been encouraged by man and not a freak developed by selective in-breeding there don't appear to be any veterinary problems associated with his unique characteristics. I suppose, though, that these will come as man selects for longer and longer hind legs and a shorter and shorter back. Until that unhappy time comes you can purchase a Manx with every assurance that you'll have a ratter second to none and a pet that is reputed to be among the most loyal and faithful of felines. And, like puddings and jellies, they come in all colours.

PS: I regret to have to report that today we are seeing a lot of these marvellous cats suffering with spinal problems. I don't know of a single breeder who is into the breed in order to make money. Most are having trouble enough keeping the bank manager at bay. They're obviously concerned. We can only hope that cooperation between them and researchers in the veterinary profession will come up with a solution.

Mastitis (*or mammitis*)

This is the dairyman's nightmare, and no wonder. The modern dairy cow is little more than a gigantic udder attached to a series of vats that convert food into milk. Cows that were meant to raise their calves with 9kg (20 lb) of milk have been developed and selected so that now they produce up to 45kg (100 lb) of milk month after dreary month. Unless conditions are spot on, the big udder flares up. It becomes sore and hot and the milk turns to a watery trickle of serum, blood and pus. This is the udder's way of saying it's had enough.

Thank goodness we rarely see the condition in cats. Despite the world's overpopulation, nobody expects the cat to feed people with its surplus milk. Its udder has been left alone. Therefore, mastitis occurs in the cat only when the udder is subjected to quite unusual stresses or injury.

For example, a cat who gets one of the infectious diseases while she is in her full flush of milk may have her resistance lowered to such an extent that she gets mastitis as well. Usually, though, the udder 'dries up' and the flow of milk stops.

143

Sometimes a kick from a cow or a man, a scratch from another cat or even an aggressive kitten, or a bite from a dog will cause an udder that is swollen with milk to flare into mastitis.

The cat may appear perfectly normal to her owners. They often first notice that something is wrong when they hear the pitiful squeals of the starving kittens or find a dead kitten in the nest. An examination of the mother reveals that the udder is swollen, hot and usually very painful to the touch. In other cases, the owner first notices that something is wrong when the mother refuses her food. Then they look at the kittens and are surprised at how weak they've become in just a few hours. It doesn't take many hours of starvation to send a kitten downhill.

However, the commonest cause of mastitis in the cat is the early loss of her litter. Many first-time mothers destroy their own litters if conditions of solitude aren't obtainable. This is a nice way of saying 'Keep the — kids away for the first few days'. Also many, too many, so-called cat lovers destroy litter after litter as they are born. Why these people don't have their pets spayed is beyond my comprehension. In fact, why they keep a cat at all I don't understand. Nevertheless, they do. They allow her to get pregnant time after time, but don't allow her to rear the kittens. Whatever the reasons or the excuses, many cats have a full flow of milk and no kittens to suckle it. The miracle is that in most cases nature 'cakes' the udder and dries it off, and all is well. But in a painful minority of cases the 'caked' udder doesn't dry off. It becomes mastitic.

What's to be done when this happens?

Well, obviously, in those cases in which the litter is still alive and you wish to attempt to rear them, the first thing to do is separate the mother from the litter. The mother has little milk anyway, and what little she has is more toxic than nutritious. And, besides, it won't help her recovery to have the kittens clawing at her tummy to get the milk that isn't there. Put the kittens in a distant room and keep the door closed. The mother will try to join them at every opportunity.

If the litter is dead, you would be well advised to keep the mother locked up, at least until you have 'dried her off' or cured the mastitis. Remember that she is quite capable of running off right then and getting bred again, and presenting you with the same problem in sixty days.

What is the safe home treatment for mastitis? Give two Epsom salt tablets and withdraw all fluids for twelve hours. Soothe the swollen udder with warmed olive oil. Don't use medicated ointments.

144

She'll just lick them off and make herself even more ill. If the udder is very painful and you simply can't get a vet (or to a vet) for several hours, an ice-pack will relieve some of the pain. If a portion of the udder is forming into a flaming red bulge you can be sure it's going to abscess and burst. Don't squeeze it. Don't put ointments on it. Bathe it with warm salt water for five minutes every hour or two.

That's as far as home treatment may be effective and humane. What the cat really wants then is professional attention. Abscesses may have to be lanced, antibiotics may have to be injected locally or into the body, and in more serious cases the animal may have to have supportive injections to ensure recovery.

Prevention: If a cat loses her litter, 'dry her off' by giving two Epsom salt tablets and withdrawing all fluids for twenty-four hours.

Memo: The vast majority of the world's cats raise their litters without problems. If you are not absolutely certain what you're doing, then you'll do less harm if you do nothing.

Mating

Cats are among the most prolific of the higher animals. Getting them mated is no problem. Just open the front door. She'll come back a few hours later slightly scarred, but smug and pregnant. She'll have been the centre of a ring of competing toms, one or more of whom will have grabbed her by the back of the neck with its powerful jaws and penetrated her for the few seconds which is the duration of copulation in the cat. One tom may have mounted her half a dozen times in an hour. She'll not have discriminated, but will have accepted each tom that wasn't too busy fighting off his competitors. Kittens in the same litter may have different fathers. The cat differs from many other animals in that during the mating season she may have several heat periods. It's the sexual act that releases her eggs. That is why, unlike the bitch, for example, you can't just lock up a cat and hope she'll return to normal in a week or ten days. Siamese in particular will keep 'calling', more or less, until nature has had its way.

Mating problems only arise when man attempts to select the sire. The same cat who would have no problem getting mated out of doors will often turn vicious or neurotic when introduced to a tom in a confined space. Obviously this is a problem that confronts the pure-bred breeder almost constantly. What advice can I offer? First, if you are a novice at the game take your queen to a tom who belongs to an experienced person. Secondly, remember the old adage about breeding a virgin female to an experienced male, and vice versa. Thirdly,

145

if your queen is incorrigibly vicious your vet may try tranquillizers. In carefully gauged doses they often work. Fourthly, a veterinary examination might reveal that she has one of the four or five common ailments of the reproductive tract. Your vet might consider this one of nature's warnings of wrong inbreeding. Fifthly, some virgin queens who simply will not mate when confined will do so after they've had one litter as a result of a natural mating out of doors. Finally remember that the best time to breed is just after the bleeding of heat has stopped but while the swelling of the vagina is still quite obvious.

Mats

If you neglect to groom a Persian his hair will clump into little hard lumps. If there are only one or two small matted bits you can generally tease them open by gently separating the larger bits into smaller bits and then combing out the dead hair. Some are easier to do if you wet the matted bits first.

I have had some long-haired cats presented to me which were just a mess of solid hair. I can't adequately describe the mess, but if you poured a large bottle of glue over your own hair and let it set you'd get the idea. All these cases aren't due to neglect by the owners. Sometimes the animal has run off and lost itself for a few days or weeks. Sometimes they've been boarded out with stupid people who just didn't realize that long-haired cats must be groomed daily.

The only practical way I've ever found to handle these cases is to administer a general anaesthetic, and clip the whole lot off. The owner is always warned to expect a half-bald cat. Even so, they usually scream in rage and one never sees them again. Maybe one of those outraged people would be kind enough to tell me a better way? *Summary:* If you can't spare a few moments every day to groom your cat, don't buy a Persian.

Meat

Raw meat was the stuff that cats lived on before the tin opener was invented. Many still do. What kind? You name it and your cat will thrive on it. Horse-meat, beef, veal, mutton, lamb, rabbit, down to its natural prey of rats and birds and even (so I'm told) insects.

Some cats don't like fat. If it doesn't agree with them, trim it off. But if they like it, let them have it because it's good for them.

Most cats can be given meat on the bone. They'll eat the cartilage bits and leave the splintery bits. But if you've cooked the chicken or the rabbit or those prime ribs, you must remove bones. Cooking makes bones brittle and dangerous. Skin, fur or feathers won't bother your cat. He'll eat or leave them depending on his mood.

If you feel that raw meat is simply too barbaric, you can cook the stuff. Baking (not too long) retains the nutrients better than boiling. But remember that some authorities state that there is something in *raw* foods that cats need.

Please don't give a hungry cat frozen, chilled or hot meat. Ideal feeding temperature is around 27 or 32°C. I know it's a gruesome thought, but that approximates a freshly killed carcass.

What parts of the carcass? Most cats will thrive on any – liver, lung, heart, brains, innards, prime sirloin, etc. There's little difference nutritionally, but vary it a bit. Some cats, unlike dogs, will get bored with the same old thing day after day.

Note: Your vet may recommend limiting the diet to certain meats. For example, kidney patients may be restricted to the white meats of veal, rabbit or chicken. Elderly patients with a tendency to constipation may be put on a diet of liver three times a week.

Meat juice

Cats with sore throats or swollen tongues or aching teeth will refuse solid foods but may be tempted by liquid meat. How do you do it? Simplicity itself. Stick the meat (lean, please) in a grinder or a blender. If you're short on machinery just mash the stuff until the juice flows free.

Menstruation

Cats like most animals (except for man and some of the higher primates) don't menstruate. They do have a vaginal discharge which occurs at the opposite end of the reproductive cycle, namely when they are in season and ready for impregnation. As cats are fastidious about licking themselves clean you may not see it. Nevertheless it does happen. Even if you don't notice it the cat will give you other indications that much as she likes you she really would prefer a tom for company (see also *Heat*).

If a cat has a thickish vaginal discharge or if that area is crusted with matter you'd better seek professional advice. It may be a symptom of pyometra which is very serious and indicates an operation to remove the infected uterus.

Milk

We all know that most cats will accept a saucer of cow's milk. How many of us know that they would prefer something much stronger? Ordinary cow's milk is not only far too dilute for the cat's nutritional needs but it often causes diarrhoea. Really rich creamy milk approximates cat's milk (as far as the butterfat is concerned) and this is the stuff to offer an adult cat. Many cats, orientals particularly, simply won't take milk or cream and that's perfectly all right. Make sure, however, that you supplement their diet of meat and fish with vitamins and minerals. A small drop of cod-liver oil and the odd teaspoon of bonemeal and of course a daily yeast tablet is ample to supplement the milk-free diet of an adult cat.

Kittens, of course, need milk, particularly in the rapid growth period between weaning and four months. You can provide this milk in one of three ways. First, you can purchase those rather expensive powders that are formulated specially for kittens. Secondly, you can economize by buying ordinary dried milk powder and mix it at double the strength you would for your own baby. Thirdly, you can use the top half of ordinary cow's milk and add an egg to each 3dl ($\frac{1}{2}$ pt) which should bring it up to cat's milk strength. How strong is cat's milk? It's almost five per cent fat and almost ten per cent protein. It's concentrated food for concentrated bodies.

Milk fever (*or calcium eclampsia or parturient tetany*)

A mother who is feeding her young may actually withdraw the calcium from her own bones to build those of her sucklings. If the mother's calcium level falls too low she may go into tetanic spasms (shivering fits), unconsciousness and then death. Veterinarians see the condition very commonly in champion milk cows, occasionally in bitches with large litters, and once in a while in well bred queens with large litters.

In the cat it usually occurs about a week or two after birth. The female is a good 'milker' but thin. She usually starts with a slight shivering which gradually grows into an unmistakable shaking. If left untreated for more than five or six hours the cat usually dies.

Treatment consists of calcium injections – preferably into the vein. Response is dramatic. Usually within minutes the shaking stops and the animal appears absolutely normal. However, relapses are common, and the vet will probably want to keep an eye on her.

Memo: Prevention consists of a proper well-balanced diet. In this day and age this means mineral supplements. Ask your vet.

Mongrels

The vast majority of cats are mongrels. They don't really know their daddies, and can't trace their pedigree. Like the majority of humans who can't trace their lineage, mongrel cats are very nice. Cats haven't been pushed in or stretched out by selective breeding for ridiculous characteristics. All of them have the same basic shape. I know there are subtle variations, but an Eskimo from Baffinland seeing a whole range of cats for the first time would consider them all, whether Siamese, Persian or back alley, as being members of the same species. The same primitive couldn't possibly consider that the Chihuahua, the St Bernard and the English Bulldog were all of a kind. That's why you can be sure that almost any old kitten is quite likely to grow into an acceptable cat. With a mongrel puppy you won't know for some months whether its going to be a monster that eats children for breakfast or a wee neurotic that's frightened of the budgie.

PS: We ourselves breed purebreds not because we are snobs or dislike mongrels. It's simply that over the years we've learned exactly the feline characteristics that we particularly cherish. The whole point about breeding purebreds is that one has a better chance of producing those desirable features. In gambling terms the odds are better with purebreds.

You might get a mongrel with a more luxurious coat than a Persian, a more demanding nature than a Siamese or a more athletic resilience than the Domestic short-haired. But don't bet on it!

Nail-bed

This is as good a term as any for the recesses in the pad in which the claws lie. Some cats get dirt in that area with which they can't cope. The area becomes infected and swollen. The pain is similar to that which you would have with a swelling under a toenail. The cat will lick the area constantly, and make it worse. Home treatment that will relieve the pain consists of bathing the feet or foot in warm salt water and then applying some fast drying antiseptic like gentian violet or mercurochrome. If there isn't considerable improvement in a day, you had better get your veterinarian to decide whether antibiotics and other treatment are needed.

Names

Call your cat anything that pleases you, because they'll come when they like and ignore you the rest of the time. I think many cats are virtually uncallable, but that doesn't mean they are stupid or untrainable. They just don't like enduring our stupidities unless they're in a particularly tolerant mood. My cat was called Mr Moss (so named by his first owner because as a kitten he liked going for car rides), and the nearest cat neighbour is called Theophila. The two looked alike, and used to sit surveying the world from the top of the mews wall. Both of them were intensely interested in everything that went on. They didn't miss a sound, a sight or a smell. But just whisper the words Moss or Theophila, and immediately they would start examining themselves with minute curiosity. They would lick and clean away as if you were dead and of no possible interest to anyone. I am convinced that cats can single out their names however complex any conversation, but that may just be cat lover's drivel, and not the scientific objectivity you might expect when you pay hard cash for a book.

With dogs it's a different story, and as dogs must be trained in order to be happy (the unhappy nervous dogs are often those who don't know what their owners want) the name must be one that can be easily repeated in training and is instantly recognizable.

Incidentally, don't use the name to admonish. They'll associate the name with punishment. Use NO to express disapproval. Use the name only to tell the cat that a command (with cats I prefer the term request) is coming.

Summary: Be as fanciful and imaginative as you like in choosing a cat's name.

Needles

I don't want to say anything to discourage the ladies from staying at home where they belong, but I do wish they'd put their sewing away when they're finished. At least once a month I'm presented with a cat and a story like the following: 'He was perfectly all right on Tuesday but he wouldn't eat on Wednesday or Thursday. On Friday I gave him liquid paraffin and an aspirin. On Saturday he didn't come home at all. And here it is Sunday afternoon and he still won't eat.'

A careful examination of the mouth reveals that a sewing needle is stuck halfway down the throat.

One gives a general anaesthetic, tries to get the needle out without ripping the mouth to shreds, follows with a shot of penicillin, and goes home to the overdone roast.

Neuter

A castrated male or a spayed female.

Nictitating membrane (or third eyelid)

The cat has a third eyelid that begins at the inner corners of the eyes. If the cat has worms, or is ill, or sometimes if she's very tired as in late pregnancy, these eyelids will creep out and partially close one or both eyes.

There's no point in plastering those lids with ointment. The thing to do is to determine the cause, and treat that.

Nose

This is a sensitive, delicate organ and you simply must never punish a cat by striking it across its nose or face. The damage you do will far outlast the memory of any misdemeanour, and the cat, quite rightly, will never forgive you.

Nosebleed is fairly rare in the cat, but when it does occur it is most distressing to the owner but usually less so to the cat. It may be caused by a sharp blow, a fall, a sharp object running up the nose, or most commonly as an extension of one of the respiratory infections. The owner usually panics and tries several first aid remedies. Ice-packs will do no good and will distress the cat. Packing the nostril with cotton will start the cat sneezing and make the bleeding worse. Elevating the head usually gags the cat, and it will panic and do its best to escape.

The only sensible home aid is to place the cat in a basket in a quiet place. Often, in less than half an hour, a clot has formed and the crisis is over.

If there's a great deal of bleeding put the cat in a basket, get on the phone and try to locate a veterinarian who is on duty. It's better to take an extra five minutes on the phone than drive around frantically as so many people do. The vet will probably give a couple of injections of stuff that helps clot formation. If the bleeding is severe he'll give a general anaesthetic and try to determine the cause. He may pack the nostrils and keep the animal 'under' until he's sure he's got the mess under control. One warning note! If the bleeding originates in a malignant growth he may advise that it's kinder not to let the cat wake from the anaesthetic.

Some cats get the ugliest growths on the tip of their noses. Sometimes these can be removed completely and they don't recur. At other times they are rapidly growing destructive tumours which destroy the life that's feeding them.

Cats who have dry scaly noses may be comforted by thrice daily applications of a bit of cod-liver oil. Even if it doesn't do much good it won't do the cat any harm. Don't keep on at it for two or three months while the condition gets worse. I don't mean that you should postpone your honeymoon or anything like that, but I do think that the earlier it's seen by a vet the more likely the chance of an early cure.

Nursing

Home nursing is often necessary. It may make the difference between saving and losing a patient. It's not a very complicated business, and is even simpler if you learn a few basic rules:

1 Don't fuss about. Do what's necessary and then allow the patient to rest.
2 Don't place the animal in a draught. Many places are warm at waist level but cold below, so bend down and make sure. Build the bed up with newspapers or old blankets. A healthy animal can move out of the cold. An ill one may not know enough to care. Some feverish cats may try to lie in a draught. It may be instinctive but it's wrong.
3 Change hot water bottles often enough to keep the temperature constant. Wrap them well to avoid burning the skin.
4 Don't force *anything* down the patient's throat without your vet's approval. This includes food and honey and brandy.
5 Change the water fairly frequently, because the cat may not wish to drink from a bowl that it has just drooled in.
6 Encourage rest by quiet and dim lighting.
7 Carry the creature to its tray three or four times a day, and support it while it does its business. If it has never used a tray you may have to carry it outdoors.
8 Patients lying flat out must be turned hourly to prevent pneumonia.
9 Bedding must be changed as it becomes soiled.
10 Grooming will help the cat keep its self respect and its interest in living. Comb and brush gently. Wipe away discharges. Bathe the eyes and nose with warm salt water (teaspoon to 6dl (1 pint)). Apply cod liver oil lightly to cracked lips and nose.
11 Wash soiled hind ends and cut away the mats. Dry gently.
12 Give pills and injections at the prescribed intervals.

Nystagmus (*or jerky eyeballs*)

The cat may appear perfectly normal or its head may weave slightly, but one, or more commonly both, eyeballs move sideways or up and down or round and round in an irregular, rapid and jerky fashion. It's a most distressing sight, and as serious as it appears. Obviously there must be brain damage to cause symptoms so severe. The cat may have fallen from a height and struck its head, or it may have taken one of those new-fangled poisons, or it may have a tumour. The only treatment until the vet arrives is rest in a dark, quiet place.

Ocelot

Ocelot (Felis pardalis) and Margay (Felis tigrina) are the two wild cats that are most often domesticated and kept as pets. They are both natives of Central America. The Margay is concentrated in Guyana and Brazil, but the Ocelot has pushed out and is found everywhere from Texas down to the Argentine.

They are downy, beautifully coloured creatures and tamed quite as easily as the domestic cat – provided one begins when they are young. I don't know if anyone has been successful at domesticating an adult.

There are three main disadvantages in keeping wild cats as pets. The first is that they remain nocturnal in habit. They sleep all day and want to be up and about at night. The second is that they are more successful hunters than the domestic cat and can tackle larger adversaries, so you may not be too popular with neighbourhood poultry or sheep raisers and possibly with owners of other cats or small dogs. The third is that if an Ocelot or Margay decides to be nasty when you're cleaning its ears or bandaging a cut they can be very nasty indeed.

In addition, there is one unanswerable reason why one shouldn't keep wild cats as pets. As long as there is a demand for Ocelots and Margays or even more exotic species the money grabbers in the animal world will go on catering for that demand.

How do you think many dealers in wild animals get their stock? I'll tell you. They go into native villages and tell everybody they're in the market for animals. The last time I heard a price list quoted was in an Indian village in Central America, some ten years ago. Snakes were about fifty cents a foot; monkeys varied from five to twenty dollars; parrots were a dollar and macaws two dollars; ant-eaters, peccarys and coati-mundis were three to five dollars, and baby alligators a dollar each. Wild cats were quoted at twenty dollars but actually a jaguar would fetch twenty-five in the villages, fifty in the local capital and three times that stateside.

I have no idea what present day prices are like. I should imagine they're all about quadruple.

There is one thing, though, that I don't think will change for a long time and that is the way primitive Indians in Central America

153

catch wild animals. They use the easiest method no matter how many other animals have to be destroyed in the process. How do you catch a baby monkey? Shoot the mother, of course. How do you capture an ocelot or margay young enough to domesticate? Shoot the adults. Make no mistake about it. Most of the cute little bundles of fluff that you see in the pet shops are the end result of the senseless murders of their parents.

If you buy one of these exotic animals you encourage the sordid trade. The only people who should be allowed licences to import exotic species are the serious workers in the field of natural history. Would that be too difficult to legislate? Surely it isn't that difficult to tell the difference between someone like Gerald Durrell or Ivan Sanderson and the people who measure the worth of a species by its catalogue price.

Orphans

The easiest way to raise orphans is by fostering them. A mother of the same species is preferable, but any nursing mother will do in a pinch. See your local newspaper for startling examples. (See *Adoption* at the front of this book if you want to know how it's done.)

A more difficult but more satisfying way is to rear them by hand. You will be rewarded by kittens who will be terribly attached to you.

Use a medicine dropper with many wee holes rather than a real squirter. Later you can use a bottle and nipple, and later still a saucer. Wash and boil between feedings. Test temperature as you would for a baby.

Frequency of feeding is more important than amounts. You'll soon get to know when they've had enough. Never push the stuff down too fast. Wait for swallowing between drops.

Feed about every three hours at first. Gradually lengthen the interval to six hours. A teaspoon is enough for a 100g ($\frac{1}{4}$ lb) kitten which is what most of them weigh at birth. When it grows to two pounds it will want about four tablespoons per feed.

The best milk is that compounded specially for orphan kittens and available at many drug stores. If you can't get it, use powdered milk, but prepare it double the strength recommended for human babies.

At two or three weeks try them on a bit of finely minced meat. As you increase the meat and decrease the milk you must add calcium pills or bonemeal to the diet.

Newborn animals are extremely susceptible to temperature change. Keep them in a draught-free box in a warm room. Modern aids (see

Heating) are both easier and better than infra-red bulbs and hot water bottles.

Orphan kittens will wake and suckle each other's tails and ears. If it looks like sores are developing it may be better to raise them separately. At ten or twelve days you may have to trim sharp claws if the kittens are damaging each other. At the same time you may have to bathe eyes with warm salt water.

At any stage you may introduce a receptive adult. Although it may not be able to feed or be interested in grooming them it may well introduce the feline arts of defence, offence, hunting and (lock up your larder) stealing.

Remember too that throughout the whole period they'll miss their mother's massaging and grooming, so give them a lick with a chamois and a bit of a rub down every time you're passing by. When they start massaging you they're ready for their new homes.

Overweight

Although we occasionally see fat cats who got that way because of a glandular or hormonal defect, most of these rounded Henrys are the result of overfeeding. Every time they miaow the owner empties the fridge. After two or three years Falstaff doesn't even bother to ask for the stuff. Everyone concerned knows that his plate must be kept brimming. One of my friends is the manager of a large dog establishment. He can tell you to the gram the daily requirements of anything from a retired lap dog to a working Rottweiller. But every day he goes to that big horsemeat fridge and pulls out a hunk of loin that would satisfy a wolf, cuts it into little cubes and feeds it to his cat. The cat doesn't do anything at all except eat. He can't. It takes him all his waking hours to work through his daily ration, and all his sleeping hours to digest it. Two or three times a day he waddles outside. His bulk looks so formidable that he's never had to assert his neighbourhood rights over other cats, but his weight has gone to his head and he resents even people occupying any space he wants. I once tried to move him from the centre of a small sofa so that I could sit down too. The only reason I didn't require stitches is because I'm not quite as fat as he is and so can move just a little bit quicker.

Is he an isolated instance? No, I don't think so. At this moment I know half a dozen cats who are grotesquely fat and are also arrogant, uncompromising bullies. They've been indulged into complete self-indulgence. The pitiful thing is that obesity in cats, as in humans, leads to all sorts of health problems and shortens life. Many people

155

make the excuse that as the animal has been neutered it's bound to put on weight. Nonsense! Thousands of neuters are trim, healthy and happy. Go along to your vet and get Blubberbottom on a supervised diet.

Oxygen

A canister of oxygen is one of the essentials of cat practice. In a busy city clinic, particularly, one sees a lot of accidents. In many of them the cat is either shocked or frightened so badly that it stops breathing. I don't understand the theory of it all, but I can tell you that many cats in shock will respond to oxygen as dogs do to an intravenous drip. It's almost miraculous the way some of those cases which appear three-quarters dead revive, and within minutes one wonders what the panic was about. Lesson? Don't mess about with accident cases trying to splint legs or force brandy. Get them in a box and take them to the vet.

We also use oxygen routinely as an aid to anaesthesia, as first aid in gas poisoning, and as an adjunct to pneumonia therapy.

Pads

A scraped sore pad may be protected until it heals by a bootee. Use a baby's sock. Tie it with a flat bandage. If you use cord you'll cut off the circulation.

If a pad is bleeding wrap a bandage tightly around the whole foot. Lay the bandage flat. Tourniquets are unnecessary unless the blood is just gushing out. They can be dangerous unless loosened every twenty minutes.

Cracked pads may be soothed with cod-liver oil. The cat will lick the stuff off but it won't do any harm.

Paint

Don't use paraffin or kerosene or turpentine or solvent to get paint off a cat. Wipe off what you can with dry cloths, and then take the animal to the vet. If there's a lot of paint he'll have to give an anaesthetic and clip off the hair that's really stuck. Don't think that just because the cat appears OK it's not a serious business. She'll spend hours licking the stuff off and poisoning herself.

Never use paint containing lead in kennels or catteries. No matter what paint you use allow kitty to escape from the fumes. If she's locked in a room that's been freshly painted she may be poisoned.

Paralysis

This is a common sequel to automobile accidents in which the spine has been injured. Often only the hind legs are affected and sometimes only the tail. The outcome depends on the extent of the damage.

Almost always these cases are best hospitalized but some owners insist that the cat would be happier and more interested in recovering if it were at home. The animal must be confined in a small area. It must be supported while it defecates or urinates. It may need enemas or catheterization if it can't pass motions or water. It must be well groomed. The diet should be fairly sloppy to avoid constipation.

If there's no improvement within a fortnight your vet will probably recommend euthanasia.

Parturition (*giving birth, having kittens*)

A day or so before a cat is due to have kittens she'll be uneasy and restless. She'll wander about looking for a dark secure place. If you take her temperature at that time you'll find it's down a degree or even two from the normal. Don't do anything much at that stage besides protecting your eiderdown quilt and trying to guide Puss where you'd rather she had her kittens. She probably won't want to eat, but if she asks for it keep it light in both quantity and quality. Allow her lots of fluids.

When she's good and ready she'll lie down and strain. Shortly afterwards there will be a kitten which she'll look after very well without your help. If she ignores it completely you can massage and slap it vigorously, and remove the stuff around its mouth. However, the vast majority are better off without you so don't rush in unless you know what you're doing.

Sometimes two kittens come at once. More often they come singly, with intervals of ten or fifteen minutes to as long as an hour and a half between each one. Don't get frightened if you see one coming backwards. Almost half of them do. If a kitten is half in, half out for some seconds and the cat has stopped straining you can attempt a gentle pull but don't be too forceful or ambitious. You may be pulling legs belonging to different kittens.

If you only have one cat you won't have much difficulty in ensuring that she has the kittens in a clean place. However, if you're breeding the creatures commercially you must be spot on with your sanitary programme. This includes scrubbing and disinfecting the kennel between occupants, having the queen checked for worms before breeding and clipping the hair around the nipples well before kittening time. If you've been shown how, and remember to wash your hands properly, you may dip navels in iodine. You probably don't agree with me that it's more for your own peace of mind than the kittens' benefit, but at least if you wash your hands you won't be doing more harm than good.

If all goes well leave them alone and go to sleep. There's plenty of time next day to oooh and aaah and conjecture about the father.

The only time you need panic into midnight phone calls to the vet is when a cat strains and strains to no purpose. She's obviously in difficulty then and needs help. Don't prolong the waiting period by poking, probing and squeezing or as many people do by offering food, hot water bottles and reassurances.

Memo: Remember that a cat may take as long as twenty-four hours to have her kittens and that ninety-nine point something of all kittens are born and thrive without man's help. So before you rush in make sure you know what you're doing.

PS: Many cats have a few kittens and appear perfectly normal. Then without any fuss produce another lot a day or two later. Don't bother reporting it to your vet or the newspapers. It's quite normal.

Also you may be interested to know that many queens go out and get pregnant within hours of giving birth. So keep the doors firmly shut.

Penis

The penis of the cat is a small organ about 2cm ($\frac{3}{4}$ in) in length and about $\frac{1}{2}$cm ($\frac{1}{4}$ in) at its base. It is carried in its internal sheath at all times except during sexual intercourse. Because it is carried internally we almost never see cats with injuries to the penis.

Like the tongue of the cat, the penis is covered with small, rough, triangular scales. We're told that the cries of pain that we hear during mating are initiated by that protective shield scratching the delicate female lining. Some authorities say that it's a cry of pleasure, and I should prefer that explanation to be the true one.

Why did nature put the scales there? No one knows for sure, but one theory is that the cat's penis, being so small, requires special protection. Any injury or inflammation could close off the very small urethra that lies in the middle of the penis, and thus prevent urination.

Perfumes

Dogs and cats get pleasure through smelling things. Dogs enjoy smells that repel most people, and are repelled by many smells that people enjoy. It's the rare flower that gets a passing sniff from a dog. Perfumes positively repel most dogs, and I have seen lap dogs put right off their appetites by owners who insisted that their dogs should smell like a boudoir.

Cats, though, appreciate odours very much as we do. Most cats will take more than a passing interest in flowers, and many cats will spend long minutes enjoying a perfume. They don't like sudden gusts of air, so don't spray it at them. A drop or two on the table will satisfy their sensuous nature. Please remember that cats don't like anything on their skin or hair. If you perfume a cat he'll immediately start licking it off.

Conclusion: If you are nicely perfumed your cat will appreciate it, but he himself prefers to smell natural – fresh, clean and healthy.

Persian (*or long-haired cats*)

If you are a cat breeder you know far more than me about the origins and history of the Persian. Whether they came from Angora or from Persia, and when they were introduced to France and then to England, seem to be opinions rather than facts all based on what authority you are quoting.

Persians or long-haired as they are now called are divided into breeds according to one factor only, and that is colour. I know it must sound unbelievable but there are rather rigid rules dividing long-haired cats into the following classifications:

Black, White (Blue Eyes), White (Orange Eyes), Blue, Red Self, Cream, Smoke, Silver Tabby, Brown Tabby, Red Tabby, Chinchilla, Tortoiseshell, Tortoiseshell and White, Blue Cream, Any other colour, Colour-point

I think that nowadays there are a few more colours I haven't kept up with. But I do know there's a rather complicated set of rules showing which hair colours go with which colour eyes and these eye colours are orange, blue, green and hazel.

However ridiculous the whole system must appear to the un-tutored it is based on sound genetic principles (which is more than we can say for most dog breeds) and some of the products are very beautiful by any standards.

As a sort of casual observer of cat behaviour, and as the recipient of scores of scratches, I feel bound to record that I find many Persians temperamentally unpredictable, and one may expect anything from nervousness to sheer spitefulness. This may well be caused by the sort of over-indulgent people who seem to favour Persians, but I can't really recommend the whole long-haired family of cats as an average household pet.

The only veterinary advice that you must not ignore is regarding grooming. If Persians are not groomed *daily* they get to be the most dreadful messes, both inside and out. The hair goes into uncombable clumps. The loose hairs get swallowed and form into hair-balls. If you are not prepared to spend ten minutes every day combing and brushing please get a short-haired cat. No matter what anyone tells you, a tablespoon of liquid paraffin is no assurance that the hair-balls won't cause trouble. The only sure way to Persian health is that daily routine with the comb and brush.

Now that I've stated the drawbacks might I also say that long-hairs are the toughest creatures in catdom. Pampered and fussed though they may be, their square cobby bodies contain nothing but flexed steel. Most of them remain efficient hunters well into old age. The only outstanding physical drawbacks one can associate with the breeders' efforts is the over-squared head which may lead to eye trouble, gummy noses, funny angled teeth and crooked jaws. These tragedies might be funny looking but let me assure there is nothing amusing about deliberately promulgating deformities.

Pneumonia

This may be an extension of an upper respiratory infection like flu. It may be a primary condition on its own. In the former the cat usually gives lots of advance warning. She coughs and sneezes. In primary pneumonia the cat may appear perfectly normal to the owner except that it's off its food and is disinclined to move. If the owner observes the cat carefully he'll notice that it's breathing with its abdominal muscles rather than its chest muscles.

In all forms of pneumonia rest is a primary consideration. Any activity at all places an additional strain on the lungs. So get out the sanitary tray and move it and the feeding bowls and water into a small room. Keep the door closed. Make sure it's a room that's adequately ventilated without draughts. Most veterinary hospitals refuse to hospitalize such cases. They are usually infectious. Professional treatment includes injections of antibiotics and supplemental feeding. In severe cases a bottle of oxygen might be laid on. The cat is usually critically ill for about a week. Convalescence takes about another fortnight. For at least a month afterwards one must pamper pussy and keep a sharp eye for any signs of relapse.

Poisons

Cats are suspicious creatures where food is concerned. They subject everything to a rigid examination which includes a sniff, a paw and taste, before they'll gulp it down. Therefore we see fewer poisoning cases in cats than in other kinds of pets. In fact, many people rush their cat to the vet certain that he's been poisoned, only to be told that he has infectious enteritis or gastric flu or chronic nephritis. Often they've complicated the case by hastily administering some 'antidote'. Sometimes they come home, find the animal is vomiting, assume he's been poisoned, and proceed to pour mustard down his throat on the assumption that a lot of vomiting is better than a bit of vomiting. They don't pause to think that it doesn't take much to empty a cat's stomach. So please try and remember that there is no reason whatever to induce an animal that is having spasms of regurgitation to heave all the harder.

On the other hand, if you are quite certain that your cat has swallowed some noxious substance, and if he is showing no signs of bringing it up, you may save his life by inducing a bout of vomiting. The easiest way is by pouring a few teaspoons of very dilute hydrogen peroxide down his throat. Of course, just when you want the stuff you won't be able to find it. Use salt instead. Mix a couple of teaspoons of salt with three or four tablespoons of water. You might, by using brute force, get half the solution down. That will be enough to start the whole lot on the backward trail. Once it's started there's no reason to repeat.

If you are certain that your cat has swallowed a poison and you're equally certain that you know the antidote (it may be printed on the package), then by all means use it. There is a first aid mixture called 'the universal antidote' which can be hastily improvised by mixing milk of magnesia, burnt toast and strong tea which approximates magnesium oxide, charcoal and tannic acid one of which may help neutralize a strong poison.

All the above measures presuppose that you can act more quickly than you can get the cat to a vet, and that you can remain level-headed enough to do more good than harm. Obviously it's better that the animal should be seen by a vet as soon as possible. Even when the emergency is over the cat should be taken along for professional treatment, because it usually requires days or weeks of treatment to repair the damaged organs. Whenever possible take the actual poison along, whether it's some in a package or was mixed in some food.

Sometimes a laboratory examination is necessary to find out what the stuff is before one can proceed with rational treatment.

I must also mention (this is a quiet book, so I won't scream) the whole host of new rat-killers and weed-killers and insecticides and pesticides, and I mustn't forget the new food preservers and growth pushers and synthetic flavours and phony vegetables and forced chickens and sunless calves which we are using just in case the big bomb doesn't go off.

Most of these things are subtle and insidious. Taken one by one you don't notice their effect, but every once in a while you get a jolt and wonder how far this chemical madness can go. I know the death of a few birds or a few cats doesn't make front page news. How many deaths should it take to make the headlines?

One day last autumn a neighbour reported that my cat had caught and practically devoured a pigeon. I replied that it must have been a very old pigeon, because he spent most of his daylight hours stalking them with a singular lack of success. That evening he was lethargic, and at midnight he was definitely off-colour. Later he started weaving and staggering. I became alarmed, and the thought of poisoning first crossed my mind. I had no idea what poison it might be, so I treated the symptoms as I recognized them. No vet can be expected to treat his own pets for a critical condition any more than a doctor should treat his own seriously ill children. One's objectivity is considerably impaired. I turned Moss over to my colleagues in the morning, and they stuffed him full of all the medicine they thought might help. It took him thirty-six hours to die. Fortunately he was unconscious most of the time. I was informed that it was one of the new-fangled neurotrophic poisons used to destroy pigeons, and there appeared to be no antidote. Subsequently we had two more similar cases. An influential novelist friend of mine wrote letters to the papers. Not one was published.

Polydactyl

If you own a cat that unkind people refer to as 'ordinary' or 'common' and nasty people refer to as 'alley' or 'stray', you might try counting his toes. If he has six on his front feet or five on the hind, then he is a genuine polydactyl. It doesn't make him valuable or even rare, but it certainly makes him different.

The normal cat has only five toes on each of his front feet and four on the hind. An extra toe (or even two), and he is blessed with poly-dactylism. Are there any virtues or faults associated with extra toes?

None at all. It's just one of those things nature provides so that we can have something to talk about.

The geneticists tell us that polydactylism is a dominant characteristic. That means that a kitten born of a tom and queen, both of whom have extra toes, will produce kittens each of which has extra toes. If the father is normal and the mother polydactyl, the kitten, when it grows up, will produce (on the average) litters half of which are extra toed. As everyone knows, the principle of all this was discovered by Mendel a century ago. It doesn't say much for our century but we don't know a great deal more today.

Post-mortems

People who don't work in medicine may think it's rather ghoulish to chop up cadavers and look at the bits through a microscope. I admit that it's not the tastiest of jobs, but the people who do it treat each case as an interesting puzzle. They bear down with the passionate detachment of a fictional detective. Without their work, medicine (whether the animal or the other kind) would be even more of an art and less of a science.

I don't think there are any valid spiritual or moral objections to doing a post-mortem on an animal. There may be aesthetic drawbacks, but surely these can't outweigh the possible benefits to other animals. Often something discovered during the post-mortem of one animal can save the lives of its contacts or its littermates. Even if the results aren't directly utilizable a system of post-mortems, related to clinical work, can show the most sceptical of practitioners that he can sometimes be wrong.

Aesthetics? Most people who object to having a post-mortem performed think that the pathologists hack their pets into mince. On the contrary, they usually dissect the tissues they need as carefully as any surgeon. When they are finished they suture it all up again. I was told about a pathologist (of humans) who, when a post-mortem was finished, casually dipped into his pocket and used his own comb to straighten the disturbed locks of the deceased. Unfortunately most veterinary pathologists are bald.

Pot belly

A pot-bellied kitten may have worms or it may be suffering from malnutrition. With proper treatment it's only a matter of days before the swelling disappears and the creature stops waddling.

In adults pot belly is almost always a symptom of kidney trouble or a tumour. Often it's so insidious in onset that the owner doesn't notice it. If your cat's middle is shaped like a triangle with the base at the top that's fine; if it's shaped like a rectangle it's probably being overfed. If it's a triangle with the base of the triangle at the bottom better take it along to the vet.

Prognosis

This is a medical term meaning prophecy. How will the case turn out? One may have a hopeful or optimistic prognosis. One may reserve one's prognosis either through fear of a client's emotional response or through a genuine doubt as to how the patient will respond to treatment.

If one has serious doubts whether the patient will respond to treatment, that is called a guarded prognosis. In cases of advanced malignant cancer or some of the kidney diseases, one must have the sad task of explaining why the prognosis is critical to hopeless.

Prolapse

Eversion of the rectum or vagina. We see it fairly commonly in kittens who are riddled with worms, or have been constipated or very loose for two or three days. Usually just a bit of the raw red rectum is showing. If one can rest the bowel for twenty-four hours and keep the kitten going on glucose and water, the organ will often slide back into place. I'm not suggesting for a moment that you should try this treatment yourself before going to a vet. Even vets often lose such cases, so give the kitten a chance. Prolapses in adults are usually such an alarming sight that even the most enthusiastic of amateur vets knows that early professional treatment is necessary.

Pulse

Have you ever noticed that while your veterinarian is blankly listening to your recitation his hand is grasping the hind leg of your cat? Observe closely, and you'll see that his index finger is placed high up inside the cat's thigh. What's he doing? Saving time by taking the pulse while you talk.

The normal pulse rate of the cat is somewhere between one hundred and one hundred and thirty, depending on its nervousness during the examination. One gets a faster pulse with fevers, pneumonia, poisoning and bleeding. A slower pulse is rarer, but is felt in older or debilitated cats, in some heart conditions and in some tumours.

The character of the pulse is more informative than the rate. A pulse may be weak and thready or strong and bounding or lots of things between. Four or five years of experience, and you too will be able to partially assess your cat's health by its pulse.

Purring

We know that cats purr when they're happy. Nobody can tell you for sure exactly how they do it. But it's a strange fact that many cats suffering from pain and indeed elderly cats on their death beds, purr in exactly the same way. I emphasize this because many people phone the vet and report conditions that vary from a broken leg to lobar pneumonia and say, 'He's been like it a week but I didn't want to bother you because he's never stopped purring.'

Purgatives

It seems to me that the English are more concerned about 'cleaning out their bowels' than are any other people. There's a multitude of bombs on the market which they swallow to blast themselves out. I think the law doesn't mind what people do to themselves. I don't know what the law says about giving these gut destroyers to cats. I can tell you that a purgative is like a laxative, only stronger and harder on the system. If a cat is only mildly constipated a laxative (a tablespoon or two of olive oil) will do the job. If a laxative won't do it, then you'd better find the cause of the constipation before proceeding further. The constipation may be due to a tumour. The only possible effect of a purgative in such a case is pain.

Pyometra

You can call it pyometra or metritis or infected womb. It means pus in the womb and although it's an unusual condition, when it does occur it's very serious. For some reason or other the uterus swells – and sometimes to an alarming size. It may be absolutely swollen with pus. The cat may have a discharge. More often the only indications she shows are an increased thirst and the odd bout of vomiting.

Owners of bitches will know that this is a common complaint of middle-aged and ageing female dogs. In both species the remedy is the same. It is an operation called an ovariohysterectomy which means that the ovaries and uterus are removed. Usually there are no complications provided it is recognized and done early. The stitches come out in ten days. Many queens who are spayed as adults develop voracious appetites and a distaste for exercise. You can't do much about the latter, but you simply mustn't cater to the former.

Pyothorax

I'm afraid there's no tasteful way of stating that this means pus in the lung cavity. Vets diagnose the condition fairly frequently in cats, but rarely in other animals.

The cat may appear perfectly normal for some days or weeks while the chest is filling. Its appetite may be good, but gradually the animal becomes slower and more reluctant in its movements. It will lie in one position for hours. Any activity causes distress. Finally even the most unobservant owner realizes that the poor creature is breathing with difficulty. Instead of its chest rising and falling with each breath the abdomen pushes in and out in an attempt to compress the lungs.

The vet will listen through his stethoscope to confirm the suspicions aroused by his first glance. He'll break the news gently, because many of these cases are quite hopeless.

Treatment includes a daily puncture of the chest wall to withdraw the stuff drowning the animal. It's a laborious, tricky business. In addition the vet may use some of the newer antibiotics. He may use oxygen to ease the breathing. Fluids may be given. Despite all efforts it's the rare case that survives, and congratulations all round are in order.

Prevention? Look to the cause, which may be a neglected abscess or flu. If your vet insists that a cat should be brought back for a couple of visits after you think it's better, this is because he wants to make sure the bacteria aren't still lurking in the body. Many clients don't bother. The condition travels along and settles in the chest. Lesson? Don't consider your cat cured of even a minor condition until your vet tells you so. And come back for that check-up a week or so later.

Quack (or empirics)

A quack is a fool without training who practises medicine for money, for self-glorification or out of a misguided love of animals or people. They've always got a store of stories to illustrate how they can save lives when the professionals give up. One can seldom check on the truth of these stories, but every doctor and every vet can tell you about the pain and suffering that quacks inflict while they postpone proper treatment.

Now I'm not saying that trained people don't make mistakes. They do. But doesn't it stand to reason that a person who takes the art and science of healing seriously enough to undergo a formal course of study is less likely to make mistakes? And besides, those mistakes are assessed by colleagues equally well trained. Who assesses the work of quacks?

Quality

Friends who are observers of such things tell me that they have noticed a steady deterioration in the quality of the everyday, common garden variety of cat. They are talking about the sort of cat that unkind people refer to as alley cats. These are in actual fact home-loving cats who, like the majority of people, can't trace their pedigrees more than a couple of generations. In other words, they're not pure-breds.

These people attribute the loss of quality (which is, I suppose, an aesthetically pleasing mixture of strength, agility and vitality) to the fact that castration is so commonly practised. People's lives are becoming increasingly circumscribed by concrete and regulations. Their cats are more and more subject to the stringencies of their owners' lives. Fewer and fewer people can keep an entire tom. Almost invariably the best of the litter find homes easily. They are, as a matter of course, neutered. The culls and the runts (if they belong to stupid or irresponsible people) are kicked out or abandoned. They become part of the roaming population of tom cats. Repeat the process for a few generations, and the majority of the toms are the offspring of runts who couldn't find homes. That's the way the theory goes. It's only a theory. Your opinion and comments are quite as valid as mine.

Quick

The upper portion of the claw, which is living tissue. It contains blood vessels and nerves. If you cut into it the animal is 'hurt to the quick'. If you're trimming claws, as you may have to in older or crippled cats, cut the points only. If you or the cat inadvertently injure the quick, it will bleed. Smear it all with ointment, and bandage the whole foot. If it's a minor injury well down the claw, it will heal in a day or two. If there's a lot of blood or if the pain persists beyond an hour or two, better get to the vet.

Quotations

Providence made the Cat that man might have the pleasure of playing with the tiger. Frank Finn BA FZS *Pets and How to Keep Them*
Paris, Buchenwald of Cats. Dr Fernand Mery *Sa Majesté le Chat*

The cat, her teeth are like a saw, and if the long hairs growing about her mouth be cut away, she loses her courage.
Edward Topsel *The History of Four-footed Beasts* published 1658

The short face which is considered the ideal in long-haired cats has been gradually produced over the last thirty or forty years, and as a consequence of this breeding practice, the skeletal changes are more marked now than they were over the first three thousand years of domestication. P. M. Soderberg *Pedigree Cats*

She merely saw, as an animal sees without speculation and almost without consciousness. George Orwell *The Vicar's Daughter*

If you want to be a psychological novelist and write about human beings the best thing you can do is to keep a pair of cats.
Aldous Huxley *Music at Night*

Unlike him she retained a kind of hope. Hope is an instinct only the reasoning human mind can kill. An animal never knows despair.
Graham Greene *The Power and the Glory*

Rabies

If you live in a rabies area have your cat inoculated when it is three months of age and every year thereafter.

If you are visiting a country that has rabid animals and you yourself get bitten try *immediately* to have the animal located and caged. If it has rabies it will die within days. A laboratory will examine its brain and confirm that it had the disease. You must then undergo the series of injections which are the only way of preventing death once you have been infected. If you shoot the animal or allow it to escape you will never know whether it was rabid. You may have to undergo the treatment, which is a long series of painful jabs, unnecessarily. Not only is the treatment painful but one is not allowed to drink alcohol throughout the course, which for some people is the worst part of the affair.

If you live in Britain or Eire or Hawaii or some other place that is rabies-free please don't carp at the six-month quarantine regulations. They are absolutely necessary. Count your blessings which include the fact that neither you, nor your children, nor your pets will be exposed to the most painful disease known to man or beast.

Radial paralysis

Sometimes, as a result of an accident or a bad bite the nerve that runs down the front leg gets injured. The cat loses much of its feeling and most of its control over the affected leg. The wrist hangs helplessly and the animal simply drags the limb. In a minority of cases time and complete rest effect a cure. Most cases, though, are incurable. One must put a light protective dressing over the wrist and paw. Otherwise it will get bruised and torn as it's dragged along. Most of the cases I've seen have been stray toms. If one can find a person to take the animal, well and good. Otherwise one must advise euthanasia as the only humane alternative to turning the animal loose. With only three useful limbs with which to fight the battle for survival (the lot of every stray) he would soon meet with disaster.

Raw food

I remember reading, some ten years ago in a manual put out by one of the largest chemical houses in America, that there was some element in raw meat, or raw fish or unheated milk that was essential for reproduction in the species. I believed it then and I believe it still. I have no dispute with the purveyors of manufactured cat foods. I use those foods to feed my cat four or five days out of seven, but I think he's better off because two or three days of the week he gets his natural food in its natural state. Oh, I know those tins have got all the elements and vitamins and minerals that we have names for. I just think there might be other qualities we don't have names for. Anyway, my cat agrees with me!

Rectal impaction

This is a special kind of constipation. The rectum gets all filled up and the poor cat, strain though it might, can't move the mess.

In the dog one of the commonest causes is a bone or bones lodged in the rectum. I can't recall seeing a case in the cat, but my colleagues assure me that they have.

Rectal impaction is commonly seen in orphan kittens. They don't have a mother to clean up after them, so the hole gets blocked with dried faeces. Prevention consists of gently washing the area every day. Dry afterwards. Treatment is usually a gentle enema of warm salt water or a glycerine suppository.

In older animals an abscess of matted hair may block the anus. Wash the whole area. Introduce a suppository. Give (by mouth) a little liquid paraffin. If the animal is still uncomfortable after six hours, better get along to the vet.

Some older animals seem to get impacted with almost every big meal. They may give a half-hearted strain, but generally they just get mopier and mopier.

Treatment is usually mechanical. One empties the rectum by a combination of enemas, suppositories and finger probings. Please don't attempt it yourself. You can do inestimable damage. Occasionally surgery is necessary. One goes into the abdominal cavity and either 'milks' the contents out or incises the actual bowel and removes the contents.

Your vet will outline preventive measures. They'll possibly include the addition of some 'bulk-makers' to the diet, and the feeding of raw liver two or three times a week.

Summary: If you can't easily clear a cat's blocked passage, get the animal to a vet.

If your animal has had one bout of impaction, take special care in grooming the area.

Refusing food

I'm not referring to those animals who simply aren't interested in food. They have either eaten elsewhere or have one of the more serious illnesses. If your cat isn't interested in food and is otherwise mopy and off colour, I'd suggest a visit to the veterinarian.

If your cat approaches food, sniffs it in his usual manner (which in cats somehow connotes interest and disdain at the same time), and then either walks away or picks a bit up and drops it, you'd better consider one of three probabilities. Either the food itself is wrong or the cat has something wrong with its mouth or it has an obstruction in the bowel.

The food itself may be too hot or too cold or too spicy or too rotten or just uninteresting. Try another batch of food. If you get the same reaction then you must have a look in his mouth. It's quite simple. Get the table and light ready. Get your current boy friend (the one who hasn't been scratched yet) to hold the beast's front feet. You gently unhinge its jaws and see if (*a*) there are great scaly messes on its teeth (see *Tartar*) or (*b*) a bone, needle, or piece of wood lodged somewhere. If there is, try gently to remove it. If you can't, get the animal along to someone who can.

A cat which has an obstruction in its bowel that has caused it to vomit its food will learn after a very short while that eating means vomiting. He'll be hungry but will refuse food. This is a serious business, of course, and any home treatment will only complicate the picture (see *Foreign bodies*).

170

Restraint

Nothing distresses me quite so much as seeing some ham-handed human turn a normal affectionate cat into a snarling ball of fury. The vast majority of household cats – and many strays – only want a bit of reassurance. They'll react in a civilized manner to civilized handling.

How do you reassure a cat? Place him on the table. Put your left hand over his shoulders and hold him firmly without squeezing. Tighten your grasp if he lunges. Loosen if he relaxes. Stroke (with the lie of the hair) over his forehead. Scratch gently behind his ears. In other words, tell him that you like him. Tell him that what you have to do may be unpleasant, but both he and you have to put up with it and the sooner it's over the better.

If he goes taut and attacks, don't try to hold some bit of skin. Let him go completely. As he turns grab him. Again try to hold and reassure. Whatever you do don't hold on as the claws and teeth dig into your hands. Let go!

During the long second while he's finding his feet, grasp him by the shoulders to control his front feet and the loin to control his hind. Talk soothingly. He may relax and let you get on with whatever you are doing.

Some cats will simply not be handled, and particularly not by a stranger.

If he's in a cage and withdraws, snarling, into a corner, you may have to don heavy gloves. Some people prefer to throw a towel and let him scratch that while they get him out. I usually use anything that's handy – like a broom or a saucepan. I shove it behind the cat and use it to shove him towards me. When he's within reach I grab his neck and force him to the bottom of the cage. Then I try to persuade him by a few soothing phrases to relax and be carried – always being careful to point his head and front feet away from my face. If he seems half-willing I then shift my grip and encompass his neck and shoulders with one hand and support his abdomen with the other.

If he's still belligerent I'm forced to hold his shoulders with one hand and his loins with the other and carry him stretched out and helpless.

The standard way of restraining a vicious cat on a table is to lay him sideways. Hold both front legs with one hand. Place your forearm over his neck. Hold both hind legs with the other hand. If he squirms free let him go all at once and then grab him again all at once.

There are some cats that have had so little contact with humans, or so little humane contact, that their only reaction is to attack with no holds barred. One can only handle such maltreated creatures by either inducing them to eat doped food or capturing them in nets and transferring them to containers where they can be anaesthetized by blocking the air holes with ether-soaked rags.

Don't be frightened because a cat snarls or growls at you. The only warning signs that really mean business are screams of rage or laying the ears flat on the head. Both are declarations of war. Get out your gloves while you negotiate a truce.

Rex

This is a curly-coated sort of the ordinary domestic cat. A male mutation, found only some thirty years ago in Cornwall, was mated back to its mother and the strain was established. Since then another natural mutation exhibiting the same curly coat was found in the neighbouring county of Devon. Curly descendants of these two unrelated phenomena of nature are now commonly exhibited at most cat shows. The Cornish sort are more square and cobby. The Devon lot are more on the slender oriental line. Both sorts have only one dense curly coat with no undercoat or guard hairs. Most I've seen look like other cats who haven't properly managed to dry themselves after an unwelcome bath. Their owners, however, declare them beautiful, find them affectionate and intelligent and say that unlike other cats, they don't shed hair all over the place. Absolutely right. They've got little to shed. And they've got to be either extra affectionate or extra intelligent to survive without the hairy protection nature intended them to have.

Don't get me wrong. Some of the nicest cats I know are Rex cats. I don't dislike their owners. I simply can't understand how people can rationalize the promulgation of a freak that must be so abhorrent to nature that without man's intervention it could hardly survive.

Spare me the letters. I had them all twenty years ago. And watching the mutation grow in popularity all over the world has only confirmed my worst fears.

But please do me one favour, you proponents of the breed. Write some really nasty reviews of this book. That might encourage somebody actually to buy it.

Rickets

Although true rickets is rare in cats there is a whole family of ricket-like conditions which we see all too frequently in kittens who don't have access to bones. Often the kitten appears sleek and well but it just lies about and won't play. If you handle it (particularly around the hind end) it may squeal in pain. Sometimes we only see these kittens when they go completely lame or when they break a leg. They usually respond beautifully to injections and tablets of calcium provided they're seen early on. Prevention includes lots of rich milk and calcium supplements.

PS: Sometimes these nutritional diseases show with startling suddenness. I recall a Burmese kitten which had only just been introduced to its new home. For two days it bounced about like an overwound spring. Then one evening it took an exuberant leap from the top of the curtains and lay in a moaning spread of misery. X-rays revealed not the suspected single fracture but a score of breaks. All the bones were as brittle as Albanian matches. Incredibly, with a few days of calcium therapy the tiny creature was on the mend.

NB: Happily the owner hadn't fussed about. Immediately after the accident she placed the cat in a basket, closed it firmly and then phoned us. Any handling at all would have caused further fractures.

Ringworm

If you have an itchy blotch on your hand and your cat has a couple of bald spots on its head, take the cat to the vet and yourself to the doctor. Either the vet or the doctor might have an ultra-violet lamp under which they can 'pick up the fungus' which is the diagnostic feature of ringworm. Unlike most parasites the fungus that causes ringworm isn't fussy at all. It will grow on almost any warm-blooded animal. Ringworm grows like a mould on bread. It spreads equally in all directions. There's no use dabbing medicine in the middle of the bald spot, because the fungus has already moved into the surrounding healthy tissue. Many drugs will arrest or kill the fungus, but only if applied to apparently healthy skin surrounding the diseased area.

Remember that any drug applied to a cat's skin will be licked off promptly. Hold the cuddly creature for half an hour afterwards and let the stuff soak in. Remember too that the medicine is meant to be applied to the skin and not to the hair. Rub it well in. Use it sparingly. If your cat has ringworm and you haven't, wash your hands thoroughly after treating him. Come to think of it, wash your hands anyway. If you have ringworm and your cat hasn't, don't handle him until you're cured. If you have children *and* a cat *and* ringworm, send them all to kennels.

Many apparently cured cases of ringworm recur. They haven't really been cured. The fungus has just moved into healthy tissue. Keep up the treatment for at least ten days after the beast looks OK.

There are some pills of recent vintage which, when taken by mouth, will cure ringworm. Why don't we use them in all cases of ringworm? First because they are very expensive, and secondly because one is suspicious (and rightly so) of anything in the chemical line that one shoves into the body's system.

I know the new drugs work, and I know that all tests show them to be safe, but why ask the body to absorb and eliminate some elaborate chemical when something far simpler just applied to the skin might do the job? If the local applications don't work, there's time enough to resort to the new drugs.

Rubber bands

Children and some SS-type adults occasionally wrap an elastic band round the legs or the tail of a cat. Often the cat simply can't get it off. It will try for some while by biting and scratching, but as the circulation is cut off and numbness takes over the cat forgets it and resumes his normal activities. He is reminded of it by an occasional stabbing pain and the numbed throbbing. A day or two later you may notice the swelling (caused by the trapped blood) and think it is an abscess or infection. The elastic by this time may have dug itself into the flesh and one sees only a line, that looks like a cut, to show its path. At this stage a general anaesthetic is usually called for to allow the necessary probing to find and release the elastic. Penicillin and bathing for three or four days afterwards is the usual treatment. Those that are not discovered for some days may cause gangrene. Amputation of the affected portion may be the only way of saving the animal.

Summary: Impress on children that they mustn't tie things around kitty. If you see a swollen extremity and a deep indent, look for a rubber band. If you can't find it, get the cat to the veterinary surgeon.

Russian Blue

His coat is really grey, and he doesn't have many cousins in Russia. In America he's called the American Blue, and everywhere some people call them Maltese cats.

Actually he's a short-haired cat and his coat, although it may be coarse, is short and lustrous. He's easily groomed to sleek perfection. Colour is an even, medium to dark shade of grey, which you might call blue without stretching your imagination too far.

His head is narrowed and pointed, his ears wide at base, large and pointed, his neck long and his body lithe, long and slim. In short, he's an oriental type.

Some people get mixed up between the Carthusian and the Russian Blue. The Carthusian has a chunkier body and yellow eyes. The eyes of the Russian Blue are always green, and ideally they should be almond-shaped.

Should you get a Russian Blue? If it attracts you, do so by all means. I know of no faults. Many people say that they have all the advantages of the Siamese and are less likely to tear the furniture to shreds or keep the neighbours awake. Like Siamese and Burmese they're easily knocked over by enteritis, so get them inoculated early.

Sacred Cat of Burma

In France this cat is called Burmese. What the English speaking world call Burmese they call Sables or Zibelines, which they quite rightly recognize as an American development of the Siamese.

The Sacred Cat of Burma has no more connection with Burma than our own Burmese. It is a long-haired cat with the massive body and powerful head that is standard for the Persian type. Its colouring is Siamese. It has a golden cream body and brown points and blue eyes. The distinguishing colour feature of the breed is the four white paws which are necessary for registration.

Although it's Siamese in colour any Siamese characteristics in the shape of the body or head are considered to be defects. Doesn't this all sound familiar? Of course! It's exactly the same as our Seal-pointed type of Colour-Point long-hair with the addition of nice white socks. The French don't mind what strange countries of origin we concoct for our cats. Why should we object to their having a Burmese Temple Cat who is about as sacred as Mickey Mouse?

Sanitation

This can be a complicated science if one is responsible for thousands of chickens or hundreds of cattle or dozens of cats. The larger the community of animals you are dealing with, the more planning is needed to avoid the introduction of disease. Numbers in themselves create their own problems. A little bug or bacterium or virus soon gets discouraged if it has but one lonely body to attack. Set the same organism loose in a crowded chicken house, and it will gleefully jump from one hen to the next, gaining in strength and growing in numbers as it travels. This is not just an abstract bit of science but a real everyday problem. For example, many dog-pounds which have a large population of transient strays will inevitably be breeding-grounds for the distemper virus. No matter how properly your dog was inoculated, and no matter how regular his booster doses, if he spends a couple of nights in those kennels he has a better than even chance of contracting the disease.

If you are the average cat owner with one or two or even three cats, you needn't go mad about this sanitation thing. After every meal soak the dishes so that the food doesn't get caked down into cement-like bits under which the bacteria can multiply. Then clean them as you do your own.

Sanitary trays are nasty things no matter how they're decorated. Use a garden trowel every single day to remove the worst of the mess. Dump the whole thing on newspapers at least once a week. Soak the tray in disinfectant once a month. Rinse it afterwards.

When dusting for fleas put newspapers down first. Burn them afterwards.

And finally a few bits of commonsense that most people forget. Don't visit friends with sick animals. You'll carry the infection home! When visiting a busy small animal hospital or clinic, keep your cat in its basket. No matter what it's suffering from there's bound to be an animal with something worse! Don't borrow or lend cat baskets. They're often used for carrying ill animals, and may in fact carry illness! And if you simply must have that adorable stray, leave him at your catless aunt's until you're certain that he's not bringing home more than just his wide yellow eyes and his wavy wavy tail.

Scratching post

Cats scratch their claws along rough surfaces to sharpen them and you must reconcile yourself to that fact or not keep a cat. The only sensible approach is to provide them with a table leg or a catnip-impregnated post or a bit of rug on a board. Every time they scratch pick them up and place them astride the scratching post. Most cats will get the idea in a few days. They'll then reserve their scratching on forbidden places to those times when they want to attract your attention or annoy you.

Incidentally most cats like to have a good stretch when they wake

176

up. If the scratching post is too far from the sleeping quarters they'll use something closer.

Scrotum

This is the skin sac that contains the testicles. Entire toms, as you know, live adventurous lives, and they can get bitten or scratched anywhere. The more unmentionable the place the more painful the bite, and the more serious the resulting swelling and possible infection.

Occasionally after castration a scrotum gets infected. The animal moves with a stilted gait, licks at the site and resents any handling or examination.

Please don't attempt any home treatment. Scrotal infections are not merely painful – if neglected they become chronic and most resistant to treatment. Get the suffering beast to a vet. He will clean up the mess and fill everybody chock full with lovely antibiotics.

Sexing

The easiest time to tell a male from a female kitten is when they are only a day or two old. But please don't attempt it unless you're quite sure that the mother welcomes your attention. At that hairless stage one can easily see the two little dots which represent the male, and the dot with the dash below it that represents the female.

Later on it's a bit more difficult. Get a good light. Examine three or four kittens at the same time because it's easier if you're comparing. The ones with slits under the anus are females – those with a circular opening under the anus are males. You may find it easier to remember by thinking of males as colons (:), and females as the letter (i) or as exclamation marks (!) upside down.

If you're not sure, you may be able to see or feel the testicles in unneutered toms. You may be able to roll (gently) the hidden barley-sized penis between your fingers in the neutered tom.

Of course you can tell an unneutered tom of four months or more quite easily. His testicles will be the size of a pea or larger. At six months his urine will start to smell strong and pungent.

Don't be too quick in making your decision.

Every few months someone brings their male cat in because 'he's getting too fat'. 'He' turns out to be pregnant. And more than one cat has been anaesthetized and placed on the operating table preparatory to spaying only to find that in fact it's a male.

Shock

Collapse which follows accidents, severe bleeding and long-standing disease. The animal lays out flat and is not aware of anything. Its pulse is weak, its respiration is slow and its temperature is down. Its feet feel cold to the touch. The only safe amateur help is wrapping the creature in a blanket. Artificial respiration and brandy and hot water bottles all do more harm than good. Professional treatment may include intravenous injections of salt and sugar mixtures. In the cat, for some reason, a few whiffs of oxygen sometimes work a miracle. Some moribund felines lift their heads within minutes and in a half an hour they're ready to lap. Others (despite the most dedicated care) simply don't respond. Shock persists and death ensues.

Siamese

There are far more Siamese cats today in Iowa or even Cornwall than there are in Siam, but most are descended from a pair brought to England in the 1880s, from the country that gives the breed its name.

There are now several recognized breeds of Siamese. These include Seal-points, Chocolate-points, Blue-points, Lilac-points and Tortie-points among others. All are based on the colours of the points which are, as you might have guessed, the extremities (tail, ears, feet and mask). My favourite remains the old-fashioned Seal-point. Many people don't like them because with age the entire body tends to darken. We've got three 'pensioners' (breeding cats who because of age or other reasons have been neutered) wandering about the place. They annoy the dogs or interrupt innocent mice at mealtime. The point is that our 'pensioners' are now so dark that uninformed visitors think they are Burmese gone wrong. But as in most breeds colour doesn't affect the temperament, so get what you like. But if you don't you'll soon like what you get.

Apart from their colouring and their lithe oriental bodies Siamese differ from most cats in their dependence on human contact. Unlike other cats they don't wait for it. They demand it – often loud and long. The Siamese will use their paws to 'know' an object, whereas most cats will sniff first. They can be easily trained to accept collar and lead. Their voices have a wider range of expression than other cats. If you have a female Siamese in heat her calling will depreciate neighbourhood housing values.

Most Siamese don't drink milk after three or four months of age. Many prefer running water to that in a bowl however fresh.

They are prolific breeders, coming into season early and averaging five or six kittens to a litter.

Medically they are no more difficult to treat than other cats though they may be more difficult to handle. If a Siamese doesn't want to take a pill he simply will not take it. I've lost every pill battle I've ever fought with a stubborn Siamese. I've watched stronger, more agile men than myself retreat in confusion after trying to force something down one of their unwilling throats.

Siamese are regarded as special anaesthetic risks partly because they are so thin and partly because they fight the stuff so hard that one just might overdose in an attempt to get them under. In sickness Siamese will respond to the human touch even more than other cats. They seem to want human reassurance before they give that extra push towards recovery.

Like all orientals Siamese must be inoculated against feline infectious enteritis and booster doses must be given before travelling or boarding or showing.

As regards breeding and in-breeding we are beginning to see many Siamese with faults that may be congenital. Too many are simply too small, too fine, too delicate and too nervous. It's partly because some people want smaller and smaller pets and it's partly because the breed is so popular that breeders can find a market for every kitten no matter how stunted or runty. Don't let me put you off the breed! Unless you've lived with one you simply can't realize how much life and character one small furry body can contain. But try to find a fair-sized example of the breed.

PS: The Balinese is simply a Siamese with a long silky coat and it has the pedigree to prove it. If somebody tries to sell you a 'Balinese' that hasn't got only pure Siamese pedigrees and/or pure Balinese pedigrees to prove its ancestry, you're being conned. It might indeed look like a Balinese but you can be sure it won't have the Siamese character which presumably is what you want. And, of course, if you intend to breed it you can't register the kittens, nor can you even hazard what they'll look like when they mature. You have been warned!

Silver Tabby

The ground colour is pure pale silver and the tabby markings are a deep jet black. Eyes are green or hazel.

This colour contrast may be found, or more often bred, in both long-haired and short-haired cats. Needless to say the body type should be appropriate to the type of coat. Therefore if you find a beautifully marked Silver Tabby among a litter born to a Persian queen and a stray tom don't bother showing it unless it's a really blocky long-hair or a typical Domestic short-hair. Of course types, like me, and your average ignorant guest, won't know the difference. We'll admire it all the same.

Smells

Cats are fastidious creatures. They clean themselves constantly. Did you read Paul Gallico's delightful book about a cat called Jennie? 'When in doubt – any kind of doubt – *WASH!* That is rule Number One,' said Jennie.

So any cat who smells offensive must be examined closely. Sometimes the cause is quite obvious. Some stupid person has dumped a noxious sticky substance over the cat or the cat has accidentally dropped into a putrefying mass. Tom cats who have been confined for several hours in a small place, or who have been frightened into urinating on themselves, will smell terrible. Don't apply solvents. Wipe off as much as you can with dry cloths, then wet. You may have to bathe a portion of the animal. Use soap and water. Rinse afterwards. You may have to cut off hair that's matted with noxious material. Sometimes tomato juice can be used to mask an odour until you can get the animal to a vet. Maybe your vet has just come from a delayed calving case, and he'll find the new odour a rather pleasant change.

Cats who have a musty odour may be infested with lice. Cats with flu have a distinctive but indescribable odour. A cat with an abscess will often give off a putrid odour, and if the abscess is in the lungs the odour can be quite overpowering. Cats with foul breath probably have badly tartared teeth. If the breath is sour your vet will suspect kidney trouble. Sometimes a noxious odour leads one to a badly infected ear.

So if your vet starts sniffing at your cat, don't think he's trying to demonstrate his social superiority.

Summary: A cat who smells badly needs attention.

Smoke

This is a long-haired breed which can look dingy and ragged if it's not really a top specimen. At its championship best, however, it combines dramatic beauty with a subtle contrast of white and black to produce the elusive Smoke. Along the whole length of its back, as well as on its head, its face and its paws, the Smoke is black. The blacker the better, although along the back the base of the hairs is actually silver. On the face and feet the hairs are pure black. The tufts of the ears and frill of the neck are silver and the sides and flanks, too, shade into silver.

Obviously it's an elusive, subtle combination, and only a great deal of luck or years of applied genetics can produce a perfect specimen. Apparently about sixty years ago there were many perfect specimens. Either those were luckier times or enthusiasm has waned, because one rarely sees a top Smoke today.

Snakebite

I'm told (in learned journals written by devoted scientists) that most cats are not susceptible to snakebites that would kill us or our canine friends. I'm further told that cats are not frightened by snakes and that some cats consider them ideal playthings. All that I can tell you from personal experience is that I've seen people, dogs, cows and horses die from snakebites but nary a cat.

Sneezing

You know what can cause a bout of sneezing in a man. Sometimes in cats, too, it's a plain simple chill or head cold, but more often it's the beginning of something far more serious. If a cat sneezes a couple of times but is otherwise OK, you can safely wait for a day to see what develops. If it sneezes throughout the day and refuses food, you know that it requires professional attention the following morning at the latest. If a cat has a long bout of severe sneezing, it may have something stuck in its nose. That, of course, wants attending to as soon as possible.

Snuffles (*or rhinitis or chronic rhinitis or feline catarrh*)

This is often a sequel of flu. Unlike flu, it's not easily treated. The cat usually refuses food because its nose is filled with thick unspeakable stuff. Every time the animal sneezes you have to clean the goo off the furniture. Rhinitis tends to become a chronic condition. It may even invade the cavities of the head and literally erode their delicate linings. Sometimes the discharges become bloody, and sometimes the cat has the most alarming nosebleeds. In other words, it's a bad condition to observe and an even worse condition to have.

Some of the newer wide-spectrum antibiotics cure some cases, but unfortunately not all. Relapses are common. Some veterinarians use surgery to drain and clean the affected sinuses, but usually as a last resort.

Prevention consists of properly treating even the mildest cases of flu from their earliest onset, and keeping up the veterinary visits until the patient has been discharged as healthy.

Spaying (*or ovario-hysterectomy or hysterectomy*)

This is the operation to remove the sexual organs of the female. The majority of owners of female cats (unlike the majority of owners of bitches) have it done. They know that an entire female cat is almost certain to become pregnant two or even three times a year. Some cats even become pregnant while they are still nursing kittens.

Some owners think they can keep the female locked in during the heat periods. They soon learn that unless she gets bred she'll seem to be always on heat. Unlike bitches, who usually have two annual heats at more or less regular intervals, the female cat can have five or six such periods, and the only thing that will give her a measure of peace is pregnancy. Unless she's kept in a proper pen or kennel she'll somehow, in sheer desperation, find a way outdoors. Once outdoors, like the famous Mounties, she always gets her man.

The operation can be done at any age, but is easier on the animal if it's done at less than six months. Many vets recommend the following schedule, and it makes sense to me. When you acquire the kitten, have a look in its ears. If they're filthy, take the kitten along to the vet. If the kitten is otherwise healthy, examine it carefully for fleas. Take a sample of the kitten's motion along to the vet, but leave the kitten at home. He'll check it for worms, and dispense the appropriate pills and a safe flea powder if it's needed. At that time he'll discuss when the kitten should be brought along for its two shots against enteritis. He'll probably book it in for spaying a fortnight to a month after its second shot.

In other words, one first rids the kittens of unwanted passengers both external and internal, and then immunizes against enteritis. After this one can be reasonably certain that the spaying is being done on a healthy subject, and that it's unlikely to succumb to enteritis while its resistance has been lowered by surgery.

The operation itself involves a general anaesthetic. Some vets use ether and air, others use ether and oxygen, and others lay on everything including an intravenous to start the anaesthesia and oxygen and halothane to maintain it. As it's a short operation it doesn't really matter. Each vet uses what he's happiest with. I know one vet who wants very deep anaesthesia and another who prefers them just sleeping lightly, and each has equally good results. The only thing that most vets consider absolutely essential is that the animal shouldn't be fed for twelve hours before the operation. If the cat has food in its stomach while it's being anaesthetized, the results can be disastrous. It may start vomiting and then inhaling the vomited food into its lungs. It's very difficult to introduce a tube into the trachea of a cat at the best of times, and it's impossible to get a tube down during those vomiting spasms. The cat may end up with a mechanical pneumonia or it may even choke to death. Don't get horror-struck and decide not to have your kitten spayed. Just follow instructions, and don't feed it no matter how piteously it miaows.

Most vets have their own favourite ways of doing the actual operation. In America many vets prefer to cut along the middle of the belly. In Britain most vets prefer to cut on the flank about an inch below the spine. Once inside the abdomen of the cat they fish out one horn of the uterus, trace it down to the ovary, clamp and ligature the ovarian vessels and pull out the ovary. They then trace the horn they have down to the other horn and up to its ovary, which is removed in the same way. Then they go back to where the horns meet, tie them off and cut them out. A couple of ligatures pull the muscles together, a couple more do the skin, and the job is finished. Most vets don't bandage, but some equally good and equally experienced ones do.

The operation is basically the same whether it's done on a four-month-old kitten or a six-year-old mother of many, but naturally the older the animal the more difficult and hazardous the operation, and the more time involved.

The skin stitches come out in a week or ten days, but many kittens pull their own out in two or three days. If they do, stick the beast in a basket and take it along during surgery hours. It's not an emergency unless it's bleeding or the insides start pushing out. Some few get infected incisions as a result of constant licking. These must be seen daily and given antibiotic injections. However, the vast majority recover uneventfully. They settle down to being happy members of the human family, and seldom express a longing for those tom-filled nights.

Spraying

Little boys on camping trips often display their prowess by urinating vast distances or in elaborate patterns. In the human, this braggadocio usually finishes with adolescence. In the male dog and in the tom cat it persists into senility. In the dog it's a harmless, if distasteful, display. A tom cat, however, can sicken other species with the odour of his spray. A tom, incidentally, may spray periodically throughout the night and day. Females and neutered toms don't spray. They squat when they urinate, and they only do it two or three times a day.

That, of course, is but the normal pattern. As any experienced cat owner can verify there are many variations. One introduces a new cat into the home. Queen Bess who has ruled alone for twelve years decides that if the upstart has the use of a litter tray nothing but the curtains are good enough for royalty. Many queens on season and some that are heavily pregnant prove beyond dispute that continental quilts contain the most absorbent material in the home. Some neutered toms display the fact that the mind is mightier than the surgical sword. And, of course, once an area has been baptized it becomes holy for all cats, even those who don't follow any particular creed. Frequent visits to such holy places can only be discouraged by thorough scrubbing and disinfection.

Cats who persist may sometimes be cured by locking them in a small cage only big enough for a bed and a litter tray. Try two or three days. Then, after release, at the first transgression back they go. It sometimes works. Many are never cured. Keep the bleach handy.

Squint (*strabismus*)

Some people think a squint makes a beautiful woman even more beautiful, and many people think that only those Siamese who squint are true Siamese. It's all a matter of opinion. A squint, however beautiful it may be, must be considered a defect. You see, it doesn't mean that the animal is seeing out of both eyes but at slightly different angles. What actually happens is that only one eye focuses on an object. If the squint is the result of an accident or injury or infection, the affected eye stays out of focus. If, as in the case of many Siamese, the animal is born with the squint, it can usually focus with both eyes – but not at the same time. Treatment for this sort of squint involves closing the lids of the 'stronger' eye to try to get the other one 'working'. This involves a general anaesthetic and careful suturing. It isn't successful in a high proportion of cases. Treatment of the other sorts of squints in cats is almost always not successful. Prevention of the congenital sort is simple: one doesn't breed from affected animals. Surprising how many people do!

Stomatitis

I know it sounds as if it should mean inflammation of the stomach, but you'll never pass your exams unless you put down that it means inflammation of the mouth.

If you've ever had a sore mouth you know how it worries you. A small blister feels like a football. By the time you've run your tongue over it a thousand times it is a football. The cat has a far more sensitive tongue than you or I, and I think his distress must be correspondingly greater.

Stomatitis may be simply a localized condition caused by bad teeth or eating something hot or sharp. Sometimes removing the tartar, bathing the mouth with diluted salt water and applying a little honey will ease the soreness. Usually, though, if the teeth are bad enough to set up an infection in the mouth a general anaesthetic is needed to clean them properly.

Stomatitis may be just part of the picture of a general condition like flu or enteritis. The earlier the treatment, the better the chances of recovery.

In both sorts of stomatitis your vet will probably use antibiotic and vitamin injections, because obviously no local medicine could act for more than a few brief seconds.

Stones

The only sort of calculi that are a common problem in the cat are the sort found in the bladder. They are usually tiny sandlike concretions. In the female they seldom cause an obstruction because they can usually find their way through the relatively large female passages. The tom though has a really tiny urethra and it doesn't take much to plug it. I've repeated this information in a half-dozen places in this book because a urinary obstruction is a terribly painful condition and if left untreated is almost invariably fatal. Many well-meaning people seeing a straining cat assume it to be constipated and fill it full of oil. The straining is much more likely to be caused by stones in the bladder and urethra. Remember too that cats keep themselves to themselves particularly if it's to do with their private body functions. Therefore when you first see the cat straining it's probably been going on for some time. Don't hesitate. Get it to the vet.

What causes stones to form? Nobody knows. Can we prevent them forming? Some experts say that toms castrated at six months are less likely to get urinary obstructions from stones than those done at three months. Many experts say that one sort of bladder stone can be prevented by increasing the salt in the diet which increases the water intake. This is very much a procedure that must only be undertaken under veterinary supervision.

Elsewhere I've outlined how your vet attempts to deal with the actual obstructions when they occur. If despite early treatment and rigid adherence to a preventive programme the condition recurs twice within a few months or a year your vet may suggest an operation to have the urine by-pass the penis. Or he may advise euthanasia. He'll base his advice on the condition and age of the animal and its history. It's not an easy decision, but one simply cannot allow an animal to go on with the certainty that it is going to have more bouts of pain, each of which will be increasingly difficult to relieve.

Stop

A slight depression between the forehead and the nose. Breeders of Chihuahua dogs and some breeders of long-haired cats (particularly the Blues) think it's a desirable feature and try to perpetuate and even accentuate it. Goodness knows why!

Stray

Any cat is a stray the minute it gets round the corner. Sometimes they go further than they intended, or get chased until they're lost. Hunger, fatigue and fright may cause a cat to lose its bearings. A couple of days of rest and food, and most will find their way home. So treat that bedraggled creature as if it were your own, but allow him his freedom when he asks for it. After a good meal and a long sleep most of them will set a straight course for home.

Cats who have been injured in a car accident or a fight may drag themselves off, and because of pain or shock are incapable of getting home. Cats with flu, enteritis or even ear mites may in the confusion of their illness lose their way. Some of them can look really moth-eaten in a matter of hours. People often assume that those pitiful creatures who creep up to them have never had a home. Genuine strays or feral cats usually won't approach strangers. Anyway, they rush the distressed animal to a vet or welfare clinic with the request that it be put out of its misery. In some cases it's quite obvious that treatment is useless and euthanasia is indicated. In many cases, however, a bit of expert attention and a couple of nights' sleep, and the cat can be restored to its frantic owner.

If your cat has been missing for more than one night and one day, you must assume it's lost. The vast majority of cats will come home for food at least once in twenty-four hours. Phone the police station in your neighbourhood, and inquire if they've 'picked one up'. Phone the vets in your neighbourhood and the welfare clinics. Don't sob a long story about how delicate she is, and how much of a reward you're prepared to pay. The people at the other end of the phone would be interested and sympathetic – if only they had the time. They just want to know the type, colour and sex of your cat. If they know of any creature resembling your description, they'll ask you to come along and identify it.

Genuine strays are tough, self-reliant beasts. They are the survivors of a rigorous, often cruel system that knocks off the weak, the slow and the stupid. Naturally they are either full toms or entire queens, and must bear the scars of many battles. You can be assured that these animals aren't the ones that pass through dealers' hands on the way to laboratories or 'fur' markets. Genuine strays are much too uncatchable for the lazy criminal types in this shoddy trade. The cat that has never learned to fear people is the one that has its trust betrayed.

Sweat glands

I always thought that cats only had these on the pads of their feet, but now I'm told by erudite colleagues that, in fact, the cat has a well-distributed system of sweat glands all over its body.

Symptoms

During the season (which for me is roughly January to December) I make my social calls heavily disguised as anything but a veterinary surgeon. The minute people discover a tame vet they regale him for hours with stories of animals and their ailments. It's not absolutely fatal if one is within arms' reach of the provender and the bottles, but often I get manoeuvred into a neutral corner. I can't fight my way out until the police come to tell us what time it's getting to be.

One of the common sentences in these one-way conversations is, 'But, my dear, my vet just looked at him and he knew immediately what was wrong.' Sometimes they say it complainingly, 'He barely looked at him and he made his diagnosis immediately – and my dear – the bill!'

Anyway for what it's worth I'll list a few symptoms and what they suggest to the vet.

I'm not saying that one symptom alone is diagnostic, but remember, that as you lift your cat out of its basket the vet is subconsciously

187

registering its approximate age, its general bodily condition and attitude, the odour it gives off, the state of its coat, its eyes and its mouth. As it's placed on the table he'll note if the animal is favouring a limb or a side. It's even easier with dogs. One can watch them walking into the surgery. I can't vouch for the mental process of my colleagues but many of them, without thinking, must chalk up a list of possibilities even before the client starts speaking.

For example, if I saw a cat that was breathing rapidly by pumping his belly in and out (rather than by using its chest) and if the cat wasn't sneezing, and had no nasal or eye discharge and no foul odour, my built-in computer would list a diaphragmatic hernia among the possibilities. If the client then said 'She went out this morning perfectly healthy and she came back like this', I'd bring that tentative diagnosis out of the list of possibles and move it up to the list of probables. Accidents or falls may cause hernias. The cat was healthy before it went out. It may have had a bad fall or been hit by a car. Its diaphragm may have been ruptured. I would then lift the cat's hind end about forty-five degrees. If the breathing became faster and more laboured that too would point to a hernia. Finally an X-ray would confirm my 'guess' or move me on to another train of possibles.

Here are some common symptoms and signs, and the condition they just *might* suggest.

Sneezing – Flu
Head shaking – Ear mites
Eyes discharging (adult) – Flu
Eyes discharging (kittens) – Vaginitis in mother
Straining (male cat) – Bladder stones
Straining (female cat) – Constipation or difficult birth
Dragging lifeless tail – Injury to spine or pelvis
Limping or soreness in one limb – Infected bite or puncture wound
Holding up one limb – Fracture
Fixed position of mouth – Fractured jaw
Fixed position of mouth – Dislocated jaw
Refusal to move – Fractured spine or pelvis
Head weaving – Concussion
Eyes jerking – Concussion
Severe vomiting – Enteritis or poisoning
Scratching – Fleas, mange or ringworm
Constant licking – Fleas, abscess or infected wound
Bald patches – Fleas, mange, ringworm, hormonal deficiency or misfeeding

188

Musty odour – Lice
Rotting odour (body) – Abscess
Foul breath – Bad teeth, pneumonia, enteritis, flu or nephritis
Refusal of food – Bad teeth, fractured jaw or enteritis
Over-affectionate, rubbing, rolling – Heat
Licking foot – Infected claw
Holding up foot – Infected claw
Holding head to one side – Middle ear infection
Licking gums – Tooth infection, trench mouth
Rubbing face – Tooth infection
Dribbling – Flu, tooth infection or ulcerative glossitis
Frequent bouts of diarrhoea in a middle-aged cat – Lymphosarcoma
Dry coat – Worms, vitamin deficiency
Body weaving – Poisoning or accident
Cold hind leg or legs – Thrombosis
Distress with any activity – Pyothorax
Yellow tissues – Liver disease, poisoning
Broken claws – Accident
Mopy, lethargic – Constipation, beginning of illness
Vomiting, no motions – Obstruction in bowel

These are, of course, all over-simplifications of the most difficult of the medical arts – namely diagnosis. If it was all as easy as memorizing some list there would be no need for laboratories and X-rays and consultants and never would there be any doubts or mistakes.

Tabbies and tigers

I'm not a naturalist, a zoologist or a biologist, all of whom could tell you far more than I can about the origin and development of the domestic cat. Veterinarians are trained to recognize and treat the ailments of animals. We know a fair bit about normal and abnormal functioning of bodies, but we don't know much about how those bodies fit into the natural scheme of things. We look to the people whose field that is.

With that preamble may I unashamedly admit that the following has been liberally lifted from minds more gifted than mine. I'm not worried that I'll be accused of plagiarism because it's all long since become part of the general knowledge about cats.

Cats who are striped are either Tabby cats or Tiger cats.

Tiger cats are striped up and down vertically. Tabby cats are striped horizontally. Tabby cats also have three oblique bars on the flanks which form a sort of a horseshoe or oyster shell pattern. The

189

incredible thing is that you never get a merging of the two types. A striped cat (even if it's the result of the mating of a Tiger striped with a Tabby striped) is either one or the other but never halfway in between. This is because each type is descended from different ancestors.

The Tiger cat is reputed to resemble and to have descended from African cats. It's been known in Europe for several hundred years. The Tabby cat has been known for only a couple of centuries, and no one knows who his ancestors were. He resembles no existing wild cats, except the European Wild Cat from which he is taxonomically distinct.

With domestication and selection the stripes disappear, and this is the explanation of solidly coloured cats. If self-coloured cats go wild after a few generations they revert to stripes. It's the brown tabby that wins this war for the survival of the fittest.

Finally just to confuse the issue may I add that many cats have sort of blodgy stripes and spots. The stripes are not distinct so it's difficult to tell if they're tigers or tabbies. The poor cat is halfway in the evolutionary scale between tiger or tabby and self-colour.

Tails

Cats use these things as a balancing rudder during fast turns and sudden drops, and as a means of expression. Siamese and other orientals have long slim tails that taper to a point. Some of them have slight kinks at the end. Pedigree short-haired cats have shorter thicker tails that taper ever so slightly. Persians have the shortest tails of all, but they are thick and have great proud flowing hair called brushes. The Manx is born without a tail and manages very well, thank you. Some people believe that a cat's tail may be a deterrent to effective hunting. They think the mouse or rat might hear it as it swishes before take-off. People who believe this amputate cats' tails, but I think it's quite ridiculous. I'm with the majority who let the cat keep and enjoy its tail.

Tails can have all the ailments of the body they're attached to, and a few more besides. Tails can harbour fleas or lice. They may get bitten and infected. They may have eczema. They can be cut and bleed. They can be strained, sprained or bruised. Senseless children might tie cord or elastic around them or attach tin cans to them. Adults, even more senseless, have been known to dip them in a can of paint. Tails can have tumours both benign and malignant.

If there's anything wrong with a cat's tail it will often turn on it and attack it as if it were a complete stranger and no part of itself. Within hours a cat can turn a minor sore on its own tail into a raging, bleeding and festering pulp. If you see it happening stick an Elizabethan collar on the cat. If you can't manage that, bandage both front paws which will provide enough distraction till you can get to the vet.

Tail fracture

If a young healthy cat fractures its tail and the bones aren't knocked out of line, his symptoms might be so slight that you won't even notice them. He'll drag his tail for a few days until a callus has formed. After a week or so the only evidence of the fracture will be a slight hard bump over the site of the injury. Some big awkward cats have three or four such mementoes to their lack of agility or judgement. Don't feel smug or superior. How many of your friends can get through a door that's being slammed by someone else?

Some tail fractures can be serious. The spinal cord runs through the middle of the series of little bones of the tail. So do the arteries and veins. If one of those little bones is displaced so that it lies over another bone, the nerves and blood vessels get pinched. Everything beyond the break loses its vital connections with the body and slowly dies. Some cases are very painful. The cat goes off and hides in a corner and refuses to eat. Others may indicate the seriousness of the fracture by gnawing or licking at it. In others you might only see a dejected individual with a dragging, lifeless bit of tail.

What does the veterinarian do? Usually he will X-ray the tail to see how bad the damage is. He might decide that he can get the bones into line by traction – under anaesthetic, of course. In many cases the only way to avoid dangerous complications is to amputate the dead or dying portion of the tail. You might think that's a very simple decision. It may be, if the cat is young and healthy and less than half of the tail is involved. But the older the cat is, and the larger the portion of the tail that must be amputated, the more serious the problem. Why? Many of the nerves to the bladder and the hind legs originate in the base of the tail. Amputation may produce a patient that can't control its bladder. Some even become paralysed in their hind quarters.

What can you do? Impress on your children and your guests that Tommykins isn't as young as he used to be. He needs time to get through the door. He might not escape falling objects. If an accident does occur, remember that any cat in pain may hide away for days. Keep him confined until you can get him to the clinic.

Tapeworms

These are flatworms, which means that they are rectangular or oval in cross-section, rather than round. The common earthworm is round in cross-section, and so are most species of intestinal worms.

The tapeworm has a head at one end and then a series of sections or segments. These segments look like grains of rice or little maggots, and you can sometimes see them just below the tail of the affected animal.

Roundworms may, if they're so inclined, spend their entire cycle within their host, but all tapeworms need to travel through at least two different creatures in order to survive and multiply. The most common tapeworm of cats, for example, needs to spend part of its life cycle in a flea. Another species of cat tapeworm spends part of its developing cycle in the mouse or rat, another in fish and yet another in the rabbit. That is why you can keep pushing worm pills down your cat and it may hatch yet another brood of tapeworms.

If, for example, your cat is infested with fleas *and* the tapeworm that lives part of its life in the flea, you must treat the cat for its tapes and rid it of fleas at the same time. I don't think it's a very complicated or difficult business – if you know what you're doing; but if you don't I think you're putting your cat through a lot of tummy-ache just to prove that you can get along without a vet.

Tartar

This is an accumulation of 'nasty' on and around the teeth. It may be scaly, hard, brown or black stuff or it may be greyish, soft cheesy stuff. Whatever sort it is, it means trouble. Under it bacteria multiply like dandelions in a neglected park. The protective covering of the teeth is eroded and the teeth decay. The gums get infected, swollen and painful. The tartar itself might accumulate to such an extent that it causes ulcers in the mouth. Sometimes a great mass of tartar will prevent the mouth from closing properly. The poor animal sits, his mouth ajar, drooling foul saliva. He may approach food and refuse it. He may paw at the side of his mouth. He may show acute pain and scratch at the side of his face or rub his cheeks along the ground. In any one of a dozen ways he'll show his owner that he's got a sore mouth. It's neglect, bordering on cruelty to ignore those signs.

What should you do? Prepare for a proper examination. Clear a big solid table and place a good lamp near it. Get someone to help hold the cat. Have that someone hold his front feet while you lift his upper jaw and have a look. There may be a fish bone or a bit of wood wedged across the roof of the mouth. There may be just one great wedge of tartar between a tooth and the gums. Place your thumbnail above it and often with a gentle pull you can dislodge it. Then allow the cat to drop it out of its mouth or fish it with tweezers and pull it out. Wipe the area with a bit of cotton soaked in saline. The whole operation shouldn't take more than a couple of minutes and you'll have relieved a painful condition. But that's as far as you can safely go in home first aid. The cat should then be taken along to the veterinarian to see if more treatment is needed.

What will the vet do? He will examine the mouth much as you did. Note how he places his light and his tools *before* he starts to handle the cat. Cats are cooperative patients – but only for short periods. The vet will decide how extensive the tartar is and whether a general anaesthetic is needed in order to do the job. If the gums are inflamed and infected he might decide that a course of antibiotic injections are needed before any extensive work can be done.

Home care after the veterinary treatment will include a soft sloppy diet like meat broths, milk and eggs and possibly a twice daily rinsing of the mouth with a weak solution of hydrogen peroxide or sodium perborate. I often advise the use of a very weak salt solution.

Prevention is largely a matter of avoiding a sloppy diet day after day. Give the creature something it has to chew. My own cat loves those crunchy biscuit things. Although there's a constant supply around he doesn't make a hog of himself like a dog would. Once or twice a week he goes over and has a crunch. I think he regards them as toothpicks rather than food. Also I don't cut his meat up into fancy bits. I throw it to him much as it is and hope he has the sense to chew it into non-choking size. Only once have I ever had to fish with the forceps to get an unswallowable piece that was choking him. It was a hunk of tendon and fat that I should have trimmed off.

The other bit of prevention I preach (and practise) is to have a look at his mouth every three or four months. Small bits of tartar that are just starting to accumulate can easily be flicked off or pulled off with the thumbnail. Be careful not to bruise the gum or scratch the tooth.

Teeth (*of kittens*)

Kittens seldom have trouble cutting their baby teeth. The kitten has twenty-six of these. At about four months of age the permanents start to shove the milk teeth out. By the time the animal is six months old it usually has the thirty teeth that are par for the game.

While the temporaries are being replaced by the permanents, the kitten might have difficulty in eating. Have a look and see if there are any loose teeth. If you can pick them out with your fingers, well and good. But don't use forceps or pliers. You may make a mistake and pull out a permanent tooth. Some people use too much force and break a tooth off, leaving the roots inside. If you've made a stupid mistake, get the animal to your vet and tell him what you've done. With the aid of a general anaesthetic he can usually dig the bits out and thereby relieve the pain.

Some kittens have teething fits. Don't panic. Grab him by the scruff of the neck with one hand and over the loin with the other. Remember he can't recognize anything and might scratch you rather badly. Transfer him to a basket or a smooth box in which you've laid a blanket. He's less likely to harm himself in a confined space than if he's allowed to fling himself everywhere. Whatever you do, don't force anything down his throat. When the fit has passed (they usually only last a minute or two) get on the phone and make an appointment with your vet.

Teeth (*of adult*)

The cat has thirty teeth. He has six sharp little incisors on the top and six below. On either side of the incisors he has big tusk teeth – four in all. These are called canine teeth, but I don't think it's meant as an insult. Then there's a little toothless gap. Behind the gap lie the premolars – three premolars on each side of the upper jaw and two on each side of the lower. Behind the premolars lies the single molar. Like this:

	3—3		1—1		3—3		1—1
Incisors ——		Canines ——		Premolars ——		Molars ——	
	3—3		1—1		2—2		1—1

Some cats only have twenty-eight teeth because two of the premolars in the upper jaw don't develop.

The cat uses his teeth to fight, to bite and to kill. He uses them for tearing and cutting but not for chewing. He just wants to get the stuff down to swallowable hunks.

Unlike horses, you can't tell the age of a cat by its teeth, but some people will hazard a guess by their condition. A cat on a soft sloppy diet will start to get tartared, mucky-looking teeth at four or five. A stray tom living by his wits and avoiding nothing fightable may have chipped some of his teeth down to the gum line by the time he's six.

What should you do to help your cat retain his teeth in shining order well into old age? Don't feed him a steady diet of sloppy foods. Give him the odd hunk of meat he's really got to work on. Allow him some of those very hard biscuits made specially for cats. But most important examine his mouth every few months to see if tartar is accumulating. If it is, rinse it off with diluted salt water. If you can't get it off, take him along to your vet.

Cats can, and do, get toothache. It's just as painful as the human kind. He may paw or claw helplessly at the affected tooth. He may rub his face along the floor, or he may just shake his head from side to side. Sometimes he'll show no symptoms except foul breath. Sometimes the poison from a rotting tooth erupts in a painful abscess.

Quite obviously the only thing to do is to get the animal to a veterinarian. He will administer a general anaesthetic, locate the offending tooth or teeth and get them out.

The strongest and most useful tooth in the cat's head is the big premolar of the upper jaw. It has three deep roots and is difficult to extract. One sometimes has to incise below the gum line to get it out. What you may think is a simple extraction is more like a minor operation. Don't be surprised if your vet asks you to bring the cat back for three antibiotic injections.

If your cat has had one bout of tooth trouble you can be almost certain that he's in for more. Take him along in three months' time for a check up.

Telegony

I think it's quite rational to love cats. Many rational people do. But many otherwise rational people will believe the most extraordinary things so long as it concerns cats.

Telegony is one of them. Telegony is the belief that one mating (or mismating) will affect subsequent matings. Your Siamese gets bred by an alley cat and produces a litter of mongrels. The next time round she is bred by a Siamese. Is that litter any less pure because of the previous mongrel litter? Not at all. But people who believe in telegony think so. If you plant carrots in a field that had been used for potatoes, would you expect the carrots to look or taste like potatoes?

Temperature

If a human being were pulled out of a packing case, stuck on a high table under a bright light and held by huge hands while a piece of cold glass was inserted in his rectum, it would be called torture.

195

When dealing with cats it's called, 'taking its temperature'. Many medical procedures are uncomfortable or even painful, but they're absolutely necessary. The difference between discomfort or pain and torture may simply be in the intent. In the case of the cat one can humanize the whole examination procedure by taking a second or two to stroke the cat or gently scratch behind his ears. One is in fact showing him that he's among friends. In my experience most cats will respond by keeping their claws where they belong.

Two people are needed to take a cat's temperature. One holds the shoulders and front feet gently but firmly. If you don't squeeze, the cat won't panic. The other person supports the abdomen with one hand while he inserts the greased thermometer. Never push the thermometer in. Rotate it gently and it will slide in.

Use only a thermometer with heavy glass all the way down. The thin human kind may break inside. A general anaesthetic is usually necessary to relax the anus sufficiently to retrieve the broken bits.

Summary: Have an assistant to help you take a cat's temperature. Use a heavy duty thermometer. Temperatures outside the range of 38°C to 39°C (100–102°F) indicate a veterinary consultation.

Tetanus

People and animals suffering from tetanus undergo the most terrible muscular spasms, and all the while their brains are conscious and alert.

Tetanus is caused by the entry of the tetanus germ (which survives in the soil) through a small pinprick or puncture wound. The tetanus germ can only grow and elaborate its killing toxin in the absence of air. Hence, small almost invisible wounds are more dangerous than large gaping wounds. Don't get worried and have your animals inoculated with the preventive toxoid. It's a very rare disease. But please treat every wound, and particularly the tiny ones, with the respect they deserve. Soak the area, clean the wound and apply antiseptic.

Thirst

Cats vary widely in their desire for fluids and their preferred source. I have had cats who would lap neither milk nor water indoors – at least while I was around. Nevertheless, day after day I would put down fresh water. Day after day they would ignore it and go outdoors, presumably to find some stagnant pool more to their liking. Many Siamese and other orientals stop drinking milk as they grow into adulthood. Many cats of all breeds will only drink water that's flowing, and some of them get handy at turning on the tap. Most cats love to play with running water even if they don't drink the stuff. And some loony cats will only drink water from one particular receptacle. In this category are cats who will only drink from the toilet bowl, and some cats on dairy farms who will only drink from the very cold vat that's used to cool the milk.

It's all perfectly normal even if it's not average behaviour, and there's nothing to worry about. The time to worry is when your cat suddenly changes his drinking pattern. If a cat who has never been much of a drinker gradually, over a few days or weeks, or suddenly, in two or three days, starts drinking copiously, you must assume it's one of the serious conditions like diabetes or nephritis or a virus infection. If a cat who normally drinks suddenly refuses all fluid, or if he hangs over the water bowl wanting water but afraid to take it, you know that he has an infection like enteritis or flu or badly infected teeth.

Summary: If your cat has a sudden increased or decreased desire for fluids, it's serious. Don't worry about it. Get your vet and let him worry.

Thorns

Take heed of thine own flesh whilst removing a thorn from a cat. It is written that more men are injured by the claws of the cat than there are cats by thorns. Therefore, temper thy benevolence with wisdom. Call upon that man whose kindness to beasts is directed by learning and experience. Surely thou knowest a vet!

Thrombus

A perfectly healthy cat suddenly gets depressed, and if handled even slightly exhibits distress and pain. He crawls into a corner dragging one or both of his hind legs. Feel the legs. One or both seem cold. This is one of the few conditions of cats where early diagnosis and treatment are absolutely essential. Your veterinary surgeon will feel the arteries of the hind legs. He may decide that it is an aortic embolism. A blood clot or thrombus has formed in the artery that feeds the legs, and they are simply being deprived of their life force. Sometimes a hurried but skilled operation can remove the clot and restore the circulation. More often (and I mean much more often), despite all treatment, death ensues in hours.

Ticks

A long time ago, when even my enemies said I was young and healthy, I walked through some jungle doing what was grandly called 'a tick survey'. I trudged through the bush dragging a sheet behind me. I was supposed to count the sheet's contents and then sort them into Smith ticks and Brown ticks and Jones ticks. The survey broke down for two reasons. The first was that I was so busy picking ticks off myself that I often didn't get around to the sheet. It took me weeks to learn that the best way to rid oneself of ticks is to jump into a river and let the fish get on with it. It's ticklish but effective. The second reason why the survey bogged down was because there are so many kinds of ticks. We had three huge and complicated volumes describing tick families. By the time I finished the third volume I forgot what was in the first volume, and anyway all three volumes were being reduced to tropical mildew and so was my ambition.

Most ticks wait until they're adults before they attack. They hang around bushes and grass and such, waiting for anything to brush them off. They don't seem to care much whether it's a buffalo, a cat or an automobile. They then cling to the warm object, locate the skin and bury their heads for a ten-day drink. If you pull them off roughly the head stays inside and starts a festering sore. The thing to do is to touch them with a bit of ether or whisky. That makes them let go. Kill them as you take them off, or they'll find their way back to the closest warm object.

If your Blue Persian comes in swarming with the things, try to brush off those that haven't got attached. Have a good look the next day and the next, because you won't notice some of them until they're engorged with blood.

Incidentally, some ticks seem to go around in couples, so if you pick off a fat juicy female look in exactly the same spot, and you may see a little male less than a quarter the size of his mate.

Tongue

In the cat this is a rough, scale-covered muscle. It's used for eating, drinking and cleaning. When Felicita eats or drinks she curves her tongue in a pretty fair imitation of a spoon. On washdays the spoon becomes a brush. It's important to remember that her tongue is covered with those little scales. You see, once she grasps something it's very difficult for her to reject it. The scales point backwards. She doesn't really want to swallow those dead hairs and needles or the end of the thread, but nature gives her little choice in the matter. So you do what you can by brushing out the loose hairs and keeping tempting objects out of sight.

Because cats are clever creatures they seldom burn or cut their tongues. On those rare occasions when they do, the best medicine is rest. The cat will rightly refuse all solid foods, but may accept broths or glucose in water. Glycerine and honey may soothe, and the honey is nutritious. Your veterinary surgeon might start a course of antibiotic injections to keep down the infection while the tongue heals itself.

A tongue that is swollen grotesquely may have an elastic band or a piece of string wrapped around it. Yes, dear reader, children and stupid adults can and do perpetrate such things. If you can see the constricting object, try to get it off, but don't mess about too long. If it's not easily cut and removed, for goodness sake get the animal to your vet. He will anaesthetize the distressed beast and remove the stuff at leisure. Sometimes too much damage has been done, and a partial amputation of the tongue is indicated. If and when it gets to that stage, your veterinarian will discuss the pros and cons with you.

Tongues may become infected either as an extension of a general infection like flu, or more commonly because they are rubbing against rotting tartared teeth. Obviously the only way to treat the tongue is to cure the flu or remove the offending teeth.

A tongue may become badly lacerated in a car accident or a fall from an open window. It's amazing how quickly they heal if they are sutured within a few hours of the accident. One must administer antibiotics for some days afterwards because the whole area is full of bacteria and it's quite impossible to maintain sterile conditions.

Finally, a reminder of the only home aid mouth rinse which you can safely use. Good old-fashioned diluted salt water. Teaspoon to 6dl (1 pint). Remember?

Tonsillitis

Tonsillitis doesn't occur as a condition all on its own in cats, as it does so often in people and in dogs. It occurs as a complication of some other conditions like enteritis or pneumonia or flu. The animal will be unable or reluctant to eat solids. It may lap broths or milk. The antibiotics that one uses to treat the primary condition will also hit the tonsillitis, and within a few days the pain and swelling should subside.

Tortoiseshell

Patches of red and black and cream, and the more distinct they are the better. There are long-haired sorts and short-haired sorts.

Obviously the latter are on the whole more attractive because the patches don't tend to merge and blur as they do in the Persian.

Almost all are female. One runs across the very odd tom, but these are invariably sterile. The females although they are quite as prolific as their unpatched cousins seldom produce patched kittens. Most people just consider a Tortoiseshell kitten a happy accidental bonus.

There is a separate breed classification in both long-haired and short-haired for Tortoiseshell and White. They've got everything the tortoise has and a bit of white besides.

There is also a Blue Tortoiseshell in which the black of the ordinary Tortoiseshell is replaced by blue. This is an official breed in America but has never been granted championship status in Britain. Yes, indeed, serious people sit down and with solemnity deliberate such things.

Training

Cats are as intelligent, responsive and trainable as dogs. Every cat lover says it, and some of them mean it. It depends on what dogs you're talking about, and even more so on the cats. For example, it would take an experienced trainer several months of patient effort to get a Pekinese to do the things that most Labradors or Alsatians would do in just a few days.

Just as there are breeds and individual dogs that are more or less difficult to train, so there are breeds and individual cats that vary widely in their response to training. Most Siamese take easily to collars and leads and walking at 'heel'. Few cats of other breeds will tolerate a lead. Short-haired tabbies will often pounce and retrieve almost naturally. Most Persians are so aloof that they make other cats look like doting Spaniels by comparison.

It can't be emphasized enough that cats vary far more widely than dogs, and even in the same litter one will find individuals with strikingly different responses to training.

The most important rule in cat training is never to punish. There are almost no exceptions to this rule (and those I will mention later). If you strike a cat once it will take you months or years to undo the damage. Everyone agrees that cats are highly intelligent creatures when it concerns their own comfort and well-being. Even if they weren't they could hardly be expected to trust someone who uses his superior strength to inflict pain. If you lived in a huge castle dominated by a giant with hands the size of your body, how would you respond to a 'short sharp blow'? You'd be a damn fool if you didn't hide under the bed every time the giant appeared. That's exactly the cat's response. Just because he reacts in the only sane self-preserving way he knows, people accuse him of being stupid and untrainable.

Why may punishment be used in training dogs but not cats? First, the best trainers don't punish dogs (except if they bite). Secondly, many dogs will forget a punishing slap in a matter of minutes, and after the crisis is over they'll join in the training with the same old eagerness. Cats just don't forget that sort of thing. Thirdly, cats bruise much more easily, and one always inflicts much more pain and suffering than you'd think possible. Fourthly, because a cat can't maim or kill you as large dogs can, there is simply no reason either to protect oneself or to retaliate with force.

How do you train a cat? It's simplicity itself. You offer rewards for an action correctly performed. If you open a tin of meat, doesn't he come? If you call him in that special tone of voice you use when you're about to feed him, doesn't he come? In my immediate neighbourhood there are four cats including my own, and each recognizes its master's call meaning that dinner's ready. To call my cat I whistle. One sort of whistle means 'food's up'. If he hasn't been fed by a neighbour he comes galloping down the mews. Another tone of whistle means, 'It's cold and it's raining, and if you want to sleep in a warm place you'd better hurry because I'm not standing here all night'.

The difference between training cats and training dogs is that a dog will usually learn or perform for no greater reward than a pat on the head or a bit of praise. Cats are much too practical to do anything just for praise. They appreciate it in limited quantities, but the reward for effort has to be tangible. It has to be food or comfort, and that has to be recognizably connected with the thing they are asked to do.

Hold a bit of your cat's favourite food in your left hand. Grasp his right paw with your right hand and say 'SHAKE'. Immediately offer it the food. Repeat two or three times that day. The next day gradually increase the interval between the shake and the titbit. The next day say 'SHAKE', but only extend your hand part-way. Usually he will extend his paw part-way. By the fifth or sixth day with just the command 'SHAKE' he will be putting his paw out for the grasp. At the end of the week most cats will 'shake a paw' once or twice without the reward being visible or smellable. You can show him off in company. But fair warning! He'll go along once or twice or three times, but after that if there's no reward he'll be bored with the whole business and simply walk away. Clever cat!

Similarly cats can be taught to retrieve objects, to roll over on their backs, to clap their paws, to jump through hoops or leap up on your shoulder. You must, of course, break complicated tricks into their component actions and teach them gradually step by step. You must never ask the cat to do more than it's physically able to do or more than it has mentally grasped. You mustn't train for more than five minutes at a time, and you mustn't train after mealtimes. The cat just wants to sleep then, and isn't interested in your stupid titbits and funny ideas.

If you are a bit bankrupt and a TV producer offers you a share of the company if only your cat will jump through a hoop, tell him you'll have the whole act in shape in ten days' time. The first day you kneel on the floor. You rest the hoop on the ground. You offer the cat a titbit. He hesitates about walking through the strange hoop. You put your hand through the hoop and give him the food. For the second titbit you don't put your hand quite so far through the hoop. By the third titbit he may gingerly poke his head through the hoop.By the sixth titbit he's walking through the hoop quite confidently.

Lesson Two begins the next day when the cat is again hungry. You place the hoop on the floor and have him walk through to retrieve the titbit in your hand. Gradually you increase the interval between his walking through the hoop and getting the titbit, but he must know that each time he goes through the hoop he gets his food. It may be as much as five seconds later but no more. Next day begin with the hoop still on the floor and a short perceptible interval between walking through it and getting the food. By the end of the session you can raise the hoop just a couple of cm so that he has to make just a slight effort to get through it. Next day you may raise the hoop 5 cm. Many cats will give the slight jump necessary to clear a hoop just eight cm off the floor. The sixth day (when you might be up to four or five inches) sorts the scholarship winners from those who couldn't care less. At that stage real effort is needed. Graduates gradually go on to greater heights as the hoop gets raised to the maximum level at which that particular cat can *easily* make the jump. Don't push beyond that because one mishap and all the work is undone. Waist level is about average.

Do I really think that my instructions should be followed to the letter? No! Not even to the paragraph. I repeat. Every cat is different. Every owner is different. You have to play it by ear and see how it goes. Generally, though, the lessons can't be too long, and not too much new stuff can be taught in each lesson.

I would like to state emphatically that all those lessons, as far as I'm concerned, are plain rubbish. I don't think cats should be trained performers. The only reason I include it all is to refute the common saying that cats can't be trained.

What training do I think a cat should have? Cats should be taught to use a sanitary tray or to ask to go outdoors. They should learn to recognize your call and to trust it. They should learn to scratch at the objects you want them to scratch. They should learn to eat in one place only and not drop food about. They should be taught to pause at street crossings and have a look around.

Some people say that a cat should also be taught to sleep only on his own bed, but I think that's carrying things too far.

All these things (except the bed bit) come almost naturally to most cats. They may need just a bit of gentle direction. Never punish. Never shout. Never push his nose in a mess he's made. Use his name and murmuring tones of approval when it does things right. Never use his name when he's doing things wrong. Say No! No! firmly but not too harshly. Don't laugh at him or make fun of him. He'll resent it, and do the opposite of what you want just to show you that he's not meant to be messed about with. I don't mean that you can't make jokes *with* your cat. You *can't* play jokes *on* your cat. For example, when my cat is in the mood he'll crawl on to my lap and let me play him like a guitar. I lay him on his side and strum gently at his rib cage, and he sings in a crescendo of rising howls. We sometimes do this when we're having a party, and the guests enjoy it immensely, tell us what a wonderful party it's been, and shortly afterwards I can feed my cat in peace. Now the point of this is that I can only play my cat like a guitar when he wants to. If I forced it on him that would be making fun of him or using him, and that's unfair. You must treat a cat as you would a human friend, with give and take and always with respect for his individuality and dignity.

Back to the boring details. Housetraining comes naturally to cats. Show them the tray or the outdoors every time they go to squat for business. Within hours or days they'll know what you want. Don't punish the odd accident. Pick him up. Say No! No! and place him on the tray.

Most cats will cover the mess by pawing the sand or peat or whatever over it. Some cats are very energetic mess-coverers, and in the process they throw a mixture of mucky sand over a wide area of the room. The only solution I know is to provide a tray with sides 8 or 9cm high.

Training a cat to come for his dinner is almost too easy. Most cats will practically drag you to the kitchen if they're the least bit hungry. Ignore them if it's not feeding time. When you wish to feed the cat call his name and say 'dinner's up' or 'fishy-fishy fishballs' or whatever strikes your fancy. The words don't matter, but the tone and rhythm do. Use the same tone of voice that means 'food', at each feeding time. You mustn't call him for dinner and then give him nasty medicine. That's not playing fair. If it's 'nasty time' better let him know. Catch him even against his own will, and get it over with. He'll respect you more if you don't lie.

If he insists on dragging his food into a corner, pick it up, gently say No! No! and replace it in his bowl. After three or four sessions he'll eat from his bowl. Make sure the bowl isn't too deep. You wouldn't like to eat by craning your head into a pail. I feed my cat great hunks of meat or liver, which I allow him to eat off a newspaper placed in his feeding corner. If he dragged it off the paper I'd place it back on the paper and tell him about his lack of consideration.

Most cats can easily be taught to use a scratching post. The best scratching posts are firm upright posts with thick textured material attached. It should be placed close to the cat's bed (if he has one) because most cats like a good stretch and a claw-scratching session to get the day rolling. If he scratches anything else he must be gently picked up and moved to the scratching post and told that he'd really be much happier using the official equipment. I have a corner of the room covered with some hideous blue carpeting, and I have trained my cat to use only that. He ignores the rather nice pile rug that lies right beside it.

Siamese are the greatest claw sharpeners in the cat world. It's their form of doodling. The earlier you start training a Siamese to use only one spot the less likely you are to find your home being gradually scratched into unsaleable shreds.

It's also very easy to teach a cat the places that he's allowed to use and the places that are forbidden. I think it's quite reasonable to ask children not to track mud across a rug, and to ask cats to keep their noses out of the guests' food. If there are too many forbidden acts or places, possibly you'd be better off without cats or children.

How do you train a cat to keep off the kitchen counter and the dining-room table? You simply tell him it's not allowed. Say No! firmly. If he doesn't move, take him off and place him somewhere else. As soon as he knows you definitely won't have him on the table he'll leave off trying. Don't allow him the use of the table one day and forbid it the next. Good teachers and trainers are consistent.

Teaching a cat to pause at the doorway or at crossings is simply a matter of communicating alarm by the tone of your voice. Open the door a crack and look out. Say something like 'Where's the horrid bogey man?' as if you mean it. Five or six repetitions, and your cat will have the idea that he's supposed to pause and pretend to be alarmed before he goes out. He'll think you're a bit crazy, but if he's at all tolerant he'll humour you along and have a look before going out. Accompany him to the road and repeat your little skit. Remember that your relatives can't have you certified so long as you're not actually dangerous. Even the police can't touch you if you don't raise your voice too loudly, and if you limit yourself to doing it only a few hours a day.

Sadly, I must mention those few occasions in which I think cats should be punished. Fortunately they rarely occur.

If a cat has been the sole pampered pet of an adult couple he may be insanely jealous of a new baby and the attention it commands. If he indicates that he means to translate that jealousy into unsheathed claws, I wouldn't hesitate to strike him on the flanks or throw a glass of water on him. If he repeats the performance later I would dump pussy on friends for two or three years or more.

If you are bequeathed an adult cat who claws at the slightest provocation, I would hold him by the scruff and flick my index finger at the offending claws until he withdrew them. Some cats have been so spoiled that they don't realize that the world is only partly theirs.

Most cats fight pills and other forms of medication. Firmness is needed. Let him know from the outset that no matter what happens he's going to get the pill. No matter if he scratches, squirms and bites. The pill will go down. Two successful performances and the cat, being essentially a sensible creature, will allow further medication with a minimum of fuss.

Strange cats who visit you without invitation or welcome can usually be discouraged by a loud hard clap. Stubborn visitors like toms trying to woo your queen are best dissuaded by an accurately aimed glass of water. It will cause neither pain nor injury, but it will be effective.

And, oh yes. Old, old cats, like many old people, will often forget all sorts of things. They may even develop a few nasty habits. I would suggest a veterinary check. Sometimes there's a physical reason. If there isn't, you'd better confine the old boy to those parts of the house where it doesn't matter. Whatever you do, please don't attempt to punish or restrain him. If you can't put up with a bit of inconvenience during his last summer or two, you're to be pitied.

Traps

Be very careful when releasing any animal from a trap. It will be in pain. Any handling will increase the pain. Soothing talk will not quieten its panic. Don't expect the injured creature to listen to reason. Get your equipment together before you start. The damage has already been done, so an extra five minutes getting prepared won't make that much difference. You need stout gloves or a thick coat or blanket, and a box or basket into which you'll quickly transfer the animal. If you don't place the animal in a box it will run off and hide. At that stage it has little reason to trust humans and their contraptions. First open the basket, then wrap the animal in the blanket or grab its neck. Release the spring with your foot if you can. Be careful you don't get caught yourself, while freeing the crushed limb. Stick the animal, blanket and all, into the basket. If you can't open the trap, transfer the whole caboodle into a box and take the problem to your vet. With the aid of anaesthetics the procedure becomes quite simple.

Travel sickness

Most cats are excellent travellers. Stick them in a basket at London Airport and they'll arrive in Montreal relaxed and refreshed after what was probably a welcome opportunity for a long undisturbed sleep. Cats shouldn't be fed or given liquids for five or six hours before a long journey. Nervous cats may be tranquillized with phenobarbs or nembutal, but get the dosage exactly right from your vet. It's just too easy to overdose. One cannot use morphine or its derivates or the chlorpromazines (largactyl and that lot) on cats without veterinary supervision, because some cats go up the wall with the stuff. On long journeys it's almost always better to put the cat in a closed basket. For shorter journeys, of an hour or so, many cats are happier if they have a window out of which they can see the horrible world.

Trench mouth

This is as uncomfortable for cats as it is for people. Affected cats will act much as we do. They will continually run their tongues over the sore gums. They may rub their faces against the wall, or they may attempt to scratch their mouths with their paws.

Treatment includes antibiotic injections and rinsing several times daily with very diluted hydrogen peroxide. Boil feeding and watering dishes twice daily.

Turkish swimming cat

In a province called Van in Turkey there is reputed to be a strain of long-haired white cats with auburn-marked heads and tails. These Van cats, we are told, love swimming. In fact, some of them have been imported, and their progeny (or those of them who breed true to type) have demonstrated their love of water for the television camera and its devotees.

It's the answer for those people who dislike Labradors and are afraid of otters, but who simply must have a furry ornament to enhance the pool.

PS: Latterly one has been able to see these cats exhibited at shows. As the average cat show doesn't provide swimming pools, they sit in little cages just like all the other cats. I must admit that I can't tell the difference between them and other cats of my acquaintance.

I'm not trying to impress anyone when I say that I have a wealthy Turkish friend. I assume he's wealthy because his yacht has more staff than the Hilton. That may be a slight exaggeration but I can state with certainty that he has good communications with all parts of Turkey, including Van Province. For six years I've asked him to get me all available information about the breed. All his contacts say either he or I is crazy. 'Even the dogs don't swim here,' they report.

Ulcerative glossitis

The tongue becomes sore and inflamed and ulcerated. Sometimes the ulcers become so deep that a portion of the tongue literally drops off. You'll have noticed it days before that stage, because the cat will be off its food and listless. He will open and close his mouth in obvious distress. He may sit by water but refuse to drink, and his breath and saliva will be offensive.

Some authorities believe this condition to be merely a milder form of feline enteritis, and others claim that it's entitled to be called a disease all on its own. Everyone agrees that the treatment should include injections to attack the disease systematically and to build up the body. Some veterinarians advise local applications as well, to soothe and heal the tongue.

As the disease usually hits younger cats (mostly between five and twelve months of age), proper and early treatment usually effects a rapid recovery. Within days Pepperpot will be lapping again. In a couple of weeks all that he'll remember of the whole affair will be the horrid human in the white coat who shoved needles into his backside.

Ulcers of the mouth

Cats are very prone to sores on the lips and in the mouth which have a tendency to become chronic and deep-seated. As the cat licks these sores they spread – often to other parts of the body and most common-ly the thighs. Veterinarians call these things granulomas. They're not malignant growths and won't kill the animal, but they can and do cause a great deal of discomfort and they can twist and disfigure the face. The cat is often so miserable with these ulcers that he's not interested in anything but licking them. To stop him doing so and thus aggravating the condition requires all of one's ingenuity and an army of medicines – right from old-fashioned gentian violet to the latest cortisones. Granulomas are the most unsatisfactory things to treat and the only advice I can give you is to get your cat into the vet's as early as possible. Then for your cat's sake don't switch from vet to vet in the hope that one knows a secret cure. All treatments for this condition are published, as indeed they are for all conditions. Every vet knows them. They'll all start with the pea shooters before bringing out the big guns.

Urination

Neutered males and all females squat to urinate. They do it three or four times a day. Full toms spray their urine and they do it as often as the fancy strikes them.

An animal that strains to pass its urine or that passes thick or blood-stained urine should be seen by a vet within hours. This is particularly true of cats because it may have been going on for a day or two or more before the creature got so distressed as to allow you to see it in the act.

Vaccination

If you prefer things by their proper names it's inoculation. In cats it should be done against Feline Infectious Enteritis (Panleucopenia) because it's a real killer. In orientals it's even more important. They succumb easily and few respond even to early treatment. The inocu-lations may be given at any age but most vets suggest a first shot at seven or eight weeks and another a fortnight later. Before boarding, travelling or showing they are repeated. Most require annual boosters.

Inoculations against the two or three sorts of cat flu are currently being widely publicized and advertised. Even as I write these words, the correspondence both for and against rages in the veterinary and cat journals. I'm afraid until it's proved beyond doubt that flu vaccines are as safe and as efficient as the enteritis vaccines, I'll leave them strictly alone. Some cattery owners and breeders I know go even further. They won't have a cat on the premises that's been done with the stuff. But, of course, neither they nor I are trained virologists. In all fairness I must point out that the real specialists are all for it. Those against it are mainly expressing prejudices and opinions. Those for it are stating facts. Maybe they'll convert us yet.

Vaginitis

This is a swelling of the vagina which becomes sore, raw and painful. I don't know why, but it's a fairly common condition in cats and is seen quite often, even in those that have been spayed. It's a relatively rare condition in dogs.

The first symptom one sees is the cat constantly licking herself around the vaginal opening. You may notice a bit of pus or blood where she has been sitting. She may strain and strain after passing water. If you examine her under a good light you'll notice the swollen red lips of the vulva and you may see a bit of caked yellowish pus. All the toms in the neighbourhood might be trying to get in, even though Jennifer is spayed.

It's a serious condition and must not be treated in an amateur fashion, for two reasons. The first is that irritating medicines introduced into the vagina may actually spread the infection. The second is that an uncured vaginitis will usually become chronic, and the bladder too will get infected.

The only absolutely safe home aid is clipping the hair from around the infected area and bathing with diluted salt water. That will soothe it, and may help to prevent the cat from doing further damage by her constant licking.

What will your vet do? He will first make sure that it's a straight-forward vaginitis, and not an infection of the bladder or the uterus.

If you've been pushing some medicated ointment into the hole he'll tell you what kind of a fool you are. Then he'll either dispense or inject a course of antibiotics to act from within the body, and he may use antibiotics in the vagina itself.

Usually there is a decided improvement twenty-four hours after the first lot of antibiotics, and then slow progress for four or five days. Your veterinarian will want to continue treatment at least two days after the animal appears to be cured, to minimize chances of a relapse or recurrence.

Vegetables

Cats are carnivores. They eat meat. In its natural state meat includes innards which are full of half-digested goodies like vegetables and grasses. Your domesticated cat might play about with a mouse (or a moose for that matter) but he probably wouldn't classify it as dinner.

He has been conditioned (or spoiled) to the point where dinner means convenient-sized familiar bits in the same old bowl at the same old time. Therefore, my dear, you may have to provide those nutritional greens the butcher shops don't handle. What sort? Almost anything except potato peelings. What quantity? Let him decide how much he wants by providing a pot of grass (see *Grass*). If that's too much of a chore mix the odd teaspoon of broccoli, peas or lettuce with his Sunday lunch. Start when he's a kitten and he'll grow to love the stuff – and he'll grow – and grow.

Viciousness

There are three common causes of viciousness in cats. The first is by far the most common and is the result of cruelty. In some countries like Spain baiting cats is considered to be a pleasant diversion during the endless hours between bullfights. In some countries and places it's considered manly to keep and love dogs and equally virile to harass other species with boots and bullets. In some countries children are allowed to vent their sadistic feelings on cats. The wonder is that more cats aren't incorrigibly vicious. But fortunately even the most tormented of creatures will, after a few weeks or months of patience learn that there are some people for whom claws can remain sheathed.

Viciousness can be caused by over-indulgence particularly during kittenhood. Like people who were incorrigibly spoiled as children it usually takes many firm lessons to teach this sort of vicious cat that the world is an oyster that must occasionally be shared.

Finally there is a viciousness that is hereditary. For over thirty years many authorities have warned us that some strains of purebred cats are simply born that way. It's rare in the short-haired breeds (both domestic and foreign) but is seen all too often in some families of Persians. I know a long-haired Blue going into his second year of ferocious life. It's quite impossible to groom him or give him a pill or handle him at all without turning him into a ball of claws and fury. Indeed if you look sideways at him – and sometimes if you're not looking at all – he'll attack, and with no holds barred. I can assure you he's been like that since he was three weeks old when his owner first acquired him. And I can assure you that his owner is an eminently sane lady who has had some fifteen years of concentrated experience with animals of all sorts. What do I recommend in such cases? If there are babies or young children in the household find another home for him. Otherwise stick with him into nasty old age. The years might just simmer him down and his scratches will keep your reflexes working. A vicious cat doesn't have to be put down as do some vicious large dogs because even the worst of them can't do that much damage. Whatever you do have such animals neutered. No matter how perfect their coat or beautiful their eyes they simply shouldn't be allowed to perpetuate their nastiness.

Virus

Bacteria are so small that they must be magnified about one thousand times their actual size before they look about the size of the period at the end of this sentence. Viruses are even smaller. One must photograph them through the very powerful electron microscope in order to study them.

Bacteria will grow on many different kinds of soups and broths and meats, but viruses will only grow in living tissues. Hence their study and their manufacture into vaccines is a tedious and expensive process.

The antibiotics like penicillin, aureomycin and terramycin, etc. will inhibit or kill bacteria, but so far there is no drug effective against viruses. Viruses as you know cause poliomyelitis and flu and colds in man, and a host of diseases like foot-and-mouth in cattle and pigs. In dogs a virus causes distemper. In cats viruses are responsible for, among other things, feline infectious enteritis. There is an effective vaccine that builds up immunity against enteritis. There is no drug that attacks the virus once it gets going in the cat's body. The conclusion is obvious.

Vitamins

We see far more vitamin deficiencies in cats than in dogs. This is partly because more cats are restricted, or restrict themselves, in what they eat. Some eat the same old thing day in day out and appear to enjoy it at least until their health fails.

The best natural source of some vitamins is liver, but even cats who get it a couple of times a week need added vitamins, particularly if they're on tinned food the rest of the week. Generally speaking a drop of cod-liver oil twice a week, and a yeast tablet every day is all that's needed. Don't go out and get a lot of high priced stuff. Overdosing with vitamins can be harmful.

There are some periods when more vitamins are needed. When the kitten is still growing it may need supplements. While a cat is suffering or recovering from any illness it can use additional vitamin A (in the form of cod-liver oil) and lots and lots of vitamin B (in the form of yeast) and any other pills your vet dispenses. Ageing cats may need supplementary vitamins. Pregnant cats, of course, need all the help you can give in order to feed those growing lives. After worming pills, additional vitamins may be indicated.

Whatever you do don't get too enthusiastic and shove all Aunt Matilda's vitamins down your cat's throat. Remember they killed Auntie.

Vomiting

Dogs, as you might know, are gluttons. They will often rush to their food and bolt it down. If they or their stomachs don't like it they casually bolt it up again. The cat, however, is most particular about what he eats. It will examine its food by sight, by smell and by touch before taking it into its mouth, and then it savours the stuff as it goes down. It's most unusual for a cat to vomit its food because it's eaten too quickly or because the food is bad.

Kittens and younger cats may vomit a few minutes or hours after eating because of the irritation or blockage of worms. Occasionally a cat will vomit a worm or a bunch of worms. Now I know this isn't a very tasteful subject, but if you can bury your sensitivity for a few moments you can help to get the beast right. Don't throw the stuff out without examining it. Get an empty matchbox and a short stick of wood. If you don't know what old-fashioned wood is you can use a new-fashioned ball-point pen – (the kind that runs dry). Sift through the disgusting stuff and transfer anything that looks alive to the matchbox. Take it along to your veterinarian who, clever chap that he is, will attach a big name to it and give you the appropriate pills.

Another common cause of vomiting is hair-balls. If your cat vomits up something that looks like soggy felt or matted wool you had better consider it a warning that you're not grooming him properly (see Hair-balls).

If your cat vomits once and refuses food the next day, you'd better take it along to your vet. It may be an obstruction of the bowel caused by anything from a hair-ball to a needle and thread or a small ball or a large button. Cats will occasionally chew the cord that butchers use to tie roasts. It can ball up inside and close off the bowel. Usually three symptoms lead the veterinarian to a presumptive diagnosis of a foreign body. The first is vomiting and subsequent refusal to eat or vomiting a little while after each feeding time, the second is a normal temperature, and the third is the lack of bowel motions. Notice that two of these three symptoms can't be seen by examining the cat on the table. You may be able to tell the vet about the vomiting, the eating and the motions. But if your cat is like my cat and goes in and out all day long it's unlikely that you'll know about the motions. So we're left with a history of vomiting and a normal temperature. The veterinarian will then examine the cat more closely. He goes through a kind of mental shorthand to try and arrive at a diagnosis which might be something like this: 'Eyes and gums look OK, a little dehydrated, nothing that points to a virus, though, hmmm, pretty tight abdomen, doesn't like it if I feel him here, ah, what's this, that feels a little hard, too hard for faeces, better have an X-ray'.

Sometimes an obstructive object will show on the X-ray plate and sometimes it won't. Further examination might include a blood count and other tests on the blood. Barium and other radio-opaque substances which are used to outline objects in the digestive tracts of dogs (and humans) cannot be given to cats, as much of it would go down the wrong way and cause a pneumonia. If a foreign body is found or there is reasonable suspicion of one, then an operation must be done to remove it. The cat will be on a liquid diet for a few days, the stitches will come out in a week or ten days, and all is well.

Sometimes a cat will have bouts of vomiting over a period of weeks or months. There may be alternating periods of constipation and diarrhoea as well. If the cat is middle-aged and losing weight, we suspect a tumour, and one of the common tumours that will cause those symptoms is a lymphosarcoma, which we can often feel as an irregular, lumpy, solid mass along the intestine (see *Lymphosarcoma*).

Vomiting of sudden onset, accompanied by diarrhoea and a high temperature, is usually caused by one of the more serious virus diseases, and the sooner proper treatment is started the better the chances of recovery.

Finally, vomiting may be a symptom of infection in the kidney, in the liver or in the uterus. Needless to say home treatment can only do positive harm.

Summary: Vomiting is a much more serious symptom in the cat than it is in the dog. Don't attempt any home treatment.

Warning

A cat who lays its ears flat and sideways has had enough of whatever you're doing. Let go!

Warts

Ugly things they are. Usually they bother the owner more than the cat. Unless they occur in some awkward location like the margin of the nose or the junction of the lips they may be best left alone. Why? Cut a wart off in one place and the nasty thing appears somewhere else.

Water

Good clean water in a clean bowl is necessary for all animals at all times. There are simply no exceptions. Even if you never see your cat lap a drop it really isn't that much trouble to change a bowl of water.

Weaning (*separation of the young from the mother*)

This is absolutely no problem provided you allow it to be a gradual process and provided that you have fed the mother properly during pregnancy and lactation. The following outline shows how simple and gradual it is.

1st week: Cull weak or deformed or surplus kittens. Daily look at navels, and a touch of iodine if inflamed or sore. If eyes are pussey or discharging call vet.

2nd week: Eyes should start opening by tenth day. More vigorous kittens might be interested in queen's bowl. If kittens are scratching each other or the mother, nails should be trimmed.

3rd week: Kittens may not be getting enough food from mother, so try them with one of the special formulae or with powdered milk at double strength plus a bit of cooked baby cereal.

4th week: Kittens should be looking forward to their own meals as well as their mother's milk. If they need it they may be wormed at this stage (but please, under veterinary direction). Check claws again because they can be really murderous at this age.

5th and 6th weeks: Kittens are gradually shifting over to their own food, and the queen is leaving them for longer and longer periods. You should be adding bonemeal and some vitamin supplements to one of their meals. Two or three of their daily five or six meals should be meat. At the end of the sixth week they may be inoculated against enteritis.

7th week: The queen won't allow them to suckle too much or too often. They'll be getting almost all their requirements from the feeding bowl. It is, however, important to leave them with the queen. She will teach them the things that they can't look up in books like this. And don't be too complacent about ear mites or fleas. Check the kittens for both every time they crawl over the dining-room table.

8–12 *weeks:* Kittens may put on as much as 225g ($\frac{1}{2}$ lb) a week during this period. Don't stint on food, milk or supplements. Make sure you write a detailed diet sheet for the new owners. It's difficult enough moving into a new environment. I've known kittens weaned on perfectly balanced tinned catfood whose new owners produced the most alarming symptoms by feeding pheasant and salmon.

Note: Many conscientious breeders leave kittens with their mothers until they are twelve weeks old.

Weight

Some oriental queens weigh as little as 2·3kg (5 lb). They're too small and shouldn't be used for breeding. Some Persian neuters weigh as much as 9kg (20 lb). They should be put on a diet. Most healthy normal cats are in the 3–6kg (7–14 lb) range. How do you weigh the brute? Weigh him basket and all. Subtract weight of the basket. Write it down because you're sure to forget.

Which species?

If you've space, time and money you can keep an elephant for all I care. Don't come crying, though, if you've acquired something that has become a bigger problem than your mother-in-law. If you are a back-slapping athletic type get yourself a brace of Boxers. If you want to impress impressionable girls you might consider a mixed trio consisting of an Afghan, a Saluki and a Chihuahua. Would you like to appear as an idealistic hard working sort of chap? Get a Collie! If you don't care what people think, find sycophancy a bore but want a creature that will fill your vacant hours you'd better have a cat. But don't get one if you think it should only be there when *you* want it. The best human cat relationships are reciprocal. If you're often away get a pair of cats – or a dog and a cat – so they can keep each other company.

Lesser creatures like budgies, canaries and rabbits and gerbils can get along without your constant presence but it's cruel to condemn them to a lonely existence. Get a pair! If your day begins in the evening, get a hamster (not a pair because they'll kill each other).

He'll be wildly entertaining at 4 a.m. and at noon he'll gently chorus your drunken snores.

Summary: Choose an animal for which you have the time and space.

Which breed?

The less exotic the less chances of trouble. Long-haired breeds require constant grooming, and number among their representatives a fair sprinkling of the most vicious creatures in catdom. They can also be the most beautiful of all cats. If you know what you're about get one. If it's just a vague sort of hankering better think again. The breeders won't mind. Practically all breeders of cats are primarily interested in finding proper homes for their kittens. I wish I could say the same for dog breeders. Oriental types (Siamese, Burmese, Abyssinian and Russian Blues) are generally far more dependent on human company, may be terribly destructive, can be embarrassingly vocal and are the poorest patients of all felines. A bug that will only mildly discomfort an ordinary cat may kill a Siamese. The most obvious reason to have an oriental is their responsiveness.

Pedigree short-haired cats (European, British or Domestic depending on where you live) are more easily kept, require little grooming, are not usually destructive or vicious, live long healthy lives and are easier and cheaper to buy. Get one or better still get two!

Summary: Just ordinary cats are wonderful.

Which sex?

Unless you have space, time and the inclination you simply can't keep an entire cat whether male or female. Toms can stink! Also they live a quite separate existence which I can't describe in a genteel book like this. Mind you, if I lived in a house with huge rooms surrounded by acres of woodland I would keep a big handsome tom and I would name him 'The Stinking Terror'. I would watch with pleasure the neighbouring cat populace, as they changed with each passing generation into mirror images of my cat, and I would repress very deeply the thought that he was living a more real existence than mine.

Entire queens will present you with many kittens at frequent intervals. You'll find yourself reduced to talking to the most unacceptable people in an attempt to get rid of them. Some people think they can keep an entire queen by confining her during her sexy periods. It's not only difficult. It's cruel. Lately we have been offered a choice of drugs with which one can postpone a heat period. I think they're OK as a temporary measure but if you don't intend to allow your queen to mate it's better to have her spayed.

There is little to choose between a neutered queen and a neutered tom. Toms are usually more expensive to buy but cheaper to neuter. Queens are usually cheaper to buy but more expensive to neuter. Of course if you want a ginger you're more likely to be landed with a male, and if you want a tortoiseshell you'll end up with a female. Some people say that neutered queens are more affectionate and neutered toms more likely to sulk in corners, but I can't bear this out from personal experience. Toms who are neutered early in life are more likely to have bladder trouble in middle age.

Summary: Most people find that a neutered cat makes a more acceptable pet than either a full tom or entire queen.

Which tinned food?

Choose only from among those whose labels clearly indicate the contents, and get the ones which offer the most protein and the least water for the money. Even the best of them, though, are best used as standbys for those days when you are too lazy to get to the butcher shop.

Which biscuits?

Many cats will refuse them all but try them anyway. They're a nice crunchy way to start the day. Unlike dogs most cats will just take a couple or three to ward off that empty feeling until dinnertime.

PS: I wouldn't advise them though as a complete diet. There is too much evidence connecting dried diets with urinary problems, particularly in the male. The manufacturers, of course, state that the incidence is very low and the evidence inconclusive. My only reply is that having treated such cases, I know how painful they must be. And that even if there's a suspicion that one single case has been caused by a dry diet, that is one case too many.

Which tonic?

None of the highly advertised tonics are necessary. Good old-fashioned brewer's yeast contains lots of good things and so does a pot or flower box of growing grass.

Which inoculations?

See *Enteritis.* See *Rabies.*

Which veterinary surgeon?

In an emergency any vet will treat any animal but obviously some are happier with and better equipped to deal with some species than with others. Distinguished old Professor Michael Q. Scope can probably remember how to castrate your kitten, but he'd really rather be left with his job of classifying the latest foot-and-mouth outbreak. Handsome Sir Thorough Bred may not be surprised when you leave an urgent call at the stables to attend your cat. You may be surprised, though, to get a bill for fifty guineas which is his normal charge for diagnosing the cause of the lameness. Your best bet is to find the vet closest to you who deals with cats routinely. Once you find him be fair to your cat by sticking to him through thick and thin.

Whiskers

I can't tell you how they work and neither can anyone else. If you are cruel enough to cut them off, the cat will lose some of its sense of balance, a great deal of its sure-footedness and most of its ability to dart into narrow openings at full flight.

White, long-haired, Blue-eyed cats

I don't know, or care, if they are more properly called Blue Eyes, White Long-hairs or where the commas and dashes should be. You'd be surprised though how many people will write nasty letters about such silly things. They have little lives, poor dears, so such details loom large.

These same people will go to great lengths defining the texture, the shading and the length of the coat and the shade of blue they expect in the eye. It would all be a harmless time-filling hobby if it weren't for the simple fact that almost all cats of this breed (and it is a recognized breed) are deaf.

Odd-eyed Whites, i.e. those with one blue and one orange eye often have impaired hearing. Orange-eyed Whites may have diminished hearing.

I know that deaf cats can compensate in other ways but is it really a good thing to keep producing a breed that is condemned to a life of silence no matter how beautiful the result? I find it all the more incomprehensible because as any experienced breeder will tell you it's very difficult to produce good specimens of the breed. Yet on they go, year after year, comparing this one and that one for the finer points of what they consider perfection. The only compensation their champions have is that they can't hear a word of it.

Windows

Cats, like Sicilians, love to stare. They can sit by the hour at a window just watching the people and the cars and yesterday's newspapers going by. If a cat is left in a room by itself for hours at a time the window is its main source of amusement. If the window is closed well and good. There is no danger. If the window is open the cat usually crawls out on the ledge. Even there he is usually quite safe – as long as he stays awake. But cats as you know are great dozers. The first ray of sunlight hits the ledge, his eyes close, and he's off in his private world of semi-sleep. A sudden sound, or perhaps a funny dream, and he may jolt back into the world and find himself falling.

Am I exaggerating? Not at all. We are often presented with badly injured cats who have fallen off window sills. Do they always fall on their feet? Usually they do but if it's a 4·5–6m (15–20 foot) fall you can be sure at least one leg will have taken the jar and one of its long bones shattered. If the cat has fallen from a greater height it may have a fractured or dislocated jaw as well as a broken leg. The leg takes the initial impact and the force is transferred to the heavy head which strikes the ground. The worst case I've seen was a Siamese who fell from a fourth storey window ledge and broke bones in both its hind legs and its jaw bone as well.

What can you do after the event? Approach him gently and quietly. Remember he's frightened and shocked, and may crawl into some inaccessible hole. Take your time approaching him. If possible get two or three people to cut off his escape routes. Grab him by the scruff of the neck and support him under his belly while you transfer him to a box or a basket. If you don't you can be sure he'll hide for hours or days. When you get him in the basket don't fool about with water and splints. Just get him to your veterinarian's office.
Prevention: Either keep the windows closed or have a couple of guard rails installed along the edge of the sill. He can see between them but he can't roll through.

Finally if you have more than one cat, or a dog as well as the cat, or an exuberant child, remember that cats when chased, will choose any convenient exit. If it happens to be an open window you can expect a serious injury.

Worms

Some mature men with high IQs spend thirty or forty years studying the intestinal worms of animals. It's quite ridiculous really because as anyone can tell you all you have to do is pop around to the local pet shop. It has a wide assortment of pills that will blast the whole lot out of man or beast. What kind of pills for what kind of worms? According to the purveyors of these things it really doesn't matter.

Now I'm not saying that you need to have a PhD from Heidelberg in order to worm your cat, but I do state most emphatically that more cats are injured by indiscriminate worming than by worms. For most practical purposes there are two sorts of worms that commonly bother the cat. The first are tapeworms and you may see them (they look like grains of rice) around the cat's anus. The second sort are roundworms and you may never see them. Affected cats may have dry scurfy skins, tight pot bellies and bouts of vomiting or diarrhoea. If you suspect this sort of worm take a sample of the cat's motion along to the vet. He will examine it under the microscope and see if it contains the eggs of the worm. It's a good idea to do this as a routine sort of check before you have a queen bred.

Right! You either see the worms, in which case you stick the actual worms in a matchbox and take them along to the vet, or you suspect worms, in which case you take a sample of the motion along.

The treatment and prevention depends on the sort or sorts of worms. For example there's no point in treating a cat for tapeworms unless you get rid of the fleas at the same time. The cat just needs to swallow an infected flea in order to start the whole cycle again. There's no point in treating for certain sorts of roundworms unless you clean out the infected area at the same time.

Some of the new worm pills require neither starvation before nor purgation afterwards. They do, however, require careful measurement of dosage, so do give the exact amount prescribed.

Most require a repetition of the treatment ten days later in order to get rid of the worms that have hatched meanwhile.

And don't phone and say you didn't see any worms come out. You often don't because they may be killed and digested inside.

Finally every once in a while there is a whole spate of publicity about some cat worm finding its way into humans. The keen young type who hands out the item advising everyone to get rid of their cats or their dogs has, in his enthusiasm, got things slightly out of proportion. If it worries you, all you need do is phone your vet and make an appointment to have your animal checked. It won't cost much in time or money. It may help the cat and it will eliminate your worries.

Yeast

Aren't brewers and distillers the nicest people? They not only ensure us mortals a constant supply of measurable happiness but somewhere along the line they produce loads of yeast which cats love and which does them a world of good. I'm not a great believer (or even a little believer) in the virtues of tonics, pills and conditioners. Most are completely unnecessary. Some may even do harm. Yeast, however, can be classified as a natural food even if it's not usually produced in a natural way. How much should one give? Oh, a tablet or two once or twice a day will provide all the vitamin B your cat is likely to need. For some reason or other yeast sometimes helps effect a cure in stubborn eczemas. Two or three tablets daily is the dosage usually used.

Zoonoses

Diseases that man gets from animals. The cow can give man some ugly things like tuberculosis and brucellosis. Pigs may be equally dangerous, if not more so. Rabid dogs often bite and infect humans. It's a long list if you care to go into it, but the cat comes out rather well. For example there are cases recorded of cats getting tuberculosis from cow's milk or from tuberculous people but none (that I know of) where man or cattle got the disease from cats. As regards rabies, although affected cats are almost invariably vicious and will bite or claw anything including a steel cage, there are comparatively few reports of man getting the disease from cats.

Once in a while there's a scare about people getting worms from cats. Don't panic. Have the cat wormed and teach your children to wash their hands. Occasionally man gets ringworm from a cat or vice versa. A bit of medicine and a bit of personal sanitation and you'll both be pretty again. If cat fleas bother you console yourself with the fact that they bother the cat more. Get out the dusting powder and the vacuum cleaner and you'll both stop scratching.

Am I treating zoonoses too lightly? Maybe I am but I think that the pedantic types who glibly advise people to 'get rid of the cat' take themselves too seriously. If there were less cats in the world there might be a few less dermatoses but there would certainly be a lot more neuroses. If you're really interested in zoonoses you'd be better doing something about the rats. Cats do.

Frank Manolson
D is for Dog £1.00

The comprehensive guide to the care, training and upbringing of all well-known breeds of dog. Written by a vet, this invaluable handbook covers everything from choosing a breed to exercising and grooming.

'An encyclopedia worth its weight in gold' DAILY TELEGRAPH

Dr Shewell-Cooper's
Basic Book of Weekend Gardening £1.25

A month-by-month guide to gardening throughout the year which is designed to help those gardeners with only limited time to spare. Dr W. E. Shewell-Cooper, one of Britain's best-known gardening writers, covers all the tasks and pitfalls likely to occur in the average year in this ideal companion for the weekend gardener.

Leon Petulengro
The Roots of Health 75p

Leon Petulengro – famous astrologer and heir to a family tradition of Romany wisdom – explains how to stay healthy by eating the right foods, describes the unique properties of individual herbs, traces the ancient link between health and astrology, and reveals beauty secrets which have made the good looks of gipsy women renowned since time immemorial.

'Fascinating and beneficial' WOMAN'S OWN

Patricia Jordan
District Nurse 70p

Born and bred in Belfast, trained in the hard school of student nursing, Patricia Jordan found her niche in a small Northern England town as a district nurse. With all the style of a born storyteller she tells of the patients and their case-histories – the comedy, tragedy and heart-warming humanity of her daily round – and of the doctors and nurses who work alongside her.

'First class . . . admirable reading' OBSERVER

James Herriot
All Creatures Great and Small £1.50

the first Herriot Omnibus Edition

Follow the career of the world's most famous vet from his arrival in the Dales countryside to the completion of his courtship of his wife-to-be, Helen. Meet the colourful Siegfried and Tristan and a host of unforgettable characters, both human and very much otherwise . . .

'Warm, joyous and often hilarious . . . there is humour everywhere' NEW YORK TIMES

James Herriot
All Things Bright and Beautiful £1.50

the second Herriot Omnibus Edition

This second omnibus takes up the story of the world's favourite vet from the closing chapters of *All Creatures Great and Small*. James is now married and living on the top floor of Skeldale House. He's a partner in the practice, and his day is well-filled with the life of a country vet, bumping over the Dales in his little car en route to a host of patients from farm-horses to budgerigars . . .

'Absolutely irresistible . . . told with warmth, charm and never-flagging good humour' EVENING NEWS

John Slater
Just Off The Motorway £1.75

Here's the handbook you've been waiting for. *Just Off The Motorway* traces all the facilities available when you turn off at every junction on every one of Britain's ten major motorways. Detailed research, careful sampling and more that 150 maps show you where you can find any service you need ... eating, drinking, overnight stops, 24 hour break down services, petrol ... cheaper and better by turning off at a junction and driving for no more than three miles off the motorway.

Norman G. Pulsford
Modern Crossword Dictionary £1.50

Norman G. Pulsford, an expert crossword compiler, 'worked his way through numerous dictionaries and reference books, making notes. He also analysed 20,000 published crosswords. The result of his labours is likely to make life more difficult for himself.'
SUNDAY TELEGRAPH

'Could reduce to a fraction the time and effort required to complete a puzzle' TIMES LITERARY SUPPLEMENT